SUCCEEDING IN LAW SCHOOL

Succeeding in Law School

Second Edition

Herbert N. Ramy
PROFESSOR OF ACADEMIC SUPPORT,
SUFFOLK UNIVERSITY LAW SCHOOL

CAROLINA ACADEMIC PRESS
Durham, North Carolina

Library of Congress Cataloging-in-Publication Data

Ramy, Herbert N.
  Succeeding in law school / Herbert N. Ramy. -- 2nd ed.
      p. cm.
  Includes bibliographical references.
  ISBN 978-1-59460-740-0 (alk. paper)
  1. Law--Study and teaching--United States. 2. Law students--United
States--Handbooks, manuals, etc. I. Title.

  KF283.R36 2010
  340.071'173--dc22

                                        2010012050

Carolina Academic Press
700 Kent Street
Durham, NC 27701
Telephone (919) 489-7486
Fax (919) 493-5668
www.cap-press.com

*This book is dedicated to my wife
Stephanie Chissler—my best friend and my favorite teacher.*

Contents

Acknowledgments

I would like to thank several people who helped to make this book a reality. Professor Elizabeth Stillman of Suffolk University Law School took the time to read every chapter of the book for content and clarity, and I incorporated much of her advice into the book's final version. Professor Kathleen Elliott Vinson and the deans of Suffolk University Law School treated this project like any other scholarly endeavor, giving me both the time and resources necessary to complete the second edition of *Succeeding in Law School*. Finally, my wife Stephanie supported and encouraged me as she always does.

Introduction

Succeeding in law school is no easy task. Classes are taught using the Socratic method, which means that students must prepare extensively every day because they may be called on to take part in a question and answer dialogue with their professors. In addition, the reading required for a single day rivals what most students are accustomed to completing for a week's worth of classes. Most importantly, law school examinations and papers emphasize analytical thinking, and most students are not used to explaining their thought process in this fashion. So how does one succeed in law school?

To perform well, students must **actively engage** the challenges presented by law school. Using a simple example, this means more than reading the assigned cases and knowing how they were resolved. Instead, you must read the assigned cases, carefully review the court's reasoning to assess *why* they were resolved in a particular fashion, and then project that result out into the future to determine whether similar cases will be resolved in the same way. In essence, you are learning to predict the future.

Law school professors reward your ability to think independently, critically, and actively. While memorization is certainly a part of performing well on law school examinations, thorough legal analysis is the difference between simply passing your courses and ending up on the Dean's List. Your professors want you to take the basic rules that you have learned, and actively apply them to factual situations you have never seen before. While the factual scenarios, or fact patterns as they are often called, will have some similarities to the cases you have read, there will also be important differences.

As you might imagine, all of this requires a great deal of hard work. Unfortunately, you can work hard in law school and not succeed unless you receive some guidance, which is why I have written the second edition of *Succeeding in Law School*. Through this book, you will learn how to best approach your classes on a daily basis. I will walk you through reading your first case, and we will dissect it together in a way that best prepares you for class. This means anticipating how your professor will use the ideas contained in the reading to promote further discussion. You will learn about the best ways to take notes in class, as well as some of the common traps that students can fall into. Then, I will show you how to use the knowledge gained through the reading and classroom dialogue as the jumping off point for developing a thorough and nuanced understanding of any legal idea.

This edition of the book has several new chapters that are geared toward success both in law school and in the job market. A new chapter on legal analysis addresses one of the most common problems professors see on law school exams—the absence of the counterargument. As for the job market, new material on interviewing techniques, creating a writing sample, and writing a résumé are designed to help students market themselves to prospective employers.

Despite the changes, *Succeeding in Law School* is still intended to give students the feedback they crave while allowing professors to assess student progress throughout the semester. Whether students are seeking advice in the summer months or looking for help once the school year has begun, this book will help them make the most of their abilities.

Succeeding in Law School

CHAPTER I

The First Days

While the entire law school experience can be intimidating, the first few days will seem particularly overwhelming. Law school will be a new experience for you, and like most new experiences, it takes a little while to get comfortable. To make matters worse, law schools do not always do a great job of letting their students know exactly what to expect. Unless you are one of the lucky ones with a helpful friend or relative who has been through law school, you can expend a great deal of energy just trying to figure out where you should be and what you should be doing. Through this chapter, I hope to place everyone on equal footing when they step into law school for the first day of classes.

Even with the benefit of my advice, you will have to engage in a bit of trial and error in order to figure out what works best for you. We are all individuals, and it should not be surprising that what works extremely well for one person may not work at all for another. Be open to the advice contained throughout this book, and try to follow the spirit of my suggestions. By doing so, you will be taking the first steps to becoming your own best teacher.

> **Herb's Hints**
> ———
> Once you receive your class schedule, take a test ride to your law school before classes begin to figure out traffic patterns and parking possibilities.

The Law School Curriculum

A good place to start our discussion is with a quick review of the typical first-year law school curriculum. Students are not allowed to choose their classes during the first year in most schools. Further, the curriculum is remarkably similar from school to school, and some of your courses will last for the entire year.[1] The first-year curriculum is designed to give you a broad base of legal knowledge, and to help you begin thinking critically and analytically.

---

1. This does not mean, however, that all law schools offer the same courses during the first year.

Contracts—In essence, this is the law that governs agreements between parties. Whether you realize it or not, you have likely been a party to several contracts. If you have ever rented an apartment, the lease you signed was a contract. Even if you did not sign a lease, the agreement between you and the landlord was an oral contract. The credit card agreement between you and your bank is a contract, as is the ticket you bought the last time you went to a sporting event or concert.

Property—Property law is the law of ownership. Most property classes are divided into three sections: real property (land ownership); intellectual property (idea ownership); and personal property (ownership of everything else). Most commonly, first year property courses focus on real property and personal property concepts, and intellectual property is often covered in upper level electives.

Criminal law—While the name is self explanatory, this is not the course that most students expect when they begin the school year. Instead of covering topics like search and seizure, which you may cover in an upper level course, you will break down crimes into their constituent parts and then address whether an individual's conduct satisfies the state's definition of the crime. For example, some states expect you to run, if it is safe to do so, before defending yourself when confronted by an aggressor while in other states you may use force to defend yourself immediately. You might spend an entire class discussing how we measure personal safety in these situations. Is it enough for you to subjectively believe that your life is in jeopardy? What if you are wrong and the "attacker" was merely a census taker at your door? Does this mean we should ignore the victim's personal beliefs and assess personal safety using a more objective standard? A single idea like this one can be fodder for an entire day's discussion.

Constitutional law—Did you ever wonder why the Supreme Court gets to decide what is and is not constitutional? You will not find the answer in the Constitution, which is silent on the question. You will find the answer to this question, and many others, as you read the cases that have molded our government and our society over the last 200+ years. As a preview, the United States Supreme Court decided in Marbury v. Madison[2] that they are

---

2. 5 U.S. (1 Cranch) 137 (1803). This is an example of legal citation. Through the use of citation, the reader is informed where to find source material supporting the writer's assertions.

the final arbiters as to what is and is not constitutional. Because of the importance of the subject matter, and the complexity of the material, some schools do not offer a course in constitutional law until the second year of law school.

Civil procedure—In your civil procedure course, you will learn the law of bringing a lawsuit in federal court. You will learn that the federal courts are courts of fairly limited jurisdiction, while state courts enjoy rather wide subject matter jurisdiction. In other words, litigants may bring only certain kinds of lawsuits in federal court while most lawsuits will take place in state court. These rules will be like the pieces of a large puzzle. You won't understand very much by looking at any piece of the puzzle. As you connect the pieces, however, the course will come into sharper focus. Many of the pieces to the civil procedure puzzle are contained in the Federal Rules of Civil Procedure.

Torts—In this class, you will cover civil wrongs. Civil wrongs can include things like striking another person, causing a car accident through your poor driving, or causing a visitor to fall because you never had a chance to fix those rickety stairs leading into your home. If you are thinking that some of these civil wrongs sound like crimes, you would be right. However, unlike in criminal law where the wrongdoer will often be punished with jail time, tort law seeks to compensate the injured party. This compensation is usually in the form of money.

> **Legal Terminology**
>
> A tortfeasor is "liable" for committing a tort, not "guilty" of that tort. Lawyers reserve the term guilty for those convicted of committing a crime.

Legal research and writing[3]—This is the class that will teach you to write like a lawyer. Unlike your other classes, where your grade is based on one or two examinations, your writing professor will likely base your grade on a series of assignments that you must complete over the course of the entire year. Be sure to take this course seriously because employers have indicated that this is the most important course you will take during the first year of law school. The skills of legal research and writing are absolutely essential to the practice of law. In practice, you will use your research skills to review hundreds of sources in order to find the rule of law. Then you will use your writing skills to communicate this knowledge succinctly and clearly, and when necessary, persuasively.

---

3. Chapter X is devoted entirely to the topic of legal writing.

Structure of the U.S. Court System

In law school, you learn the law through a discussion of cases. To understand why we spend so much time reviewing cases, however, you need to have a basic understanding of the United States court system and our system of government. Unfortunately, students who do not come to law school with this knowledge can struggle to keep up during the first several weeks of classes.

I am sure that you remember from your high school civics class that there are three branches to our system of government: executive, legislative, and judicial. Once you learned the three branches of our government, your teachers taught you that the legislative branch makes the law, the executive branch enforces the law, and the judicial branch interprets the law. This notion is fine as far as it goes, but as law students you have to be aware that a level of complexity lies behind most general statements. For example, the executive branch of the government also generates laws, or rules, through various executive level administrative agencies.

As for the judicial branch, judges make law that we call **common law**.[4] Some use the term in a general fashion to cover every decision a court makes, and this would include interpreting statutes and rules created by the executive and legislative branches. Technically, however, common law is a somewhat narrower category of law, and is defined as law created and developed solely through judicial opinions. How judges create common law, and what it means for litigants in cases before the court, is an important aspect of why we emphasize case law in most first-year classes.

The structure of the United States court system is both vertical and hierarchical. This means that there are different levels to the court system, and as you progress up the structure, each court has progressively more power. To complicate matters even further, there are two independent and parallel court systems in the United States—the federal courts and the state courts. The information in Chart 1 on the facing page will help us continue our conversation.

Trial Courts

Much of the information we are about to discuss will be the focus of your civil procedure class. Therefore, don't expect to have a complete understanding after a few pages of a topic that you will cover for at least a semester and

---

4. Terms appearing in **bold** are also explained in the glossary.

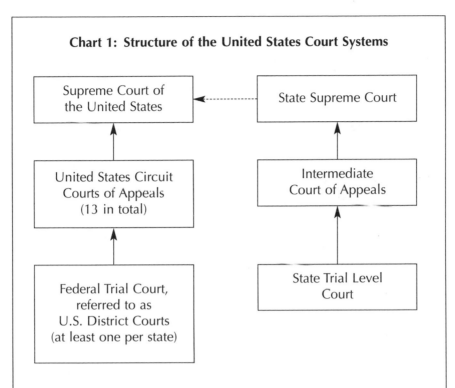

Chart 1: Structure of the United States Court Systems

Supreme Court of the United States

State Supreme Court

United States Circuit Courts of Appeals (13 in total)

Intermediate Court of Appeals

Federal Trial Court, referred to as U.S. District Courts (at least one per state)

State Trial Level Court

Here are a few additional points about this chart.

- This is an *extremely* simplified version of the federal and state court systems. On the federal side, for example, I have excluded any reference to appeals from administrative agency decisions, the United States Claims Court, or the Court of International Trade.
- For the most part, the state and federal court systems operate independently from each other. For example, most cases that are begun in state court cannot be appealed to the federal courts.
- On the state side, not all states have an intermediate court of appeals. In these states, appeals proceed directly to the state's supreme court.
- The dashed line leading from the state supreme court to the United States Supreme Court is meant to indicate that, in most instances, a state's supreme court is the final word on a matter of state law. In rare instances, however, a matter may be appealed from a state supreme court to the United States Supreme Court. This typically occurs where the state court has reviewed some aspect of federal law, including the United States Constitution.

likely the entire year. Instead, view this as background information that will help you better understand the cases you will be reading as a first-year student.

The first level in either the state or federal court system is the trial court. Trial courts are where the parties go to have their disputes resolved. On the federal side, we refer to trial courts as United States District Courts. Each state, the District of Columbia, and other U.S. Territories have at least one United States District Court. When a state has more than one federal district, however, a geographic designation is added to the name. For example, there is only one district court in Massachusetts, the United States District Court for the District of Massachusetts. In Iowa, where there are two district courts, they are referred to as the U.S. District Court for the Northern District, or Southern District, of Iowa. On the state side, the trial courts go by a variety of different names.

Trial courts hear two broad categories of disputes—criminal and civil. Criminal cases are just what you imagine they are. One party, a state or the federal government, is alleging that the other party, the defendant, has committed some crime. It is the government's burden to prove beyond a reasonable doubt that the defendant committed the crime.

In criminal cases, the government is a party to the matter and will be represented by a lawyer. In federal criminal cases, this lawyer will be an Assistant United States Attorney. In state criminal cases, the lawyer can go by many names but the most common designation is Assistant District Attorney or simply "A.D.A."

A lawyer, referred to as defense counsel, may represent the defendant as well. If the criminal defendant cannot afford a lawyer, then the court will appoint a lawyer to represent the defendant at no cost.[5] The requirement that the government appoint a lawyer to represent indigent criminal defendants applies in both state and federal criminal trials. A defendant may choose, however, to proceed without a lawyer and defend himself. In these rare instances, we say the defendant is proceeding *pro se.*

Civil cases cover all other disputes that are not criminal in nature. Disputes over the terms of a lease, disagreements over the terms of a contract, and demands for compensation for injuries suffered in a car accident are all civil matters. In most instances, civil lawsuits are between individuals or corporations, and the government is not a party to the lawsuit. Here, the party alleging that they have been harmed, the **plaintiff**, files a lawsuit against the other party, the **defendant**. While both parties are often represented by an attorney, it is

---

5. The Supreme Court established an indigent's right to counsel in a criminal case in *Gideon v. Wainwright*, 372 U.S. 335 (1963) based on the Court's interpretation of the 6th and 14th Amendments to the U.S. Constitution.

not required. If you cannot afford an attorney to help defend you in a civil case, the government does not have any obligation to appoint one for you.

Civil Cases

The first big decision the plaintiff in a civil action must make is whether to bring the lawsuit in a federal or state court. In some instances the plaintiff will have the option of starting the lawsuit in either. Whether the plaintiff has the option depends on whether the trial court has **subject matter jurisdiction** over the lawsuit. Subject matter jurisdiction is the power of the court to hear a particular type of lawsuit. State trial courts have very broad subject matter jurisdiction and plaintiffs may initiate most types of civil lawsuits in state court. In contrast, federal trial courts have relatively limited subject matter jurisdiction. In most instances, subject matter jurisdiction in federal courts will be based on the matter "arising under" federal law or the fact that the plaintiff and defendant are from different states.[6] In legal terminology you would say that the parties are **domiciled** in different states. The requirement that the litigants be domiciled in different states is also known as **diversity jurisdiction**, and was originally based on the notion that an out of state defendant might have difficulty obtaining a fair trial in the plaintiff's home state. In addition to the parties being domiciled in different states, the amount in controversy must exceed $75,000 for a federal trial court to have diversity jurisdiction.

Civil cases are initiated by filing a document called a **civil complaint**. A civil complaint is the first of many **pleadings**, or documents, that the parties will file during the course of a lawsuit. In a civil complaint, the plaintiff gets to tell his side of the story. The plaintiff provides the court with essential information through individually numbered paragraphs. Each paragraph contains important information such as the names of the parties, the location of the dispute, what happened, and why the plaintiff is entitled to some form of relief based on what happened. In federal civil cases, the plaintiff must lay out the basis for the court's jurisdiction over the matter.

Upon receipt of the civil complaint, the defendant will typically respond through another pleading called the **answer**. Through this document, the defendant responds to each of the complaint's numbered paragraphs by agreeing or disagreeing with the plaintiff's assertion. In some instances the defen-

---

6. These are the two most common aspects of federal subject matter jurisdiction that you will discuss in law school, but there are others. For example, federal courts have jurisdiction over cases in which the U.S. government is a party or where the controversy is between two states.

dant can decline to respond or simply note that he has no basis from which to agree or disagree with the assertions contained in the complaint.

After the pleadings phase, next comes **discovery**. Discovery is an investigative process where the attorneys obtain information necessary to the case. This information can come from any number of sources, including the opposing party. In addition to conducting your own research or even hiring a private investigator, some discovery devices allow a litigant to obtain information from opposing counsel. The most common discovery devices include depositions, interrogatories, admissions, and requests for production of documents ("RFPs").

A **deposition** is formal question and answer session with a witness. Typically, the witness swears to tell the truth during a deposition, so a lie may amount to the crime of perjury. Either a stenographer is present to document the questions and answers, or the responses are recorded electronically. Most witnesses and parties to a civil lawsuit may be deposed, including the opposing litigant. This process allows the attorney to obtain important information, and forces the witness to tell a consistent story. If the witness tries to tell a different story during the trial, then the attorney may be able to use the deposition testimony in an effort to discredit the witness.

Interrogatories are just what the term implies—a series of questions. Both the plaintiff and defendant are allowed to send a certain number of questions to opposing counsel, and the party must respond if he knows the answers. As with most rules, however, there are some exceptions. For example, a party does not have to respond to an interrogatory if the answer involves a privileged communication between a lawyer and his client.

While interrogatories are questions, **admissions** are statements of fact that a litigant is asked to declare as true. While no litigant would admit to liability through this discovery device, admissions are a helpful way of narrowing the contested issues for trial. For example, the plaintiff in an auto accident case might request an admission that the defendant owns a "green sports car." If the defendant answers in the affirmative, this fact is no longer in dispute for purposes of the trial.

The final discovery device, a **request for the production of documents,** allows a litigant to obtain and view important papers from the opposing litigant. Business records, a deed to a parcel of land, and tax returns are a few examples of the kinds of documents that an attorney may be able to obtain through an RFP.

Once started, trial court cases can end in one of three ways: by agreement of the parties; by motion; or by trial. Most civil cases are resolved through an agreement between the parties. The parties will often negotiate some type of settlement where each party gets some part of what they want. Most often this means that the plaintiff receives some percentage of the amount of money being sought. If the parties are sufficiently satisfied with the settlement they have negotiated, they will voluntarily consent to the dismissal of the case.

If negotiations fail to produce a settlement, then the case may be resolved through a **motion** brought by one of the parties. Any request for a judge to take an action during the course of a lawsuit is done through a motion. Two types of motions, a motion to dismiss[7] and a motion for summary judgment, can end the lawsuit before it ever reaches the trial stage. I will not spend a great deal of time discussing these motions because to truly understand them you will need to spend several weeks in your civil procedure class reviewing them. For now, simply remember that a motion to dismiss is brought fairly early during the course of the lawsuit, and the moving party is saying that even if everything stated in the complaint is true, the plaintiff still cannot win. When a party files a motion for summary judgment in a civil case, they are arguing that the material facts are not in dispute and that the law dictates the moving party should win.[8] If these motions are denied by the court, then the matter will proceed to trial unless the parties settle the case.

Whether dealing with a civil or criminal matter, a trial is the vehicle that we use in this country to resolve legal disputes. The trial process addresses two types of questions—questions of fact and questions of law. A question of fact arises when the parties disagree as to what happened. For example, in a car accident case one party might testify that the car was traveling at 75 miles per hour in a 40 mile per hour zone while another party might place the speed at 40 miles per hour. The conflicting testimony as to the speed of the vehicle creates a question of fact. The next question is "who resolves questions of fact?"

The **trier of fact**, who will be either the judge or the jury, resolves questions of fact. If the parties agree to a jury waived trial, then the judge will be the one who listens to the testimony and decides what really happened. If not, then a jury will be the trier of fact, and will get to resolve the factual disputes brought up by the case. Regardless of whether a judge or jury acts as the trier of fact, their roles will be the same.

The trier of fact reviews the evidence and decides what actually happened. The evidence can take many forms—witness testimony, photographs, video,

---

7. For purposes of this discussion I am referring to a motion to dismiss for failure to state a claim upon which relief can be granted. *See* Federal Rule of Civil Procedure 12(b)(6).

8. Under Rule 56(c) of the Federal Rules of Civil Procedure, the moving party in a motion for summary judgment prevails if "there is no genuine issue as to any material fact and that the moving party is entitled to a judgment as a matter of law."

etc.—and will often be contradictory. By that I mean the evidence introduced by the defendant will likely contradict the evidence introduced by the government or plaintiff, and vice versa. In addition to testimony of the witnesses, the trier of fact is entitled to consider the witness's body language on the stand, and any motivation the witness might have to lie. A judge or jury's resolution of factual dispute in a trial is called a **finding of fact**. For example, if the jury concludes in a traffic accident case that the light was red and not green, we say that the jury has found that the light was red.

During the course of a trial, questions of law will often arise and it is the judge's job to answer these questions in the form of **conclusions of law**. The most typical conclusions of law include decisions on the parties' motions, rulings on the admissibility of evidence, and rulings on the parties' objections. When the judge comes to a decision on a question of law, the jury may not reconsider the question. For example, if the judge decides that a certain piece of evidence should be excluded from the trial, the jury may not choose to consider that evidence when it deliberates.

In a civil case, the plaintiff has the burden of proof. This means the plaintiff has alleged that the defendant has done something wrong, so the plaintiff has to prove the case to the jury. It is the plaintiff's job to prove her case by a **preponderance of the evidence**, not the defendant's job to prove that she did nothing wrong. Under the preponderance of the evidence standard, which is the standard of proof in most civil matters, the plaintiff must convince the jury that the evidence weighs in her favor. If we were actually using a scale to weigh the evidence, it would only need to tip slightly in favor of the plaintiff for her to win the case.

Because the plaintiff has the burden of proof, she will be the first one to present evidence during the trial. When the plaintiff's attorney brings in witnesses and asks them questions, she is performing a **direct examination** of a witness. Once the plaintiff has finished asking questions, it is the defendant's turn to ask questions in the form of a **cross examination** of the witness. Once the defendant has finished, the plaintiff may ask the witness additional questions through a **redirect examination** of the witness or may introduce additional evidence.

The plaintiff will **rest** once she has finished introducing evidence. Once the plaintiff has rested, it will be the defendant's turn, but the defendant does not have to introduce evidence of her own. If the defendant does not believe that the plaintiff has met her burden of proof, she can decide not to introduce any evidence of her own. More typically, however, the defendant will attempt to introduce evidence that contradicts the plaintiff's version of events and that tells the defendant's side of the story.

Once both sides have rested, the defendant will typically make a motion for a **judgment as a matter of law** or, depending on the jurisdiction, a **directed verdict**. Regardless of the name, the point of this motion is the same. The defendant is asserting that the evidence is so weak that no reasonable jury could find for the prosecution. *See* Fed. R. Civ. Proc. 50(a). Therefore, the judge should end the case in favor of the defendant without allowing the jury to deliberate. If the judge allows the motion, the case is over and the jury will not deliberate. The plaintiff's only option would be to appeal the case to a higher court. If the court denies the motion, the case proceeds. In jury trials, the judge will next instruct the jurors as to the law, their role in the process, and what they may consider when coming to their decision. The jurors are then **sequestered** and they attempt to decide the case relying on the facts provided by the litigants and the law given by the judge. Once they have finished their deliberations, the jurors will return to the courtroom where their verdict will be announced.

If the jury finds in favor of the plaintiff, the defendant may renew her motion for a judgment as a matter of law. In some jurisdictions, this is referred to as a motion for a **judgment non obstante veredicto**, Latin for judgment not withstanding the verdict ("JNOV"). The only real difference between this motion and the original motion for a judgment as a matter of law is timing. Counsel makes a JNOV motion after the jury returns a verdict while a motion for a judgment as a matter of law is made before the jury begins deliberating. If the judge denies this motion as well, the trial court phase of the case is over and the only option left to the parties is an appeal to a higher court.

Criminal Cases

Criminal cases follow a path similar to civil cases, but with some important differences. For example, some criminal matters can also be initiated by a type of complaint called a **criminal complaint**.[9] One important difference, however, is that the state initiates the lawsuit through the criminal complaint, not the victim. A criminal complaint lists the crime(s) the defendant is being charged with, as well as some very general information supporting the charge. In many jurisdictions, however, prosecutors utilize criminal complaints only when charging the defendant with relatively minor crimes. In these states, and

---

9. In some jurisdictions, this document is referred to as an **information**.

in the federal system, more serious criminal prosecutions are initiated through a grand jury proceeding.

Through a grand jury proceeding, the prosecution is seeking to obtain an **indictment** based on the defendant's alleged criminal conduct. To obtain the indictment, the prosecution must convince the grand jury that there is probable cause to believe that the defendant committed the crime in question. The probable cause standard used in the grand jury is far easier to meet than the **beyond a reasonable doubt** standard used in criminal trials. Therefore, it is easier for the government to indict an individual than it is to obtain a conviction. If a majority of the grand jurors vote favorably regarding the indictment, they are said to have returned a **true bill**. We refer to a negative vote by the grand jury as a **no bill**. If the grand jury returns a true bill, then the case will end through the one of the same three mechanisms used in civil matters—settlement (plea bargain), motion, and trial.

While the amount of money changing hands is usually the deciding factor in whether a civil case is settled, the level of crime agreed to by the defendant is most often the main issue in criminal settlements. In these cases, the government will have charged the defendant with committing a specific crime that carries a punishment in the form of jail time, a fine, or both. The government's lawyer and the defendant can negotiate a settlement where the defendant will agree to having committed a lesser crime. The defendant gets a lesser fine or a shorter jail sentence and the government can avoid the uncertainty of a trial where the jury may find the defendant not guilty. While the government's lawyer and defense counsel are the ones who work out the settlement, the trial court judge must still agree to it. If the parties cannot settle the case, then the case may still be ended before a trial takes place through a motion brought by the defendant.

Similar to the parties in a civil trial, the defendant in a criminal matter may also make a motion to dismiss the case. In a criminal motion to dismiss, defense counsel is arguing that the grand jury did not have enough evidence to establish probable cause that a crime was committed by the defendant. The probable cause standard is relatively easy to satisfy, however, so the defendant is unlikely to prevail on this motion. The defendant may have a better opportunity of success with a motion to suppress. Through a motion to suppress, the defendant is alleging some constitutional irregularity with the evidence gathering process. If the court allows the motion, the prosecution is precluded from using some or even all of the gathered evidence at trial. Technically, a motion to suppress does not end the trial process. As a practical matter, however, a case is likely to be dismissed if the court suppresses much of the prosecution's evidence.

In a criminal matter, the trial proceeds in much the same way as it does in a civil case. As noted earlier, it is the state through the district attorney's office that is trying to prove the case. Just like the plaintiff in a civil case, the DA will be the first one to present evidence. The DA will not, however, be able to call the defendant to the stand as a witness. Under the Fifth Amendment to the United States Constitution, the defendant in a criminal case has a right against self incrimination. Therefore, while the defendant can choose to take the stand in her own defense, the state cannot compel her to do so. If the defendant chooses not to testify, the judge will instruct the jury at the end of the case that they are not allowed to draw any negative inferences from this decision.

After the prosecution finishes introducing evidence, the defendant may make a motion for a **required finding of not guilty**. While the terminology used can vary from jurisdiction to jurisdiction, this motion is quite similar to a motion for a directed verdict or a motion for a judgment as a matter of law. In each of these instances, the moving party is asserting that the evidence is insufficient to prove the case as a matter of law. As such, the judge should rule in favor of the defendant and end the trial. If this motion fails, the defendant has the option of introducing evidence or allowing the matter to go to the jury.

Once the defendant has rested, the judge will instruct the jury on the law and then give them the case for deliberation. If the jury returns a verdict for the defendant, the trial is over and the prosecution cannot file an appeal. This is the end of the line for the prosecution. If the prosecution prevails, however, the defendant may once again move for required finding of not guilty, or in some jurisdictions a JNOV. The denial of this motion leaves the defendant with only one more option—appealing the matter to a higher court.

The Intermediate Court of Appeals

Because all litigants have a right of appeal,[10] appellate courts are necessary in both the federal and state system. If you look back to Chart #1, you will see that an intermediate court of appeals is the next level of court in our hierarchical system. On the federal side, the courts are referred to as United States Circuit Courts of Appeals. There are 11 numbered circuits (1st Circuit Court of Appeals, 2d Circuit Court of Appeals, etc.), and each hears appeals originating in the federal district courts within the circuit they cover. (See Chart #1). In

---

10. In criminal matters, the state may not appeal a verdict of not guilty.

addition, the D.C. Circuit Court of Appeals hears appeals from federal trial cases originating in the District of Columbia and hears appeals from many federal administrative agencies. Finally, the Federal Circuit Court of Appeals has jurisdiction over the U.S. Court of International Trade, U.S. Claims Court, the Court of Veterans' Appeals, and patent appeals.

On the state side, there is a great deal of variation from state to state. Maine, for example, does not have an intermediate court of appeals and all appeals proceed directly to their court of last resort, the Maine Supreme Judicial Court. Due to the number of appeals being filed by litigants over the last several years, more and more states do have an intermediate court of appeals that handles the bulk of appeals.

The Court of Last Resort

The highest level court in either the state or federal court systems is occupied by the court of last resort. In the federal system, the court of last resort is the United States Supreme Court. While all litigants have a right of appeal, this right in the federal system is usually satisfied by an appeal to one of the United States Circuit Courts of Appeals. In most instances, an appeal to the United States Supreme Court is a matter of discretion as opposed to a matter of right. Parties seeking review by the Supreme Court must file a petition *for writ of certiorari with* the court. Through the petition, the party seeking the writ will lay out why the U.S. Supreme Court should grant certiorari and hear the case.[11] A writ of certiorari "will be granted only for compelling reasons."[12] Examples where the Supreme Court may grant certiorari include instances when: (1) the Circuit Courts of Appeals are in conflict on an issue; (2) a state court of last resort has ruled on a matter of federal law that should be resolved by the Supreme Court; or (3) a state court has ruled in a way that is contrary to established federal law.[13] When the United States Supreme Court hears a case, its ruling is the final word on interpreting federal law including the United States Constitution.

On the state side, the courts of last resort go by different names but they all perform the same basic function. On matters of state law, which covers most of the issues that come before state trial courts, a state's court of last resort is the final word on interpreting the law. If a state does not have an intermediate court of appeals, then trial court litigants have a right to appeal

---

11. Supreme Court Rule 14.
12. *See* Supreme Court Rule 10.
13. *Id.*

their case directly to that state's supreme court. In states with an intermediate court of appeals, appeals to the court of last resort are often accepted as a matter of discretion and not as a matter of right.

The Role of the Appellate Court

An appellate court has two main functions. One is to resolve questions regarding unsettled points of law and the other is to correct a trial court's incorrect application of a settled point of law. Another way to put it is that appellate courts deal with issues of law, not issues of fact. During the trial, the judge and jury were in the best position to review the evidence, so an appellate court will defer to their conclusions regarding the resolution of factual disputes. However, if a question arises as to whether errors of law were made during the trial, for example an incorrect ruling on an objection, then the appellate court may be asked to review that ruling. The *Mary v. John* fact pattern contains both questions of law and questions of fact.

Mary v. John
Questions of Fact and Questions of Law

John is driving through an intersection when he hits Mary's car. They cannot agree on what happened, so they go to trial to resolve the dispute. During the jury trial, John testifies that the light was green as he was passing through the intersection. Mary's witness testifies that he was standing on the corner with a friend on the date of the accident and the friend told him that the light had just turned red as John entered the intersection. John's lawyer objects to the witness' statement, arguing that it not be admitted into the trial because it is **hearsay**. The judge disagrees and allows in the witness' testimony. Mary wins the case and John later appeals the decision to an appellate court.

In the above example, the jury will get to decide who they believe, Mary's witness or John. Whether the light was red or green is a question of fact, and the jury's decision on this point cannot be reviewed by an appellate court. However, the appeals court may review whether the trial judge correctly admitted the statement into evidence or whether it should have been excluded as hearsay. This decision is a question of law, and an appellate court has the power to address questions of law. If the appellate court decides that the trial court judge made a mistake, it could order a new trial. While the appellate court's decision is certainly important to the parties in the lawsuit, it is important for another reason.

A decision by an appellate court not only binds the litigants in that dispute, but it may also bind litigants in future disputes. Decisions that must be followed by litigants in future lawsuits are called **binding precedent**. Whether a decision is binding precedent depends on the level of the appellate court in the hierarchy and where the original lawsuit took place.

For example, let's say that the *Mary v. John* case took place in Kentucky, and that John is now appealing the matter to the Kentucky Court of Appeals. The Kentucky Court of Appeals hears arguments from both John and Mary, and agrees with John and **holds,** or decides, that the witness' statement was hearsay and that it should have been excluded from the trial. This decision by the Court of Appeals is now law in Kentucky, and all judges in the Kentucky trial courts must follow the decision when dealing with the same facts.[14] Judges in other states and in the federal system, however, are free to come to a different conclusion even if presented with similar facts. Finally, while the decision binds trial court judges in Kentucky, the state's court of last resort, the Kentucky Supreme Court, is free to rule differently.

Continuing with our sample case, the appeals court would not have decided *John v. Mary* in a vacuum. Instead, the judges will look at other legal authority to help answer the question before them. The judges would likely start with earlier decisions from both the Kentucky Court of Appeals and the Kentucky Supreme Court. If cases from their own jurisdiction are not helpful in resolving the case, the Court can look to decisions from courts in other jurisdictions and, potentially, legal treatises when coming to its conclusion. These forms of legal authority fall into two broad categories, **primary authority** and **secondary authority**, and each category has a number of subdivisions.

Simply stated, primary authority is the law, and the law can take many forms. Whether the law takes the form of a statute, a constitution, a judicial decision, a rule of procedure, or an administrative agency decision, it is all primary authority and the law. Primary authority can be further divided into binding (or mandatory) primary authority and **persuasive primary author-**

14. A lower court in Kentucky would not have to follow the decision, however, if the material facts of the new case were distinguishable from those in *Mary v. John*. For example, a lower court might rule differently if a witness used different words or if the words were introduced for a different purpose.

Types of Authority

	Mandatory/Binding Authority	Persuasive Authority
Primary Authority *The law. This includes statutes, appellate court decisions, rules of procedures, and constitutions.*	Primary authority is mandatory or binding if it originates in the same jurisdiction where the court making the decision is located. For example, Minnesota statutory law and rulings from the Minnesota State Supreme Court MUST be followed by throughout the state of Minnesota. When referring to mandatory case law, lawyers tend to use the term "binding precedent" as opposed to binding authority.	Primary authority is persuasive authority if it originates in another jurisdiction. For instance, a decision from the Texas State Supreme Court is binding authority in Texas, but is only persuasive authority in Rhode Island.
Secondary Authority *Any other material that a court relies on coming to a decision. Examples include legal treatises and law review articles.*	Secondary authority is never, by itself, mandatory authority. The most brilliant legal scholar in the world may write a universally praised article in a legal journal, but no court or legislature would be bound to follow her opinion. Legislatures can adopt secondary authority, the Uniform Commercial Code for example, and then it becomes law and binding authority.	All forms of secondary authority are persuasive authority. All sources of persuasive authority are not created equal. For example, decisions from well-respected appellate courts sitting in a different jurisdiction tend to be more persuasive than law review articles written by academics.

ity. **Binding primary authority** is law that must be followed. Persuasive primary authority is also the law, but likely originates in another jurisdiction and the court is under no obligation to follow it. Thus, a court may be persuaded by the logic behind another jurisdiction's law and choose to follow it, but the court will not be required to do so.

Whether primary authority is mandatory or not depends on the state where the litigation is taking place, where the law was created, and which court within the state is hearing the matter. For example, if the Massachusetts Supreme Judicial Court interprets a dog walking statute to require leashes that are at least 4 feet long, this new law is primary binding authority for litigants in Massachusetts but has no impact on California litigants. In future Massachusetts cases, the issue of how long a leash must be has been resolved. In California, the law would be considered persuasive primary authority because the decision is law, but from another jurisdiction. As such, the legislature or courts of California may be persuaded to adopt a similar rule, but they are not required to do so. Courts are not limited to considering primary authority, however, and often review secondary authority when deciding a case.

Secondary authority includes materials that comment on the law or suggest the future direction of the law, but these materials are not law themselves. Therefore, secondary authority is never mandatory and may only be persuasive authority. Forms of secondary authority include **legal treatises, restatements of law**, legal encyclopedias, legal dictionaries, and **law review articles**. While these are examples of the most common types of persuasive authority relied upon by courts, almost anything can be persuasive authority. The only requirement is that it helps persuade the court to adopt a particular position. Keep in mind that not all persuasive authority is created equal. For example, secondary materials published in leading law journals by recognized experts in a field are more likely to persuade a court as to a particular point of view than short articles appearing in local legal newspapers. While the basics of primary and persuasive authority apply to case law, the terminology used may be different. For example, appellate court decisions are often referred to as **precedential authority**. Precedential authority is simply law derived from an appellate case. If you happen to be a litigant within this appellate court's jurisdiction, then the decision is considered **binding precedent**.

A corollary principle to that of binding precedent is *stare decisis*, which is Latin for "to stand by things decided." Under this principle, courts must follow binding precedent when confronted by similar facts in later cases. Without *stare decisis*, there would be no consistency within our judicial system.

New judges would be free to review and change settled points of law for no reason other than they disagreed with the original decision. While *stare decisis* is a powerful concept, it is not without its limitations. Courts do not blindly follow established precedent when to do so no longer makes sense due to other changes in the law or to changes within our society.

One of the most famous examples of a court departing from *stare decisis* is the doctrine of "separate but equal." In *Plessy vs. Ferguson*,[15] the United States Supreme Court upheld the segregation of African Americans so long as they were provided with "separate but equal" education and transportation facilities.[16] Although it took nearly 60 years, the Supreme Court overturned *Plessy* in the case of Brown vs. Board of Education,[17] in which the court reasoned that separate education facilities were "inherently unequal."[18]

Federalism

One of the more confusing aspects of the United States system of government is the concept of federalism. The division between the state and federal court systems is but one aspect of federalism, a concept that you will review in your civil procedure and constitutional law courses. Federalism involves the relationship "among the states and relationship between the states and the federal government,"[19] and is governed by the United States Constitution. While there is a great deal of nuance to this concept, a basic understanding of the idea is all that is required at this point.

Simply remember that each state is entitled to make and interpret its own laws without interference from the federal government. In most instances, a state's supreme court is the final word regarding interpretations of that state's law, and the United States Supreme Court may not review the issue. This comes as a surprise to many people who are under the mistaken belief that federal courts always trump state courts. There are a few instances, however, where federal courts do have the final word.

When state courts are required to interpret the United States Constitution, and this does occur, the state court must follow the decisions of the United States Supreme Court in coming to its conclusion. Importantly, decisions

---

15. 163 U.S. 537 (1896).
16. *Id.*
17. 347 U.S. 483 (1954).
18. *Id.*
19. Black's Law Dictionary 627 (7th ed. 1999).

from other federal courts, including the various Circuit Courts of Appeals are only persuasive authority. In this scenario, the United States Supreme Court is the final word on interpreting the U.S. Constitution.

Also, the U.S. Constitution bestows certain rights on individuals. No state may interpret its laws in such a way that citizens of that state receive fewer rights than those guaranteed by the U.S. Constitution. In interpreting its own state constitution, however a state may bestow additional rights on its citizens. For example, the United States Supreme Court decided in Miranda v. Arizona[20] that officers must inform criminal suspects of certain rights. These rights are laid out through the now familiar *Miranda* warning—the suspect has a right to remain silent, the right to an attorney, and the right to have an attorney appointed if the defendant is indigent. The Supreme Court was interpreting the United States Constitution when it decided *Miranda*, which is why police officers throughout the U.S. must read the Miranda warning to a suspect or run the risk that evidence will be excluded from the trial. No state court may overturn the *Miranda* decision, but state appellate courts can expand upon *Miranda*.

A state appellate court may decide that the Miranda warning is fine as far as it goes, but that it doesn't go far enough. For example, in addition to warning the defendant that he has a right to remain silent, a state court may require that officers explain that the defendant can stop giving a statement to the police at any time. A ruling like this one does not run afoul of the Supreme Court's decision in *Miranda v. Arizona* because the state has given the defendant an additional right.

Casebooks and the Casebook Method

Typically, your law school casebooks contain appellate court decisions as opposed to trial court decisions. Why? Think back to our earlier discussion about the role of the appellate courts. Because appellate court decisions bind the litigants in future disputes, they are viewed as law that must be followed.

For many students, law school casebooks are their first hint of the uniqueness of the law school experience. Prior to the beginning of the semester, many dutiful 1Ls go to the bookstore to purchase their casebooks to "get a jump" on everyone else. After they get over the sticker shock of spending several hun-

---

20. 384 U.S. 436 (1966).

dred dollars for a semester's worth of materials, they go home and open a casebook to page 1 and start reading. After about five minutes, some of these students will question their decision to come to law school!

As the term implies, law school "casebooks" are quite a bit different than most college "textbooks." While textbooks provide further explanation of the concepts that a professor might have lectured on in class, casebooks contain little more than cases. Instead of explaining concepts, your casebooks are the jumping off point for your exploration of most legal concepts. In fact, cases often generate more questions than answers. You will review some of the answers in class, but many concepts will require further review after class either on your own or with your classmates.

In part, we use casebooks in law school to teach you about judge made law. There is, however, more to the story. If we simply wanted to teach you the law, we would not bother with casebooks. We could simply hand every 1L a list of rules on the first day of class and have them memorize those rules in time for graduation. If the cases are not simply about memorizing rules, then why we do we use them? Part of the answer can be found by reviewing our definitions of stare decisis and binding precedent.

Remember, courts are bound to follow decisions from the appellate courts within the same jurisdiction if confronted with similar facts in later cases. If the facts are different, then a different conclusion may be permissible or even required. If you were about to ask "how different," then congratulate yourself on actively engaging the topic with me. There is no simple answer to this question. Instead, one must carefully review the court's decision to determine which facts the court deemed important, or material, to its conclusion. Finding the **material facts** is no easy task, and you may spend an entire class dissecting a case in order to extract a single kernel of information.

In addition, the casebook method allows you to review a single concept from multiple perspectives. You might read three cases with essentially the same facts where the courts arrive at different conclusions. The reason can be as simple as the time frame for the decisions or that the cases originated in different jurisdictions.

Elements — Pieces to the Law School Puzzle

In law school, you will spend a great deal of time breaking rules down into their constituent parts. In many instances, these individual pieces of a rule are called elements. Independently, each of these elements may be viewed as a rule of its own. If you are truly dealing with the elements of a rule, then each piece must be proven in order to establish the broader rule. If one piece of the puzzle is missing, then the rule has not been proven. This concept will be a bit easier to understand if we use an example.

One of the rules you will likely learn about in your criminal law class is larceny. A fairly typical definition of larceny is:

> The trespassory taking and carrying away of the personal property of another with the intent to deprive the other of that property permanently.[21]

To convict the defendant of a larceny, the state would have to prove beyond a reasonable doubt that the defendant's actions fell within the above definition. So far, so good. You may not realize, however, that this rule of larceny is actually comprised of several smaller rules or pieces. In this instance, these pieces are elements because the state *must* prove all of them to establish a larceny. If we break this larger rule down into constituent parts, we end up with the following.

A larceny is the:

- Taking
- And Carrying Away
- Of the Personal Property
- Of another
- With the intent to deprive the other of that property
- Permanently

Remember, the state must prove all of these elements in order to prove that the defendant committed a larceny. This means that the state must prove beyond a reasonable doubt that there was a taking. The state must also prove beyond a reasonable doubt that the defendant carried something away. Then, the state must prove beyond a reasonable doubt that the item carried away was indeed personal property, and so on.

The concept of elements is not limited to criminal matters. For example, if you are suing a homeowner after you fall on their rickety stairs, you will be suing for the civil wrong of negligence. The concept of negligence is also divided into elements, and those elements are:

- Whether the homeowner had a **duty** to maintain the stairs properly, and
- Did the homeowner **breach** that duty through the manner in which he maintained the stairs, and
- Did the homeowner's breach of his duty **cause** the alleged harm, and

---

21. Joshua Dressler, Understanding Criminal Law § 32.02 (3d ed. 2001).

- Did you suffer **harm** or **damages** as a result of the homeowner's breach of duty

You must prove all of these elements in order to prove the tort of negligence. Your failure to prove even one of these elements means that you have not established the tort of negligence.

There is one important difference between the prosecution's burden in a criminal trial and plaintiff's burden in a civil matter. In most civil matters, the plaintiff must prove their case by a preponderance of the evidence as opposed to beyond a reasonable doubt. As noted above, a preponderance of the evidence means that the trier of fact is over 50% sure that the plaintiff should win. From the very wording of these standards, you probably realize that the beyond a reasonable doubt test is much more difficult to satisfy. Judges do not use numbers when explaining beyond a reasonable doubt. Instead, judges explain that beyond a reasonable doubt means that you are sure to a "moral certainty," understanding that the defendant may lose his liberty based on your decision.

So, what does the concept of elements mean in the context of law school? It affects everything from how you read your cases to your exam writing. For example, you might spend an entire class period reviewing how one case interprets a single element of the crime of larceny. After class, you will review your understanding of this single element and try to incorporate this knowledge into a broader understanding of criminal law in general and larceny more specifically. Finally, when you are confronted by a larceny issue on your criminal law examination, you will be sure to address each element separately to determine whether a larceny took place.

Review Questions

To test whether you truly understood the ideas contained within this chapter, try answering the following questions. Some are quite simple and are merely testing whether you remembered some term or definition. The more complicated questions use the basic information provided in this chapter as a starting point, but require active thinking on your part.

True or False

1. _____ The United States Supreme Court is always the final word on matters of state and federal law.

2. _____ Federal trial courts are referred to as United States District Courts.

3. _____ Appellate courts resolve questions of fact, not questions of law.

4. _____ A *pro se* litigant is one who has decided to handle his case without the assistance of a lawyer.

5. _____ All litigants in a civil trial have a right of appeal.

6. _____ In the federal system, the court of last resort is the United States Supreme Court.

7. _____ A litigant unhappy with a decision handed down by the United States First Circuit Courts of Appeals has a right to have the matter heard by the United States Supreme Court.

8. _____ All state court systems include a trial court, an intermediate court of appeals, and a court of last resort.

9. _____ Primary persuasive authority is not law.

10. _____ Generally, courts must follow primary authority that originates in the same jurisdiction where the court sits.

Short Answer

Provide a brief explanation for your answer when responding to these questions.

1. Must the government appoint counsel for an indigent defendant in a civil matter?

_____

_____

2. During a trial, the witness tries to testify that she heard the defendant say "I'm going to shoot," but defense counsel objects because the testimony falls under the legal definition of hearsay. Despite the objection, the trial judge allows in the testimony. May an appellate court review the trial judge's decision?

   _____

   _____

   _____

3. May an appellate court use case law from other jurisdictions to support its opinions?

   _____

   _____

   _____

4. What is the difference between primary mandatory authority and primary persuasive authority?

   _____

   _____

   _____

5. Under the doctrine of *stare decisis*, must an appellate court always follow its earlier decisions?

   _____

   _____

   _____

6. Name two types of secondary authority.

   _____

   _____

   _____

7. May an appellate court use secondary authority as support for its decisions?

   _____

   _____

   _____

CHAPTER II

Maintaining a Healthy Mental Approach to Law School

Law school can be an extremely stressful environment, and you must maintain a healthy approach throughout the year if you expect to perform well and enjoy your time as a student. While students enter law school suffering from clinical stress and depression at a rate that mirrors the national average, this number skyrockets during the first year of law school. Studies have shown that law students suffer from clinical stress and depression at a rate that is three to four times higher than the national average.[1] Should you think that the problem is confined to first-year law students, these same studies indicate that student stress rises steadily through the third year of law school and then improves only moderately after graduation. New graduates show signs of stress that is twice the national average. These numbers are quite sobering, but it is not my intent to frighten you. These statistics are intended as a warning. Do not neglect your mental health during law school. If you do, debilitating stress and/or depression is a possibility. It is a problem, however, that you can prepare for and protect yourself against.

Dealing with the Unknown

New situations in life can be stressful, and law school is full of new experiences. For example, while every law student has graduated from a college or university, few have any idea of what law school will be like. Attempts to familiarize yourself with the unique aspects of a law school education before you arrive for the fall semester can help you deal with stress before it ever begins. In fact, one of the reasons I have written this book is to help students

---

1. Stephen B. Shanfield & G. Andrew H. Benjamin, *Psychiatric Distress in Law Students,* 35 J. LEGAL. EDUC. 65 n.1 (1985).

acquaint themselves with law school. Law school itself is not the only new thing that students may have to deal with.

For example, consider your law school's location. If your law school is located in an urban environment and you are used to living in a more rural setting, the hustle and bustle of the city can be unnerving. On the other end of the spectrum, city dwellers can become frustrated by the quiet found in law schools located in more bucolic settings. Also, is your law school located in your home state or in another part of the country? Regional differences can be enjoyable to experience while on vacation, but may not be so much fun when one is confronted by them for months at a time. Also, quick trips home may not be a viable option if you take into account cost, distance, and the fact that law school studies consume so much time. I am not suggesting that these differences, and dozens of others like them, are unique to law school students; any college student who has experienced a bit of homesickness will attest to that. When these issues are coupled with some of law schools unique stressors, homesickness can turn into something far more serious.

Law students also face the unknown in the form of a lack of feedback from their professors. In many law schools, students receive feedback through midterm and final examinations and nothing more. With competition for grades so high, a point that will be discussed shortly, a lack of feedback can lead to extremes in studying. Some students engage in hyper studying. These students are convinced that they know so little about their classes that they must study to the exclusion of all else, including sufficient eating and sleeping. Other students are paralyzed into inaction by the lack of feedback. These students are also convinced that they know little about their classes, but do not know where to begin their studies. Instead of starting something, they accomplish little or nothing.

Grading and Competition

Law school students can be extremely competitive. This is not surprising when one considers that offers from the highest paying and most prestigious legal employers are based heavily on first-year grades. Unlike college where students can adjust to a new environment at a relatively leisurely pace, the push for law school grades can generate a more frenzied approach to studying where students try to obtain every edge possible.

In addition, good grades can be more difficult to come by in law school than in college. First, law students quite often represent the very best students from their respective colleges and universities. Students who were accustomed to being the smartest or hardest working members of their college classes are suddenly thrust into an environment where their classmates are similarly intelligent and hard working. Second, many law schools grade on a curve. While colleges and other graduate programs are subject to a fair degree of grade inflation, this phenomenon is not as prevalent in law schools. This leads to many law students receiving the first "C" in their academic careers.

Students can deal with stress rooted in grades by channeling it into a more productive form of competition. For example, many students want to be in the top 10% of their class. The need to achieve this goal is often perpetuated, both explicitly and implicitly, by faculty, administrators, and placement offices. If every law student "needs" to be in the top 10% of the class, then 90% of them are doomed to failure by their own standards. Instead of striving for a particular spot in the academic pecking order, students should attempt to achieve their personal best.

Asking the best from yourself is no small task. It requires that you do everything within your power to succeed. Consider this for a moment. How often in your life have you done everything possible to succeed? Keep in mind that your personal best may not translate into "A's" or even "B's" on your examinations. However, by definition your personal best means that you had nothing left to give. Anyone whose grades represent their best work has to be satisfied. Keep in mind that doing your best is not the same thing as working yourself to the point of exhaustion. Law school will require a great deal of time and effort, but you must have a life beyond law school if you expect to do your best in your classes.

The Fall Doldrums

While the pace of law school can be a bit daunting during the first few weeks of class, it can also be exhilarating. Your new environment, new challenges, and new friends all contribute to a sense of excitement that, hopefully, will never disappear. Unfortunately, it usually does.

About midway through the first semester, many students begin to feel a mounting sense of anxiety. From the outside looking in, the reasons for this are fairly obvious. First, most classes start off the semester at a relatively slow pace, and begin to pick things up in late September or October. Your professor will suddenly go from covering 1 or 2 cases per class to 5 or 6 cases. In addition, the days are getting progressively shorter, and for those of you in more Northern latitudes, significantly colder. In some schools, mid-term examinations are getting closer every day, and because of this some students adopt a more competitive approach to their studies. Together, all of these things start to wear away the sheen from the law school experience. You have officially entered the fall doldrums. Thankfully, there are a number of ways to avoid the doldrums and maintain a healthy outlook throughout the entire academic year.

Self Help for Law School Stress

The first step to maintaining a healthy mental approach in law school is to treat yourself well. Later in this book I will discuss the need to approach law school in a scheduled fashion, and part of that schedule must include making time for yourself. At times, law school can seem all consuming and that you will have to work constantly in order to stay on top of your studies. I won't lie to you—law school will demand a great deal of your time and energy. If law school starts taking up all of your time, however, your studying will become counterproductive.

Studying more is not always the solution. There is a limit to the amount of information your mind can assimilate in a single day. Once you have reached this limit, additional studying produces less in the way of returns for your efforts. Have you ever pulled an all night cram session before a college exam? Did you find yourself having to re-read sentences, paragraphs, or even whole pages of material because you seemed to forget the information as soon as you read it? Did you notice that other ideas would intrude into your mind, sapping your focus and energy? When these things start to happen, it is because your brain is sending you a message, and the message is ENOUGH! Hopefully, you will rarely reach this point.

One of the best pieces of advice I ever received about law school is that you should treat your studies like a job. Comparing your law school studies to a job may sound like I'm making things worse rather than better! In certain important respects, however, treating a typical law school day like a work day will lead to a more scheduled and balanced life.

Start Your Day Early and On Time

Unless you work third shift at the local manufacturing plant, the work day typically begins between 8:00 and 9:00 AM and so should your study day. Human beings are diurnal creatures, which means that we work best during the daylight hours. As the day progresses, our energies slowly dissipate making it more difficult to accomplish complex tasks. This first aspect to treating your studies like a job is the most difficult for many students to accept.

When I make this point during my law school orientation lectures, several students will comment that they are night owls. They studied during the evenings throughout college, performed reasonably well and see no reason to change. Certain study habits are unique to each individual, and I don't doubt the truthfulness of students who tell me that they've always studied in the evenings and still performed well. Further, I am not saying that it is impossible to study evenings and perform reasonably well in law school. My point is that you will be more efficient in your studying if you begin early in the day.

Becoming efficient in your study habits is no small thing. Studying efficiently means you will accomplish more in less time. Most professors will tell you that you need to spend three hours studying for every hour of class time. This translates into between 55 and 65 hours per week studying pre-class, in class, and post-class. Considering the number of hours you will spend studying, the need for efficiency should be apparent. Night time studying works in college, in part, because you rarely spent 55–65 hours preparing for class. These kinds of hours were reserved for the week or two before exams. It is one thing to spend long evening hours studying if you are doing it for a week or two. It is another thing entirely to work in this fashion for several months, particularly where most of your classes will begin between 9 and 10 in the morning.

Don't Allow Yourself to Become Bored

At times, studying can be boring. Despite the fact that your professors will expose you to new ideas and concepts on a regular basis, it is quite easy to become bored and frustrated with your studies. This is particularly true if you spend too many hours studying for a single class.

Our minds begin to wander after we spend between 1 and 1.5 hours on a single topic. This is part of the reason classes from the first grade through graduate school last less than 1.5 hours. For example, your college history class could have met for 3.5 hours on one day a week, but it probably didn't. Can you imagine sitting still and listening to a professor lecture for 3.5 hours? How long before your attention would begin to wander? If 3 and 4 hour classes make little sense, then 3 to 4 hour study sessions on the same topic are similarly counterproductive.

On a given day, you may need to spend 2, 3 or even 4 hours studying for a single class. Too often students make the mistake of trying to complete their studying all at once. By this I mean that they spend 4 hours in a row studying, for example, their contracts materials. Instead, take a break from studying for a single class, move onto studying different material, and then come back to the original material.

You may think that this is counterproductive because it will take you several minutes to get up to speed with the new material each time you change gears. There is some truth to this observation—it will take you some time to get yourself up to speed each time you shift gears, but the benefits of moving on to a new topic outweigh the costs. This simple change will help keep you from becoming bored and frustrated with your studies. When you come back to studying the original material, a strange thing sometimes happens. The ideas that were causing you so much trouble initially now makes more sense. While you were consciously studying for class "B," your unconscious mind was continuing to process information regarding class "A." Have you ever gone to bed after trying to work with a difficult problem, and the answer comes to you in the middle of the night or when you wake up in the morning? If so, this is the same process at work. Moving on removes your frustrations from the studying equation and allows your mind to work more productively.

Finish at a Certain Time Every Day

One of the most beneficial aspects of scheduling your study time during typical work hours is that you will be finished relatively early in the day. Obviously, this is only true if you schedule your day appropriately. If you begin your day at 8:00 or 9:00 AM and then work an 8 to 10 hour day, you will be finished with your studies no later than 7:00 in the evening. "Finished" in the context of law school is a relative term. At the end of the day, there will always be additional things that you could be doing. If you have already worked 9 or 10 hours and you have finished your assignments for the next day, then resist the temptation to do additional work. This may sound strange coming from an educator, but you must embrace the long view as a law student. If you finish studying at a relatively early hour every day, then you will wake up the next day refreshed and ready to tackle new things.

A Healthy Body Promotes a Healthy Mind

So what should you do with your free time? Just about anything unrelated to law school that you find relaxing. As we have already discussed, law school will be stressful and mentally taxing. At the end of the day, you will need to clear your head in order to help alleviate the stress. There is no complete list of approved stress relieving activities because we are all unique, but some form of exercise should be high on your list.

If your goal is to make the most of your law school studies and to do well on exams, then you need take care of your physical self. You do not need to be a marathoner to derive some benefits from exercise. Any form of physical exertion is quite a bit different than your mostly cerebral law school studies. This difference is exactly what most of us need to put law school out of our heads for an hour or two. Also, exercise allows you to focus on both your physical and mental well being at the same time. Too often students focus so heavily on their studies that they allow themselves to become physically run down.

Of course, exercise is not the only way to take your mind off of your schoolwork. Almost any activity that you enjoy can provide an escape from the stress of law school. Going to a movie, drinking coffee with friends, or going for a walk with your significant other are all simple ways of relaxing. What you do to break away from law school is much less important than simply doing something to relax.

Another great way of avoiding stress is to maintain your ties with friends and family. Doing so, however, can be a little bit tricky. I've already alluded to the fact that your studies will take up a great deal of your time. In addition, you will be encountering new ideas and making new friends during your time at law school. Naturally, your friends and family will start to feel left out or left behind. On one level, this is unavoidable. You are changing, so it is natural for some of your relationships to change as well. It may be difficult to integrate your new circle of friends into the old. And, in some instances, you will have to be selfish with your time, meaning you won't be able to attend every party, birthday, or wedding.

Your family and good friends will understand if you give them plenty of warning and if you meet them part of the way. Before the academic year begins, be sure to discuss the rigors of law school with your friends and family. They are more likely to be understanding if you have apprised them in advance of the time commitment law school requires. In addition, you can rearrange your schedule at times or even attend a celebration a little bit later than the rest of the guests. Remaining connected with friends and family will help ensure that they will be there for you when you need a break from your hectic schedule.

If you still aren't sure about what I am saying, then consider this. If your entire day is devoted to your law studies, you will quickly grow to despise everything associated with law school and the study of law. Obviously, despising law school is not a recipe for doing well on your exams! You are more than a law student, so you have to make allowances in your day for the other facets of who you are. If you don't, your studies will suffer.

Warning Signs of Stress

Despite your best efforts, stress (or even depression) can rear its ugly head. If it does, you must address the problem before it becomes debilitating. Before you can make some changes, you have to be aware of the warning signs of stress.

Physical Signals of Stress*
How Your Body Is Functioning

- Tension, or migraine, headaches
- Upset stomach, problems retaining food
- Change in appetite
- Tightness in chest, back, shoulders
- Aching jaw, tight forehead
- Shortness of breath, dizziness
- Excessive sweating
- Sweaty palms
- Tingling sensation in fingers, toes
- Nervous tension all over; heart palpitations
- Diarrhea or constipation
- Constant low grade fever
- Cold, or sore throat
- Rashes, hives, skin irritation
- Increased blood pressure
- Always tired
- Menstrual problems, missed menstrual periods

Behavioral Signals of Stress
What You Are Doing

- Change in eating habits
- Eating more or less
- Sleep problems (too much, too little)
- Difficulty talking to, holding, loved ones
- Isolating self from others
- Staying at home or staying at work
- Complaining more
- Increased use of alcohol, drugs, coffee, tobacco
- Change in general activity level
- Pacing
- Change in sexual activity, either more or less
- Increased nervous habit, such as nail biting or hair twisting
- Loss of temper: yelling, throwing, and kicking
- Increased recklessness, risk-taking
- Bossiness or inflexibility with others
- Grinding teeth
- Stuttering
- Sudden outbursts of crying, laughing, or anger

* The warning signs of stress are reproduced with the permission of Paul R. Korn, Psychologist, Suffolk University Counseling Center.

Intellectual Signals of Stress
How Your Mind Is Functioning

- Having difficulty remembering recent information or details of recent situations
- Less able to make decisions
- Difficulty concentrating
- Attention span shortens
- Feeling confused, especially with familiar tasks
- Repetitive thoughts
- Racing thoughts
- Continually thinking particular thoughts
- Misunderstanding what others tell you
- Increasingly poor judgment
- Thoughts of escaping, running away
- Unable to slow down thought process
- Loss of objectivity

Emotional Signals of Stress
What You Are Feeling

- Less interest in hobbies, familiar fun activities
- Upset by the unexpected
- Sudden shifts in mood
- Frequent and/or recurring nightmares
- Vague feelings or uneasiness, restlessness
- Feelings of being swamped, overwhelmed
- Feelings of anger, resentment
- Intolerance, irritability with others
- More easily frustrated
- Increased fear of failure
- Feelings of inadequacy, powerlessness, hopelessness
- Changed interest in sex, either more or less
- Apathy, general dissatisfaction
- Desire to cry
- Reduced confidence
- Fear that everyone except you is doing fine
- Worry that you are asking for too much help or too much time from others

As you can see from these lists, stress can manifest itself in many forms. The important thing to remember is that you can do something about your stress. I have already addressed ideas like exercise, making time for yourself, and spending time with family and friends as ways to avoid becoming overly stressed in law school. If you find yourself becoming overly stressed, then it may be time to review your schedule to see if you are actually utilizing these stress reducers. In addition, there are number of very simple stress reducing techniques that can produce results in as little time as five minutes.

A quick breathing exercise is an excellent way of clearing your mind of stress and unwanted clutter. Here are two variations on this exercise that you can use whenever you feel the need to relax and clear your head. In fact, I recommend that you make some form of these exercises part of your daily routine.

Counting Exercise

To begin this exercise, you must put away your pens, pencils and computers and find a reasonably quiet place to sit. Place your back against your chair and have your feet planted firmly on the ground. You want to be comfortable, but keep in mind that you won't be taking a nap! Next, close your eyes, take a deep breath from your diaphragm, and try to empty your head of all thoughts. As you breathe in, count slowly up to 4. Pause briefly when you reach 4, and then start counting again to 4 as you exhale. Repeat the breathing and counting for between 5 and 10 minutes. You will likely notice that other thoughts are intruding in your mind. This is natural, so don't worry. The counting is there to help you focus and keep other thoughts out. When an unwanted thought enters your head, do not get angry. This negative reinforcement can destroy the calm you are trying to create. Instead, gently move the thought out of your mind and continue counting and breathing. With a little practice, fewer and fewer thoughts will intrude. After 5 to 10 minutes, take one last deep breath and open your eyes. I guarantee you will feel refreshed, relaxed, and ready to continue your work.

Trouble Sleeping?

This next breathing exercise is one that I started using during the first month of law school. Prior to beginning law school, I used to have trouble falling asleep on occasion. Once law school began, however, it was not uncommon for me to spend hours tossing and turning prior to finally falling asleep. My brain was full of new ideas that it wanted to explore, and I had a great deal of difficulty quieting my mind so that I could sleep. After a particularly poor night of sleep, one of my friends asked me about my ragged appearance. I told her about my difficulty falling asleep, and she recommended that I try a breathing exercise to clear my mind. I was somewhat dubious of new age cures like meditation and yoga, but I needed to give something a try. The following simple exercise worked so well that I continue to use it to this day whenever I have trouble sleeping.

First, be sure that you have stopped studying for at least 30 minutes before you even get into bed. Your mind needs to shift from awake to sleep mode, and a break during which you start relaxing prior to bed is a good intermediate step. Of course, you will have completed the days studying hours earlier if you followed my advice from earlier in this chapter.

Once you are in bed, start off with a deep breath. Continue inhaling and exhaling slowly and focus your mind on your breathing. Again, you will lose focus at times as thoughts jump in and out of your mind. Acknowledge these thoughts, move them aside, and again focus on your breathing. If you find it difficult to focus on your breathing, then you may need to provide your mind with something more to focus on. As you breathe in, think of the word "inhale," and then think "exhale" as you breathe out. You may also use the counting exercise discussed above to help. These simple changes should give you enough focus to move other ideas out of your head.

These breathing exercises will take a little practice, but will pay dividends almost immediately. After using these exercises on a few occasions, you will find it easier to clear your mind. Eventually, few if any thoughts will enter your head as you use these relaxation techniques.

Reach Out If You Need Help

Even if you follow all of my advice, you may still find yourself experiencing debilitating stress or even depression while in law school. This is not something to take lightly, so do not be afraid to ask for help. I started off this chapter by warning you that stress and depression are, unfortunately, relatively common in law school. Because they are relatively common, you should not feel any embarrassment when seeking help. Do not let your ego get in the way of you obtaining the help you need to perform up to your potential.

Of course, knowing who to turn to for assistance can be difficult. Family and close friends are often those that we naturally turn to for assistance. If your family and friends have helped you through life's rough spots before, then they can do so now. If family and friends have little experience with law school, however, they may be unaware of how stressful the environment can be. While well intentioned, they may minimize the situation in a way that is counter to your needs. In addition, you may need more help than a layperson can provide.

If you need to talk with someone who might have a better understanding of what you are going through, consider making an appointment with someone in your academic support office or your dean of students. Quite often, these people are both lawyers and educators who can provide you with valuable perspective, options, and guidance. If these folks can't help, they will likely know someone who can.

Many law schools and universities offer counseling as a part of the services you pay for along with your tuition. Quite often these counseling sessions are provided at a reduced rate or even free of charge to students. For example, at Suffolk University Law School where I teach these services are provided by the

University Counseling Center. These professionals, and others like them at schools across the country, are dedicated to your mental well being and will do everything in their power to help. If you are concerned about confidentiality—don't be. Psychologists and psychiatrists are bound by rules of confidentiality that preclude them from telling anyone about your situation.

In the end, maintaining a healthy mental approach to law school is just as important to your success as are studying and going to class. The challenges you face as a law student can be draining at times. If you spend time taking care of yourself, you will be able to face these challenges head on and succeed.

CHAPTER III

Reading and Briefing Cases Efficiently

In order to be an active participant in your law school classes, you must learn how to read and understand case law. In addition, case briefing is an essential step in learning the individual legal principles necessary for success on your final examinations. As we discussed in Chapter I, most of your classes will emphasize the casebook method of learning.[1] You will review literally hundreds of cases during your first year of law school, so you must have a plan in place so that you can assimilate, understand, and categorize everything you are learning. I have developed a multi-step process that will help you master this information. My active method of studying is no magic formula, and will require a great deal of work on your part. Mastery of your law school subjects is a process that will happen over time. My active studying methodology takes this into account, and allows you to address every topic slowly and from multiple perspectives. The individual steps in the active study method are:

- Read Your Cases Twice
- Write a Case Brief and Then Correct It
- Take Complete Notes, But Listen to the Lecturer
- Review and Type Your Notes Within 24 Hours of Class
- Incorporate Your Notes Into Your Course Outline

More broadly, these steps can be summed up as pre-class preparation, in-class work, and post class review. While each of these steps is crucial to your overall understanding of the law, my method requires you to study in a way that may be unfamiliar to you. You will still spend time preparing for class, but a great deal of your weekly work will revolve around reviewing ideas after class is over. This notion of backloading your studies will be further discussed where applicable.

---

1. Some classes are more case driven than others. For example, you will review certain cases in your civil procedure class, but you will spend much of your time learning the Federal Rules of Civil Procedure.

Reading Cases Efficiently

One of the more time consuming aspects of law school life is the reading of cases. At the start of the semester, much of the terminology within the cases will be new and you will spend a great deal of time turning to your legal dictionary for help. While you will understand more of the terminology as the semester progresses, your professors will take this into account and begin assigning additional and more complex materials for you to read. There is no substitute for reading the cases, but there are ways to maximize the return on your time.

The first step is to place the case in context and understand why your professor is having you read a particular case at a particular time. Cases are full of information that, while relevant to the litigants in that case, may not be relevant to your professor's purpose in assigning it. Thankfully, you already have the material necessary to place your cases into a broader context.

Your syllabus and casebook contain information that can help provide some of the context you need. For example, most casebooks are organized into chapters that cover individual concepts. Before reading the case, take a quick look at the casebook's table of contents. If the case is listed under the chapter on negligence, then any material on the intentional tort of battery is, at best, marginally relevant. Similarly, the course syllabus likely contains information about the topic being covered on a particular day. Once you have finished perusing your syllabus and the casebook's table of contents, you are ready to read the case with a more focused approach.

A thorough understanding of the cases you read is so important to your success as a law student that I encourage all students to read each case twice. Once you receive your course syllabus and realize the number of cases you are assigned for each class, you will realize that I am making no small request of you. I know this method works from my experience with hundreds of students, so let me take you through why it works.

First, law school is difficult because of the volume of material we expect you to master in a detailed and nuanced fashion. To master all this material, you must review it multiple times, and in multiple ways. By reading the case twice, with a different focus during each read, you will have a better understanding of the case's meaning before you step into class for the day's lecture.

Second, you must get into the habit of teaching yourself the law. While you will learn a great deal from each professor's lectures, you will have an even deeper understanding of the topic if you come to class better prepared. Ultimately, your professors are teaching you how to extract the critical information from caselaw as much as they are teaching you about the law contained within a single case, so do not expect to be spoon fed what is important. You must become your own best teacher

Your first reading of the case is the easy one. To prepare yourself, put down your pen, pencil, or highlighter. Do not worry, as you will take notes during the next read when you are trying to extract specific information from the case. During the first read, your only task is to get a general sense of what the case is about. With this as your only task, the first read should go fairly quickly.

All law students take notes about the cases they read. We call these notes case briefs, and I will be covering the topic shortly. A problem associated with briefing cases is that most briefs are much too long. The reason? The student is trying to write down all of the important information, but it is difficult to be sure of what is and isn't important until you reach the end of the case to discover the court's conclusion. If you treat the first read as if you are reading a short story, by the end you will be able to look back and realize what was truly important. Next, you proceed on to your second, but much more focused read of the case. Skim the marginally important material, and take time writing notes on the critical aspects of the case.

Not only does the "two reads per case" method help lead to a deeper understanding of the material, it does not take nearly as long as you might think. Many of my students who try the method assume that it will take twice as long to read the case, but they are pleasantly surprised that it does not. Because you are emphasizing different things each time, neither read of the case takes as long as a single read where you are trying to accomplish everything. Obviously, reading the case twice does take more time initially, but by giving yourself a more thorough understanding of the material before you even listen to your professor's lecture, you are actually saving time in the long run.

In general, do not read your cases any more than twice prior to class. This advice may seem counterintuitive. If reading a case twice is better than reading it once, then wouldn't reading the case a third time be better still? On the surface, there is a simple and attractive logic to this assertion, however, my experience of working with several hundred law students has taught me that there are flaws in this reasoning.

Even if you are able to extract additional information from the case after a third read, consider the notion of diminishing returns. You will extract a great deal of information from the cases by reading them twice, which necessarily means that there will be less left to find if you read them a third time. By reading your cases twice, you will have extracted the information necessary to be an active participant in class.

Even after a second read, however, you may feel that there are still subtleties within the case that are eluding you. You are probably correct, but reading the case a third time is not the answer. For one thing, there is no guarantee that you will understand the case any better after reading it a third time. You might find something new after reading each case 100 times, but your time is too precious a commodity to waste in this fashion. The study of law is extremely time consuming, so it is important to maximize the returns on your studying at every step in the process.

Finally, remember that your pre-class preparation is only one aspect of your law school studies. Next, you will go to class where your professors will further discuss the cases you've been working on. This in class discussion will clear up most of your questions. Then, you will have time to further explore these ideas during the post-class review of your class notes and case briefs.

Case Briefing

Case briefing is a formalized way of taking notes on your reading in preparation for class. When lawyers read cases, we are looking for specific useful information. Case briefs are broken down into several parts that correspond to the important information we are looking for. As a law student, you will be briefing cases for two specific reasons. First, you will need the brief in order to have the essential information at your fingertips should your professor call on you during class or to simply follow along with the class discussion. Second, your case briefs are an important study tool that you will use later when you prepare for your mid-term and final examinations.

Herb's Hints

You must create your own case briefs! The ability to pull out the salient points from a given case is an essential skill that every lawyer must develop. You will struggle to keep up at times, but the struggle will prepare you for final exams and, ultimately, to be a lawyer.

As we start our process, keep in mind that there is no such thing as a perfect case brief. Case briefs will vary from student to student. In fact, your own case briefs will evolve over time, likely getting shorter as your understanding of the law increases during the semester. In addition to varying from student to student, case briefs should vary depending on your professors' teaching styles. Be sure to mold your case briefs to the requirements laid out by each of your professors. For example, some professors review each case in excruciating detail. Case briefs for these professors need to be correspondingly longer or they will not fulfill their role of providing you with easy to find information should the professor call on you during class.

In most law schools, students are taught to brief cases during the first few days of orientation. While the format can differ somewhat from school to school, most case briefs contain the following sections.

- **Case Name, Judge, and Citation**
- **Facts**
- **Procedural History**
- **Issue**
- **Holding**
- **Rule**
- **Reasoning**
- **Disposition**
- **Notes**

The easiest way to describe the various sections of a brief is to do so in conjunction with a case. The case I have chosen is *Garratt v. Dailey*. It is a case that most students will cover during the first few weeks of their torts class. After you finish reading the case, we will create a case brief one step at a time. Before you start, however, let me try to address a few typical questions that students have about reading cases.

How long should it take me to read this case? This is likely the first case you have read, so do not be surprised if it takes you a long time to get through it. You will develop the skill of separating the important from the unimportant when reading a case, but it is a skill that takes time to develop.

How long are most cases? *Garratt v. Dailey* is average in length. Some cases, particularly those in your constitutional law class, will be significantly longer.

Will the case use language I can understand or will it be filled with legalese? The law, like many professions, has its own peculiar language that you must learn. Buy a good legal dictionary, the unabridged *Black's Law Dictionary* is the standard, and look up any word that you are unsure of. We do not expect you to know the meaning of every legal term when you start law school, but we do expect you to learn the meanings while you are here.

How long should the brief be? Try to keep them under one page long. Any longer, and the brief will not be as helpful to you in class or as a study aid. Also, longer case briefs are an indication that you need to do a better job of noting only the critical information.

Garratt v. Dailey[2]
46 Wash. 2d 197, 279 P.2d 1091 (1955)

HILL, Justice. The liability of an infant for an alleged battery is presented to this court for the first time. Brian Dailey (age five years, nine months) was visiting with Naomi Garratt, an adult and a sister of the plaintiff, Ruth Garratt, likewise an adult, in the back yard of the plaintiff's home, on July 16, 1951. It is plaintiff's contention that she came out into the back yard to talk with Naomi and that, as she started to sit down in a wood and canvas lawn chair, Brian deliberately pulled it out from under her. The only one of the three persons present so testifying was Naomi Garratt. (Ruth Garratt, the plaintiff, did not testify as to how or why she fell.) The trial court, unwilling to accept this testimony, adopted instead Brian Dailey's version of what happened, and made the following findings:

> 'III. * * * that while Naomi Garratt and Brian Dailey were in the back yard the plaintiff, Ruth Garratt, came out of her house into the back yard. Some time subsequent thereto defendant, Brian Dailey, picked up a lightly built wood and canvas lawn chair which was then and there located in the back yard of the above described premises, moved it sideways a few feet and seated himself therein, at which time he discovered the plaintiff, Ruth Garratt, about to sit down at the place where the lawn chair had formerly been, at which time he hurriedly got up from the chair and attempted to move it toward Ruth Garratt to aid her in sitting down in the chair; that due to the defendant's small size and lack of dexterity he was unable to get the lawn chair under the plaintiff in time to prevent her from falling to the ground. That plaintiff fell to the ground and sustained a fracture of her hip, and other injuries and damages as hereinafter set forth.

> 'IV. That the preponderance of the evidence in this case establishes that when the defendant, Brian Dailey, moved the chair in question *he did not have any willful or unlawful purpose* in doing so; that *he did not have any intent to injure the plaintiff, or any intent to bring about any unauthorized or offensive contact with her person* or any objects appurtenant thereto; that the circumstances which immediately preceded the fall of the plain-

---

2. I have removed portions of this case not germane to the central issue. This is a common practice in case books.

tiff established that the defendant, *Brian Dailey, did not have purpose, intent or design to perform a prank or to effect an assault and battery upon the person of the plaintiff.'* (Italics added, for a purpose hereinafter indicated.)

It is conceded that Ruth Garratt's fall resulted in a fractured hip and other painful and serious injuries. To obviate the necessity of a retrial in the event this court determines that she was entitled to a judgment against Brian Dailey, the amount of her damage was found to be $11,000. Plaintiff appeals from a judgment dismissing the action and asks for the entry of a judgment in that amount or a new trial.

The authorities generally, but with certain notable exceptions, see Bohlen, 'Liability in Tort of Infants and Insane Persons,' 23 Mich.L.Rev. 9, state that when a minor has committed a tort with force he is liable to be proceeded against as any other person would be. Paul v. Hummel, 1869, 43 Mo. 119, 97 Am.Dec. 381; *Huchting v. Engel,* 1863, 17 Wis. 230, 84 Am.Dec. 741; *Brics v. Maechtle,* 1911, 146 Wis. 89, 130 N.W. 893, 35 L.R.A.N.S., 574; 1 Cooley on Torts (4th Ed.) 194, §66; Prosser on Torts 1085, §108; 2 Kent's Commentaries 241; 27 Am.Jur. 812, Infants, §90.

In our analysis of the applicable law, we start with the basic premise that Brian, whether five or fifty-five, must have committed some wrongful act before he could be liable for appellant's injuries.

The trial court's finding that Brian was a visitor in the Garratt back yard is supported by the evidence and negatives appellant's assertion that Brian was a trespasser and had no right to touch, move, or sit in any chair in that yard, and that contention will not receive further consideration.

It is urged that Brian's action in moving the chair constituted a battery. A definition (not all-inclusive but sufficient for out purpose) of a battery is the intentional infliction of a harmful bodily contact upon another. The rule that determines liability for battery is given in 1 Restatement, Torts, 29, §13, as:

'An act which, directly or indirectly, is the legal cause of a harmful contact with another's person makes the actor liable to the other, if

'(a) the act is done with the intention of bringing about a harmful or offensive contact or an apprehension thereof to the other or a third person, and

'(b) the contact is not consented to by the other or the other's consent thereto is procured by fraud or duress, and

'(c) the contact is not otherwise privileged.'

We have in this case no question of consent or privilege. We therefore proceed to an immediate consideration of intent and its place in the law of battery. In the comment on clause (a), the Restatement says:

> 'Character of actor's intention.' In order that an act may be done with the intention of bringing about a harmful or offensive contact or an apprehension thereof to a particular person, either the other or a third person, the act must be done for the purpose of causing the contact or apprehension or with knowledge on the part of the actor that such contact or apprehension is substantially certain to be produced.' See, also, Prosser on Torts 41, § 8.

We have here the conceded volitional act of Brian, i. e., the moving of a chair. Had the plaintiff proved to the satisfaction of the trial court that Brian moved the chair while she was in the act of sitting down, Brian's action would patently have been for the purpose or with the intent of causing the plaintiff's bodily contact with the ground, and she would be entitled to a judgment against him for the resulting damages. *Vosburg v. Putney*, 1891, 80 Wis. 523, 50 N.W. 403, 14 L.R.A. 226; *Briese v. Maechtle*, supra.

The plaintiff based her case on that theory, and the trial court held that she failed in her proof and accepted Brian's version of the facts rather than that given by the eyewitness who testified for the plaintiff. After the trial court determined that the plaintiff had not established her theory of a battery (i.e., that Brian had pulled the chair out from under the plaintiff while she was in the act of sitting down), it then became concerned with whether a battery was established under the facts as it found them to be.

In this connection, we quote another portion of the comment on the 'Character of actor's intention,' relating to clause (a) of the rule from the Restatement heretofore set forth:

> 'It is not enough that the act itself is intentionally done and this, even though the actor realizes or should realize that it contains a very grave risk of bringing about the contact or apprehension. Such realization may make the actor's conduct negligent or even reckless but unless he realizes that to a substantial certainty, the contact or apprehension will result, the actor has not that intention which is necessary to make him liable under the rule stated in this section.'

A battery would be established if, in addition to plaintiff's fall, it was proved that, when Brian moved the chair, he knew with substantial certainty that the plaintiff would attempt to sit down where the chair had been. If Brian had any of the intents which the trial court found, in the italicized portions of the findings of fact quoted above, that he did not have, he would of course have had the knowledge to which we have referred. The mere absence of any intent to injure the plaintiff or to play a prank on her or to embarrass her, or to commit an assault and battery on her would not absolve him from liability if in fact he had such knowledge. *Mercer v. Corbin*, 1889, 117 Ind. 450, 20 N.E. 132, 3 L.R.A. 221. Without such knowledge, there would be nothing wrongful about Brian's act in moving the chair and, there being no wrongful act, there would be no liability.

While a finding that Brian had no such knowledge can be inferred from the findings made, we believe that before the plaintiff's action in such a case should be dismissed there should be no question but that the trial court had passed upon that issue; hence, the case should be remanded for clarification of the findings to specifically cover the question of Brian's knowledge, because intent could be inferred therefrom. If the court finds that he had such knowledge the necessary intent will be established and the plaintiff will be entitled to recover, even though there was no purpose to injure or embarrass the plaintiff. *Vosburg v. Putney*, supra. If Brian did not have such knowledge, there was no wrongful act by him and the basic premise of liability on the theory of a battery was not established.

It will be noted that the law of battery as we have discussed it is the law applicable to adults, and no significance has been attached to the fact that Brian was a child less than six years of age when the alleged battery occurred. The only circumstance where Brian's age is of any consequence is in determining what he knew, and there his experience, capacity, and understanding are of course material.

From what has been said, it is clear that we find no merit in plaintiff's contention that we can direct the entry of a judgment for $11,000 in her favor on the record now before us.

Nor do we find any error in the record that warrants a new trial.

* * *

The cause is remanded for clarification, with instructions to make definite findings on the issue of whether Brian Dailey knew with substantial certainty that the plaintiff would attempt to sit down where the chair which he moved had been, and to change the judgment if the findings warrant it.

Costs on this appeal will abide the ultimate decision of the superior court. If a judgment is entered for the plaintiff, Ruth Garratt, appellant here, she shall be entitled to her costs on this appeal. If, however, the judgment of dismissal remains unchanged, the respondent will be entitled to recover his costs on this appeal.

Remanded for clarification.

Congratulations! You have just finished reading one of your first law school cases. At this moment, there is a great deal of information coursing through your brain about *Garratt v. Dailey*. Now that you have finished reading, we can use our case briefing categories to organize all that information.

Case Name, Author, and Citation—This may be the easiest section of a case brief to complete. In this example, the name of the case is *Garratt v. Dailey*. A tougher question associated with the case name can be: "Who is the plaintiff and who is the defendant?" Oftentimes the plaintiff, the party who initiated the civil lawsuit, is the first name listed. In this instance Ruth Garratt is the plaintiff and the minor, Brian Dailey, is the defendant. The plaintiff will not always be the first party listed, however, so you may have to rely on a careful read of the case to determine who is suing whom. As for the remaining information in this section, Justice Hill wrote the opinion, and the citation for the case is 46 Wash. 2d 197, 279 P.2d 1091 (1955).

Case citations are extremely important in that they inform the reader where they can go in order to find the source material. In this example, the citation tells us that *Garratt v. Dailey* can be found in two different sources. The first is in volume 46 of the Washington Reports, Second Series on page 197. The case may also be found in volume 279 of the Pacific Reporter, Second Series on page 1091. The "Wash. 2d" portion of the citations also tells the reader that the Washington state supreme court wrote the opinion. You will learn a great deal more about the intricacies of citation and the case reporter system in your first-year writing and research class.

Herb's Hints

A fact is critical or material if it was necessary to the court's conclusion. A change to a critical or material fact may cause the court to come to a different conclusion.

Facts—This is the section of the case brief where students tend to include too much information. When writing the facts section, focus on the essential or critical facts as opposed to merely retelling the entire story contained within the case. Remember, a lawyer defines critical facts as those that are relevant to the court's final conclusion. In *Garratt v. Dailey* for example, the defendant's action of pulling away the chair is certainly relevant, but how about his relationship to the plaintiff? Does it make a difference that the chair was made of wood and canvas or that the incident occurred on July 16, 1951? To answer these questions, ask yourself whether these facts made a difference. The easiest way to do this is to change the fact and determine whether the court would have decided the case differently.

Exercise 1: Facts Exercise

Focusing on critical facts, try to write the facts section to a case brief for *Garratt v. Dailey*.

_____

_____

_____

_____

_____

_____

_____

_____

_____

_____

_____

_____

Now that you have completed the exercise, compare your facts section to the one provided below. When comparing your answer to the sample, look to see whether you have included information that I have left out or whether my version contains facts missing from your account. Remember, there are no perfect case briefs!

> *The plaintiff, Ruth Garratt, filed a lawsuit against a then five year old child for battery. She alleged that the defendant child, Brian Dailey, deliberately pulled a chair out from under her as she was about to sit. She hit the ground and fractured her hip. The trial judge found that the child moved the chair in order to sit in it, and then tried to move the chair back when he realized the plaintiff was about to sit down.*

So, what does your facts section look like? If you are like most new law students, your facts section is longer. If it is, do not panic! Initially, you are better off writing a slightly longer facts section until you figure out exactly how detail oriented your professors will be. You are better off including a little more than is absolutely necessary than possibly leaving out something important.

With that in mind, let's review my facts section to see if we can make it even leaner. First, I refer to the parties by name, but I also designate them as the plaintiff and the defendant. Are both necessary? In most instances, the actual names of the parties will be irrelevant to the issue the case stands, so this information could come out. Next, did you happen to notice that I am really telling two stories in my facts section? First, I provide the victim's version of the events and then list what the judge found. Are both versions needed? The short answer is "no," but see if you can follow along with me as I explain why.

> ### Herb's Hints
> ---
> Consider using bullet points when writing out the facts portion of your brief. The facts section tends to be the longest part of your brief, and can be hard to sift through quickly when you are called on in class.

This was a jury waived trial, which means that the judge was the trier of fact. The trial judge listened to the conflicting evidence and then decided what actually happened. The judge listed his conclusions as to what happened in the form of findings of fact. The appellate court's decision, which is the version of *Garratt v. Dailey* you read, focused on questions of law and did not disturb the trial judge's findings. In fact, as far as the appellate court was concerned, the trial judge's version of events *is* what happened, and the appellate court based its conclusions on these facts. Therefore, the victim's version of events cannot be considered critical. So, we could remove from the facts section the sentence about the plaintiff's allegations as to what happened.

Procedural History—The procedural history section of a brief is fairly straightforward. In this section, you are to describe how the case ended up before the appellate court. In most instances, the appellant, who is the party seeking the appeal, is alleging that some error of law occurred in the trial court or that a lower level appellate court ruled incorrectly. In some instances, aspects of the procedural history may be missing from the cases you read. When available, however, your procedural history should include how the case began, the outcome at trial, which party is bringing the appeal, and whether there were earlier appeals of the same case.

> *The plaintiff (Garratt) filed a civil action alleging that the defendant (Dailey) committed a battery when he pulled away the chair in which she was about to sit. In a jury waived trial, the judge found for the defendant. Ms. Garratt is now appealing "from a judgment dismissing the action and asks for the entry of a judgment ... or a new trial."*

The Issue—The issue should be viewed as the question(s) the appellate court is seeking to resolve. While this definition may seem simple on its surface, it is actually quite difficult to articulate the issue as a reasonably short, easy to understand question.

Your statement of the issue should be a single sentence and written in the form of a question. Also, when writing your issue statement, be sure that it can be answered with a simple "yes" or "no." In addition, try to be as specific as possible when formulating the issue. The reasons for this are twofold. First, it will force you to work through the case in an active fashion. The more you dig into which facts are material, the closer you will get to the narrow question before the appellate court. Second, a general statement of the issue is not helpful when trying to figure out what a case truly means. For example, one could say that the issue before the court in *Garratt v. Dailey* was whether the trial court had correctly dismissed the case. While this is accurate as far as it goes, it is applicable to most every appellate case! Moreover, it does nothing to enhance your understanding of the central problem the court was seeking to resolve.

When you read through *Garratt*, it becomes quite clear that the court is grappling with the issue of what intent means in the context of a battery. Even more specifically, the appellate court reviewed whether intent in the battery context should be defined as merely intending to cause a harmful or offensive contact or something more. The court was compelled to engage in this review based on the trial court's decision.

Remember, the trial court found that the defendant moved the chair in order to sit in it, and that he did not intend to injure the plaintiff or play a prank. Based on these findings, the trial court concluded that the plaintiff could not establish that a battery had occurred because a battery requires the intent to cause a harmful or offensive contact.

The appellate court, based on a review of its own case law and on some very persuasive secondary authority (The Restatement of Torts), became concerned that the trial court had applied the incorrect definition of intent to the situation. The trial court's definition required that the boy intend to injure or play a prank on his aunt. So the issue, or question, before the appeals court was:

> *Did the defendant's action of moving plaintiff's chair as she was about to sit down, which resulted in her falling and being injured, satisfy the intent element of the tort of battery even though the defendant did not intend to harm or play a prank on the plaintiff?*

In this example of an issue statement, notice how I have used facts from the case to focus my sentence. Also, did you notice that I adopted the trial judge's version of what happened? I have done so because the trial judge was the trier of fact, and the appellate court is very unlikely to disturb these factual findings. As far as the appellate court is concerned, the trial judge's findings are what happened.

By using the facts, you are more likely to write an issue statement that accurately reflects the issue before the court. Without the facts, issue statements often become too broad. Including the facts is the preferred method of creating an issue statement, but it is not an absolute requirement. For example, the following issue statement is more general, but still accurately reflects the issue before the court.

> *Is a desire to cause a harmful or offensive contact the only way to establish the intent element for the tort of battery?*

The Holding—After you have figured out the question, the next logical step is to answer it. Lawyers call this answer the holding. If you have spent time carefully framing your statement of the issue, then your answer to the question should be quite obvious. In fact, you should be thinking about your holding when writing your statement of the issue. The only difficult aspect of coming up with your holding is figuring out what your professors mean when they use the terms holding and rule.

When we were working on creating a statement of the issue, I noted that the question should be answerable with a "yes" or "no." For some professors, this simple answer and nothing more represents the court's holding. For these professors, the next section of our case brief, the rule section, is much more important than the holding.

For other professors, a yes or no response in the holding is merely the first part of the answer. That yes or no would be followed with a rule that supports the answer. Unlike the issue statement, which should be written narrowly in order to accurately reflect the question before the appeals court, this expanded version of the holding should be written more broadly. Why? This broadly stated rule is what you are to take away from the case. It is the principle of law the case stands for, and it will be applied to future cases. For students, it is the rule you will memorize and then use when analyzing the factual scenarios you see on your examinations. If you incorporate too many facts into your holding, you are in effect narrowing and making it applicable to fewer situations. To help you see my point, let's revisit our issue.

> *Did the defendant's action of moving plaintiff's chair as she was about to sit down, which resulted in her falling and being injured, satisfy the intent element of the tort of battery even though the defendant did not intend to harm or play a prank on the plaintiff?*

The simplest answer to this issue statement would be "**Yes.**" Remember, the appeals court noted that a desire to cause harm was not the only way to satisfy the intent element of a battery. The young boy in *Garratt v. Dailey* could still be liable if he knew to a substantial certainty that a harmful or offensive touching would result from his actions. If we tried to incorporate a number of facts into the holding, it would read something like this.

> *Yes, Dailey's action of grabbing the chair in order to sit in it could satisfy the intent element of a battery.*

While this holding gives us the answer to the question before the court, it does not give us any idea as to how future cases should be resolved, unless that case has the same facts. What is missing from this holding is a principle of law. If you revised the holding by adding such a principle it might read as follows:

> *Yes, when Dailey pulled the chair away in order to sit in it he could still satisfy the intent element of a battery if he knew to a "substantial certainty" that his actions would result in the plaintiff hitting the ground.*

This version of the holding gives us both a principle of law (knowledge to a substantial certainty that harm would result) and the essential facts. I have also placed the words "substantial certainty" in quotes to indicate that this is a specific legal term that should not be paraphrased. Lawyers refer to these phrases as terms of art.

The holding can take one more form. If you remove the facts entirely, then you are still left with the principle of law. If you keep in mind that the holding will appear immediately after your statement of the issue in your case brief, then you may not need to state the facts a second time. To wrap up this discussion of the holding, let's take one more look at the issue statement, and our three acceptable versions of the holding.

> *ISSUE: Did the defendant's action of moving plaintiff's chair as she was about to sit down, which resulted in her falling and being injured, satisfy the intent element of the tort of battery even though the defendant did not intend to harm or play a prank on the plaintiff?*

> *HOLDING:*

> *(1) Yes. (Short version)*

> *(2) Yes, when Dailey grabbed the chair in order to sit in it he could still satisfy the intent element of a battery if he knew to a "substantial certainty" that his actions would result in his aunt hitting the ground. (Facts plus principle of law version.)*

(3) Yes, if he knew to a "substantial certainty" that his actions would result in harm to the defendant. (Principle of law version.)

The Rule—As we have already touched on, the rule is the idea from the case that the reader can take away and apply to future cases. When writing the rule section of your brief, be sure to differentiate between the rule, or principle, that the case stands for and other rules that the court might reference or use. For example, the *Garratt v. Dailey* court references the entire rule of battery, but the case is really about the definition of intent.

In many instances, the rule will expand upon, refine or explain an existing legal principle. Here, the court was refining the definition of intent to include the concept of knowledge to a substantial certainty. If the case represents binding precedent in your jurisdiction, then it will help you determine how the court might resolve a new factual scenario. In law schools where professors prefer the short version of the holding, the rule is broken out into its own section of the case brief. For *Garratt v. Dailey*, the rule could be stated as follows:

A party may satisfy the intent element of a battery if he knows to a "substantial certainty" that his actions will result in a harmful or offensive contact.

Notice that this statement of the rule is relatively broad. The idea is to state the rule in such a way that it is useful in future cases.

The Reasoning—The court's reasoning is the "why" behind its decision. Understanding the court's reasoning is essential if you are to truly understand the case and the principle of law it represents. The importance of the court's reasoning can be traced back to our earlier discussion of binding precedent and *stare decisis*.

Lawyers use cases to help them predict how a new controversy should be resolved. To do this, we must pay careful attention to not only how the court resolved the dispute, but why the case came out as it did. Once you understand why a court ruled in a particular fashion, it is much easier to predict whether that case will be applicable to your new controversy.

Looking at *Garratt v. Dailey*, it seems that the court remanded the case for clarification based on the definition of the term intent. The trial court found that Dailey never intended to harm his aunt, and was merely trying to sit down. For this reason, the trial court dismissed the action for battery. The appeals court, however, noted that this finding touched on only one aspect of the definition of intent—desiring to bring about a particular result. The appeals court went on to explain that a defendant could also be liable for an intentional tort if he knew to a substantial certainty that his actions would bring about an actionable result. Bringing all of this together, a statement of the court's reasoning in *Garratt v. Dailey* would look something like this:

> *The trial court's finding and ruling were based on only one aspect of the definition of intent. The appellate court reasoned, however, that Dailey could still be liable for a battery if he knew to a "substantial certainty" that his actions would have resulted in a harmful contact.*

The Disposition—The disposition is the appellate court's decision as to what to do with the case, and this resolution can take a number of different forms. You will find the appellate court's disposition at the very end of the opinion, and typical dispositions include: reversed, remanded, affirmed, overruled, or some combination of these terms. Each of these terms has a specific legal meaning, so be sure to consult your legal dictionary.

In *Garratt v. Dailey*, the appellate court remanded the case for clarification. To remand a case means to send it back to the trial court for further action. In this instance, the appellate court "remanded for clarification, with instructions to make definite findings on the issue of whether Brian Dailey knew with substantial certainty that the plaintiff would attempt to sit down where the chair which he moved had been, and to change the judgment if the findings warrant it."

If you are wondering why the appellate court did not make this decision on its own, remember that the trial court and appellate court have different roles. The trial court, not the appellate court, makes findings of fact, and a determination as to what Dailey did or did not know is a finding of fact. So, the disposition for this case would be:

> *The case was remanded back to the trial court for clarification. More specifically, the appellate court instructed the trial court to make specific findings as to whether the defendant knew to a "substantial certainty" that the plaintiff would hit the ground as a result of moving the chair. This new finding might require the trial court to alter its original judgment.*

Notes—This final section of your case brief is something of a catchall category. Here, you will note anything that you think is worth remembering about the case, but that does not fit neatly into any of the other categories. For example, the definitions of new legal terms could go here.

In *Garratt v. Dailey*, you could note that the rule might be applicable to cases involving intentional torts other than battery. There are several other intentional torts, and it is possible that the appeals court's broader definition of intent could be applied to all of them.

That's it! We have now covered all of the sections of a case brief. Remember, learning to brief cases effectively is a prerequisite to success on your law school examinations. Through the act of briefing, you will discover the legal principles within each case. Then, this legal principle becomes part of your overall understanding of how an area of the law operates. In addition, the brief will force you to consider which facts are material to the court's reasoning and conclusion. With this information in your possession, you will have a better understanding of whether to apply this legal principle when confronted by a similar factual scenario on your exams.

As a quick review, let's take a look at what the various sections of our case brief would like when viewed together.

Case name, Author, and Citation—*Garratt v. Dailey, 46 Wash. 2d 197, 279 P.2d 1091 (1955). Justice Hill, author.*

Facts—*The plaintiff, Ruth Garratt, filed a lawsuit against a then five year old child for battery. She alleged that the child, Brian Dailey, deliberately pulled a chair out from under her as she was about to sit. She hit the ground and fractured her hip. The trial judge found that the child moved the chair in order to sit in it, and then tried to move the chair back when he realized the plaintiff was about to sit down.*

Procedural History—*The plaintiff filed a civil action alleging that the defendant committed a battery when he pulled away the chair in which she was about to sit. In a jury waived trial, the judge found for the defendant. Ms. Garratt is now appealing from that judgment and is seeking a new trial or for the appellate court to enter judgment in her favor.*

Issue—*Did the defendant's action of moving plaintiff's chair as she was about to sit down, which resulted in her falling and being injured, satisfy the intent element of the tort of battery even though the defendant did not intend to harm or play a prank on the plaintiff?*

Holding—*Yes.*

Rule—*A party may satisfy the intent element of a battery if he knows to a "substantial certainty" that his actions will result in a harmful or offensive contact.*

Reasoning—*Trial court's finding and ruling were based on only one aspect of the definition of intent. The trial court reasoned, however, that*

Dailey could still be liable for a battery if he knew to a "substantial certainty" that his actions would have resulted in a harmful contact.

Disposition—*Remanded to trial court for clarification. Trial court to determine whether Dailey knew to "substantial certainty" that his actions would result in harmful touching.*

Notes—*Definition of intent used by appeals court may be applicable to other intentional torts, not just battery.*

As you look back at our case brief, take note of how much shorter it is than the case on which it is based. One skill that all good lawyers possess is the ability to separate the important from the unimportant. Through this distillation process, you are left with, hopefully, only essential information.

Exercise 2

Read the following case, *Ransom v. State*, and try to complete a case brief. Remember that there is no such thing as a perfect case brief, so do not spend hours completing this assignment. Once you have finished, we will review my version of the brief for comparison purposes.

Ransom v. State
460 P.2d 170 (Alaska 1969)[3]

BONEY, Justice. This case arises out of the same assault which is the subject of the appeal in *Berfield v. State*, 458 P.2d 1008. Both Ransom and Berfield were convicted by a jury of assault with a dangerous weapon, i.e., their boots. Many of the issues raised by Ransom on appeal have been disposed of by this court's opinion in Berfield; however, there is one issue which has been raised by appellant Ransom which requires that the appeals be considered separately.

Ransom was charged with assault with a dangerous weapon in a joint indictment which reads in part as follows:

That on or about the 8th day of July, 1967, at or near Anchorage, in the Third Judicial District, State of Alaska, Christopher Anthony Ransom and Lowell Bernard Berfield, being then and there armed with danger-

---

3. I have redacted portions from this case for purposes of the exercise.

ous weapons, to wit, their boots, did willfully, unlawfully, and felo-
niously assault David Baker by kicking him about the head and shoulders with said boots.

Ransom asserts that the charge as described in the indictment was not proved
at trial because there was no evidence that he was wearing boots at the time of
the assault. The state's response to this claim of error is threefold: (a) there was
sufficient evidence for a jury to conclude that Ransom was wearing boots; (b)
the evidence at least showed that Ransom was wearing some kind of footgear
and the difference between 'footgear' and 'boots' is not material; (c) since
Berfield was wearing boots and both Ransom and Berfield were guilty as prin-
cipals in the crime, it doesn't matter if Ransom was wearing boots or not.

The totality of the evidence concerning what Ransom was wearing on his
feet at the time of the assault is contained in the testimony of one of the vic-
tims of the assault and is as follows:

Q Do you know what kind of footgear Ransom had on?
A No, I couldn't be sure.
Q As to Mr. Ransom, you're uncertain as to what footgear?
A Yes.
Q Let me ask you this, was he shod in some sort of footgear?
A Yes.
Q He wasn't barefooted?
A No.
Q Were you able to observe what Ransom was wearing?
A Not for sure.
Q Type of footgear?
A No, not for certain.
Q Did you observe any boots on Ransom?
A No, I didn't—I didn't even know what kind of footgear he had.

From this evidence it is clear that no reasonable person could conclude that the
state had shown beyond a reasonable doubt that Ransom was wearing boots at
the time of the assault.

Susan Bailey testified for the defense. During her testimony the defense attempted to introduce into evidence the shoes that Ransom was wearing in the
courtroom. Susan Bailey was asked on voir dire if she could positively identify
the shoes as the ones Ransom was wearing at the time of the assault. She stated
that she could not but that they looked like the same shoes. The shoes were not
allowed in evidence nor were they described by the witness. We have no way of
knowing if the entire jury saw the shoes which were offered as evidence, and

we have no way to judge what kind of shoes were offered. The jury was instructed, of course, to only consider the exhibits which were in evidence.

This evidence is also insufficient for us to conclude that the variance between 'boots' and 'footgear' is immaterial. It is true that many kinds of shoes could be considered the rough equivalent of boots. However, the state did not show that Ransom was wearing shoes; at best it was shown that he was not barefooted. One of the questions the jury was to answer was whether the 'boots' of Ransom were dangerous weapons. Because of this required determination, the physical characteristics of Ransom's footgear cannot be considered immaterial. The term footgear could include such a variety of shoes, sandals, slippers and mukluks besides boots that we cannot see how a jury could reasonably decide whether Ransom's 'footgear' was a dangerous weapon. We believe that bare hands and feet cannot ordinarily be dangerous weapons. It is true that a blow with a bare hand or foot can cause serious bodily injury under certain circumstances. However, since Alaska does not have an aggravated assault statute such a blow by an ordinary person must be classified as a misdemeanor assault. If a person were wearing a soft leather glove a blow from his fist could still cause serious bodily injury; yet the possibility of injury would not be attributable to the use of the glove but rather to the fist itself. Such a case would still be a misdemeanor assault. For the crime of assault with a dangerous weapon to be shown, it must appear that the use of the weapon, rather than just the blow, had the capability of producing serious bodily injury considering the manner in which it was used. Thus, we believe that most types of ordinary wearing apparel cannot be dangerous weapons. Yet, under some circumstances a heavy-soled boot such as used in the *Berfield* case, could be a dangerous weapon. As we stated in *Berfield*, whether an object is a dangerous weapon depends upon the object's capability for harm considering the manner of its use. If nothing is known of the object's physical characteristics, its capability for harm cannot be reasonably determined.

There are some cases in which it is possible to infer from the nature of the victim's injuries that a dangerous weapon was used even though there is complete absence of evidence as to what the weapon was. However, such is not the present case. See *State v. Farmer*, 156 Ohio 214, 102 N.E.2d 11 (1951).

★ ★ ★

We therefore reverse the conviction and remand for proceedings not inconsistent with this opinion.

———————

Case Brief, Ransom v. State
Case Name, Author, Citation:

_____

_____

Facts:

_____

_____

_____

_____

_____

Procedural History:

_____

_____

Issue:

_____

_____

_____

Holding: (For purposes of this exercise, phrase the holding as a simple "yes" or "no.") _____

Rule:

_____

_____

_____

_____

Reasoning:

_____

_____

_____

_____

_____

Disposition:

_____

_____

_____

Notes:

_____

_____

_____

Exercise 3: Discussion Questions,
Ransom v. State

Now that you have completed and reviewed your case brief for *Ransom,* you need to consider how the case might be used in class. Your professors will spend a great deal of time asking follow up questions based on the case to see if you truly understand its ramifications. Read the questions below and write out your answers, being sure to consider any counterpoints to your assertions. Remember, your professors are often less concerned with the "answer" to a question than they are with how you arrived at and supported your conclusion.

Question 1—What arguments can you think of, both pro and con, for treating hands and feet as dangerous weapons if the defendant has been specifically trained to use them to harm others (e.g. boxer or martial arts expert). How do you think the Alaska Supreme Court would rule if they were confronted by these facts?

_____

_____

_____

_____

_____

_____

_____

_____

_____

_____

Question 2—If the witness testified that the defendant had been wearing "boots," would this change in the testimony have altered the Alaska Supreme Court's holding? Why?

_____

_____

_____

_____

_____

_____

_____

CHAPTER IV

What Your Classes
Will Be Like

In the last chapter, we discussed reading cases and creating a case brief, skills that are important to your pre-class preparation. Obviously, all students strive to be well prepared so that they can make the most out of their education. In law school, there is another reason why pre-class preparation is so important. In law school classes, students participate a great deal through a dialogue with their professors called the Socratic method. Through this dialogue with your professors and your classmates, you will begin to learn that there are multiple answers to most law school questions. Each answer will have some strengths and weaknesses, and some answers will be better than others. Eventually you will come to realize that your thorough explanation of these strengths and weaknesses is the real answer to the question being asked.

The Socratic Method

The Socratic method is as integral to the law school experience as studying case law. In fact, the two concepts really go hand in hand. You will spend most of your classroom time reviewing cases in an almost excruciating level of detail. What you may not realize is that student ideas are an important part of that review. In the introductory section to this book, I noted that active class participation is an important difference between college and law school. The Socratic method is an important aspect of that participation.

In a typical Socratic method scenario, a professor will call on a student to provide some of the essential information about an assigned case. After hearing this information, the professor will continue asking questions to flesh out the student's, and the class', understanding of the principles for which the case stands.

Professors employ the Socratic method in any number of ways. Some inform students in advance that they will be called on, others randomly pick a student, while still others adopt a middle of the road approach and "randomly" pick students in alphabetical order. Once a student has been chosen, there are still more variations. On one end of the spectrum, the selected student will be on the hot seat for the entire class and must respond to all of the professor's questions. The professor may ask other students questions as well, but their answers or questions will simply generate additional questions for the student on the hot seat. Using those answers and opinions as a springboard, the professor will explore the issue from every conceivable angle. On the other end of the spectrum, a professor may call on dozens of students during a single class. Your answer to a question will generate additional questions from your professor, but it will be your classmates who will have to respond. By the end of the period, over half the class may have spoken.

One of the more unnerving aspects of the Socratic method is that, regardless of how hard you try, it seems almost impossible to perfectly respond to your professor's questions. The reason for this is quite simple. There is rarely one perfect response to any question in law school, and this is part of what you are being taught. Instead of looking for the one right answer, your professors will force you to consider alternative ideas and points of view. This thorough discussion of all points of view, including their strengths and weaknesses, is the right answer. Therefore, do not be unnerved when you still don't know "the answer" to the professor's question at the end of Socratic dialogue. You are learning that there may not be an absolute answer to every question. And, even when there is a right answer, your professors will be more concerned about the process you went through in arriving at your conclusion as opposed to the conclusion itself. Therefore, the Socratic dialogue itself becomes the answer to your professor's question.

So, why do professors use the Socratic method? For one thing, its use tends to ensure a certain level of preparation from every student. More important, however, is that the Socratic method is an extremely helpful way of teaching students to think like lawyers. You will likely hear the term "think like a lawyer" dozens of times during your first year, and it means to think analytically. Thinking analytically means to look at an idea from every angle, and to consider the pros and cons of each possible outcome. The Socratic method helps you to develop this extremely important skill by forcing you to reconsider some of the basic assumptions you used in arriving at your answers to the professor's questions. While your professors will certainly be interested in hearing your answers, their careful questions will force you to confront "why" you came to a particular conclusion. As you and the professor begin exploring the "why" behind your answer, you may come to realize that there are unintended consequences to what you have put forward.

A certain amount of stress will accompany every Socratic dialogue between you and your professor. That is natural and should be expected. This is particularly true for those of you who are terrified of public speaking. If you are, you are in good company as public speaking is a very common fear.

Being aware that you are about to encounter a stressful situation is the first step in dealing with it, and the best way to deal with it is through preparation. Case briefing is one aspect of that preparation. Here are a few additional hints for helping you deal with speaking in class. Notice how each of these hints involves some form of active preparation or practice on your part.

Herb's Hints

If you are like most people and afraid of public speaking, just remember this old joke to keep things in perspective:

Through a recent survey, Americans identified their two greatest fears. Coming in first was public speaking and coming in second was death. I guess this means that more people are afraid to give a eulogy than to be the guest of honor at the funeral!

- **Actively participate and be proactive**—Accept the inevitable, that you will be called on in class, but do it on your own terms. If you know the answer to a question, raise your hand and participate as opposed to looking away and hoping that you are not called on. The stress you feel while answering a question that you know the answer to is nothing compared to being called on when you are unprepared. However, be ready for the professor to ask you follow up questions.
- **Create your own questions**—Another way of being proactive is to create your own questions. Write down any questions that occur to you as you read the day's assignment, and then bring these written questions with you to class. While you will not get any points for extemporaneous thinking, having written notes to consult as you ask a question can be a helpful security blanket.
- **Practice, practice, practice**—Make it your goal to speak regularly in your classes. While you may fumble through your first few efforts, it will get easier each time you speak. Do not make the mistake of believing that you will never need to hone this skill because you do not plan on being a trial attorney. Even if you never appear in a courtroom, your supervising attorney, your colleagues, or your clients will sometimes expect a quick oral summary of an issue you are working on.
- **Anticipate where your professor is going**—Answering a professor's questions becomes much easier if you know what she is going to ask,

and you do not need to be Nostradamus to pull off this neat trick. Based on a careful reading of the day's material, a review of the prior week's lecture notes, and a glance at the syllabus, you should have a pretty good idea of what concepts the professor is trying to get across. You will not be right all of the time—if you were you would be teaching the class. You will be surprised at how often you come close, however, and this exercise is also an outstanding way of preparing for your examinations.

- **Your professors have no interest in making you look foolish**—Some students have a hard time believing this, but professors are not out to make you miserable or make you feel foolish. Calling on you in class is simply one way that we can ensure you are engaged in the topic. We do not expect you to be right every time we call on you—far from it. In fact, incorrect answers are an important way for us to determine how well we are getting across the day's material. We do, however, expect you to be prepared. Your clients will certainly expect this as well.

Classroom Hypotheticals

One of the most common methods for generating classroom discussion is the hypothetical. Once you have finished dissecting a case in class, your professor will want to see whether you truly understood the rationale underlying the court's decision. To do this, the professor will use the recently discussed case as a starting point, but will then change some of the facts. The professor will then ask you to determine whether this new fact pattern, or hypothetical, will lead to a different conclusion. If the conclusion is different than the court's conclusion to the case you have been discussing, then the professor changed **material facts**. Facts are material when they are essential to the reasoning supporting a given conclusion. If the conclusion does not change once you have changed some of the facts, then the professor did not change material facts. Figuring out whether facts are material is an important aspect of performing legal analysis, and is part of the reason you will spend so much time briefing and dissecting cases for class.

At this point, you may be concerned about your ability to consistently come up with right answers to your professor's questions—don't be. An incorrect answer will not earn your professor's wrath—unless of course the answer indicates a lack of preparation on your part. In fact, it is often impossible for students to come up with the "right" answer time and time again. Why? There will not always be right or wrong answers to the questions.

Professors are more interested in the reasons behind your answer than the answer itself. Regardless of your response, your professor will force you to consider the rationale behind your answers and will suggest alternative rationales that you may not have considered. Then, once you have finally distanced yourself from your original conclusion and adopted the professor's point of view—WHAM! Suddenly your professor will change gears and what seemed like the wrong rationale a few moments before will now seem to be the correct point of view. Eventually, the professor may paint you into a corner so that regardless of your response, you feel like you are wrong. Usually, this is when class will end. There will be no resolution to the hypothetical posed by your professor, and you will walk out of class vaguely dissatisfied and wondering whether you just learned anything. The answer to this question is a resounding YES. You have learned to be fluid in your thinking. You have learned to consider alternative points of view. Finally, you have learned that, in some instances, there is no single "right" answer to a question.

In addition to all of the above, there is one more very important aspect to the Socratic method that you should keep in mind: the Socratic dialogue is an important way of preparing you to take law school examinations.

The most common method of testing first-year law students is the essay examination. In this type of examination, your professor will provide you with a lengthy fact pattern. The fact pattern will often be written in the form of a narrative in which the professor describes a series of events, and the narrative can be a few paragraphs or several pages long. The luckless individuals in these fact patterns will do everything from commit murder, to get lost and end up in a neighboring state, or even drop a piano on their neighbor's head. At the end of the fact pattern, the professor will likely ask an extremely open ended question along the lines of, "What are the rights and liabilities of all the parties?"

While these exams are far from easy, your professor has prepared you for just this sort of test. These fact patterns are simply lengthier versions of the hypotheticals discussed in class throughout the entire semester. Sorting out the various issues and organizing a thoughtful and complete response will take a great deal of time, but remember the Socratic dialogues from class whenever you start to struggle. They will remind you to support your conclusion with thorough analysis and to consider every issue from multiple points of view.[1]

---

1. I will discuss law school exams more fully in Chapter XI.

To give you some idea of what a Socratic dialogue feels like, here are a few exercises to work through. Without a full classroom and professor expectantly waiting for your answer, I cannot recreate the stress you will feel when called on in class. Still, these exercises will give you some idea of how each time you answer one question, you are actually generating addition questions for the professor to ask.

Exercise 1A

Let's use the first case we briefed from Chapter I, *Garratt v. Dailey*, as our starting point. In *Garratt v. Dailey*, the court noted that the defendant could still be liable for a battery if he knew to a substantial certainty that his actions would result in unwanted contact. Does this standard allow the trier of fact to take into account the defendant's age, and if so how?

_____

_____

_____

_____

_____

Exercise 1B

Assuming for a moment that the standard does allow for consideration of the defendant's age, should this be applied objectively or subjectively? In other words, should the trier of fact be asked to determine whether this specific child knew that his actions would result in unwanted contact (subjective) or should the emphasis be on whether an average child of the same age and background should have been aware of the ramifications of his actions? Explain your answer.

_____

_____

_____

_____

_____

Exercise 2A:
Consider the Following
Classroom Hypothetical

In your state, a statute requires that all cars come to a complete stop at a stop sign before proceeding. A complete stop requires a full two second pause after the stop before proceeding. The legislature in your state passed this law because drivers were quickly rolling through stop signs without coming to a complete stop. This resulted in several accidents and a large number of fatalities. A violation of this statute carries with it a $1,000 fine and the loss of a driver's license.

John has come to you seeking your help to avoid paying the fine and losing his license. He was recently pulled over for failing to come to a complete stop at a stop sign. He claims that bushes were obstructing his view at the intersection and that he had to keep edging his car out into the road in order to see the oncoming traffic. He did not accelerate until he was sure that there was no traffic. The police officer's report confirms that John was moving extremely slowly when he edged out into the road and that there were no cars approaching.

Pretend that you are John's attorney. Based on the law and on these facts, construct an argument as to why John should not have to pay the fine or lose his license. If you come up with more than one argument, list the ones you feel most strongly about first. Remember to fully explain the rationale supporting your conclusion.

_____

_____

_____

_____

_____

_____

_____

_____

Exercise 2B

Now, switch gears and pretend that you are the prosecutor! This is an old law school trick that is designed to force you to consider all points of view. If you haven't taken the opposing arguments into consideration when coming up with your answer, then your answer is incomplete. This time, come up with an argument as to why John should be treated no differently than anyone else who violated the statute. In your answer, be sure to address the defense arguments and why the prosecution's position should prevail.

_____

_____

_____

_____

_____

_____

_____

_____

_____

_____

CHAPTER V

Taking Notes:
A Three-Step Process

Everyone has taken notes during their college classes, and everyone has a system that works for them. You will be tested differently in law school than you were in college, however, which means that you will need to modify your note taking skills.

The most important thing to keep in mind about taking notes in law school is that it is a three-step process.

- First, write down what is said in class.
- Second, review those notes within 24 hours of class to make sure that everything still makes sense.
- Third, incorporate your notes into your course outline.

Step 1: Write Down What Is Said in Class

This first step, writing down what is said in class, is what most students think of when they think of taking notes. On the surface, the idea of note taking is a simple one. The professor speaks and then you write down the professor's words. However, this simple view of note taking is premised on the notion that your examinations will require you to parrot back your professor's words in order to receive a good grade. As I have already mentioned, law school examinations emphasize critical thinking as opposed to rote memorization. Therefore, as your law school examinations have a different emphasis, it only makes sense that you should modify the way you take notes.

Let's start with the fact that you took notes before you came to class. We called these notes a case brief, but they are still a form of notes. Avoid simply rewriting information about the cases that is already contained within your case briefs. Instead, correct or add to your briefs so that they accurately reflect what your professor and classmates are saying about the case. In fact, you can purchase a certain type of note paper that is made specifically for this purpose. It is referred to as "briefing" or "law ruled" paper, and its main distinguishing characteristic is a single line that runs from top to bottom that divides the paper into roughly 1/3 and 2/3 sections. The larger section is meant for your case brief and the smaller section is meant for your notes and corrections about the case. While I am not advocating that you purchase this kind of note paper, students who have used it indicate that it is an easy way to synchronize your notes with your case briefs.

So, are there any absolutes as to what you should be writing down? Thankfully, most professors give you clues as to which ideas from class are more important than others. For example, if you hear your professor say "these are the four (or any other number) factors that courts consider when addressing this issue," pay attention. One aspect of thinking like a lawyer is breaking larger ideas down into their constituent parts. When your professors start numbering ideas, they are showing you that an individual rule may actually be comprised of several smaller rules. Another example is the hypotheticals used in class. As we discussed earlier, your professor is exploring the limits of a particular rule through the use of hypotheticals and is testing your understanding of each new legal principle. These hypotheticals will be important later when you are studying for your exams as they are examples of how to analyze a particular rule of law.

Laptops vs. Handwritten Notes

The use of laptop computers for taking notes has exploded in the last few years. The reasons? First, the current generation of law students has grown up around computers, and these students are more comfortable at a keyboard than they are with a pen or pencil in their hand. Second, once you understand the basics of touch typing, you can take down information more quickly at a computer than you can writing in a notebook. Finally, the newest law schools place a great deal of emphasis on their high tech capabilities. Oftentimes, every seat has a power and data port so that students can plug in as soon as they enter the classroom. With all this going for the use of laptops in class, no one has really asked the question if there is a negative side to their use as a note taking tool. Allow me to suggest that there is a potential negative side to the use of computers in the classroom, but this does not mean you have to throw away your new laptop.[1] At the end of this section, you may conclude that

---

1. While reading this section, please keep in mind that I am limiting my discussion to the use of laptops in the classroom for taking notes.

handwriting your notes has some distinct advantages. However, if you keep a few things in mind, you can still take notes with your laptop efficiently and effectively.

Let's start with the most obvious downside to using a using a laptop in class—they can be a distraction. The most egregious example is students playing the hottest computer game when they should be paying attention to the professor's lecture. This is a waste of your hard earned money. If you doubt me, divide your tuition bill by the number of class sessions you will have by the end of the year to see just how much money each wasted class period is costing you. It is also unprofessional and can be a distraction to your classmates. Past generations certainly wasted time in class by playing hangman, but this decidedly low tech diversion never seemed to catch on the way gaming has in recent years. Because you are reading this book in order to help you prepare for law school, you are unlikely to be the kind of person who would play video games during class. Still, even students with the purest of motives can be lured to their doom by the siren's song of the internet.

If your classrooms come equipped with data ports at each seat, your natural inclination will be to plug into the internet as soon as you sit down—avoid this temptation. Unless your professor has specifically noted that you will need to access the internet during class, there is simply no reason to log on. Once you have logged on, it will be difficult to avoid the billions of distractions provided by the web. I am not suggesting that you will immediately log on and go view the newest movie trailers. Instead, it will begin with something as seemingly innocent as checking your e-mail during a free moment. Putting aside the fact that there are no free moments in class, an hour delay in checking your e-mail is hardly a reason to distract yourself from your professor's lecture. Then, once you have checked your e-mail, instant messaging your classmates won't be far behind. Let's assume, however, that you are quite diligent and that, during class, you use your laptop solely for taking notes. Even still, there are reasons to consider handwriting your notes.

When students use a laptop in class, they are tempted to write down every word said by their professors and their classmates. As a professor myself, I like to think that every syllable that comes out of my mouth is pure gold and worthy of immediate transcription. Honesty, however, forces me to admit that not everything I say is worth taking down. Remember, your overriding goal is to take an active role in your education. You cannot reach this goal if you turn yourself into a stenographer. Students who take down every word feel as if they are being active. Their fingers are ticking away at the keyboard, and at the end of class they will have several pages of notes on which to reflect. This kind of note taking can give you a false sense of security. If you focus on taking down every word, you will miss the substance and the nuance of what the professor has to say.

<table>
<tr><td>

Herb's Hints
___

Are you truly engaged in the professor's lecture? Here is a quick test. Stop taking notes to see if you could engage the professor in a dialogue on her lecture topic. If you can't, then you are not actively participating in your education.

</td><td>

As we have discussed, your classes are in many ways a dialogue between professor and student. During the course of this dialogue, your professor will introduce ideas that you may later discard. At other times, ideas that seemed incorrect initially will turn out to be the focus of your class. If you write down every word as it is being said, you are likely to lose track of what you are supposed to take away from that day's class. More importantly, you won't be a part of the dialogue because your focus will be on the words you are hearing and not on the ideas being tossed

</td></tr>
</table>

around. If you handwrite your notes, you know at the outset that you won't be able to take down every word. Therefore, you are more likely to listen carefully and remain engaged in the classroom dialogue.

I am not suggesting that the use of laptops as a note taking device will lead to failure during the first year of law school. In fact, now that you understand the pitfalls associated with the use of laptops in the classroom, you are much less likely to take notes incorrectly. Handwriting your notes during class, however, may help you during the next step in the note taking process, the post class review.

Step 2: Post-Class Note Review

Regardless of how you take notes during class, it is essential that you review those notes as soon as possible after class. A good rule of thumb is that you should review your notes no later than 24 hours after class. Even better, review the notes later that same day.

Your goal when reviewing your notes is to make sure that you understood every aspect of that particular lecture. In a sense, this is the "micro" view of your class. At this point, do not be concerned with the bigger picture of where these concepts fit into the course as a whole. Fully understanding a single lecture is enough work by itself, and do not fool yourself into thinking that this step will only take a few minutes.

While you are sitting in class, most everything your professor has to say will make perfect sense. I know this because I have been on both sides of the podium. As a student, my professors would often pause during their lectures to ask me and my classmates whether we had any questions, and most of the time we did not. The material being discussed was clear in our minds, at least while we were sitting in the friendly confines of the classroom. A week or two later when I would begin reviewing my notes, I would have dozens of questions. Ideas that I did not bother writing down because they seemed so elementary at the time had been forgotten. In addition, I could no longer follow the reasoning behind the resolution to the hypotheticals we had worked on in class. Without these ideas, my notes appeared fragmented and disjointed.

From the other side of the podium, I see the same thing happening to my students. Just as my professors did, I will often stop and ask my class for questions. During class, it is quite rare for someone to raise their hands. After class, I will receive e-mails with questions on ideas that we had discussed weeks earlier and that were essential to understanding the more recent topics. Suddenly, these students are weeks behind in their understanding of the material, and may not even realize it.

To avoid this danger, you must review your notes as soon as possible after class. One of the little secrets about law school, and something that is true of most graduate programs, is that much of your learning occurs outside of the classroom. You need to be your own best teacher, and the post-class review of your notes is an important step in this process.

The review itself is a multi-step process. First, you read the notes, but you must do so with a critical eye. Look for gaps in your understanding and for ideas that can be stated more concisely and clearly. Also, review the hypotheticals discussed in class.

As you review your notes, additional questions will occur to you, and this is the time to answer those questions. If you do not understand a concept, do not type it into your computer. Go to the library and conduct additional research, consult a legal treatise, or e-mail your professor a well thought out question, but be sure to answer your questions then and there. There will be a temptation to put off difficult questions until later, but you will be so busy later with other work that your questions will go unanswered. This will lead to what I refer to as the "snowball" effect.

Legal learning is a cumulative process where each class builds on the concepts learned in previous classes. If you do not understand the first week's lectures as well as you should, then it will be impossible to understand next week's lectures to their fullest because next week's concepts will build on this week's ideas. This effect multiplies itself over time, or snowballs, so that it is impossible to see the nuances in the principles discussed in class. Instead, you will only understand your lectures on the surface. What is truly insidious about this snowball effect is that you won't necessarily realize that it is happening. You will still be reading your cases, and you will understand the professor's lecture on a general level. Seven or eight weeks into the semester, however, you won't realize that you are missing the deeper level of the professor's lecture because you will not have learned the information necessary to realize that there is even a deeper level to be learned. The only hints will be your classmates writing notes furiously regarding a concept that you regard as quite basic or questions from your classmates that make little sense to you. The good news is that you can make the snowball effect work for you.

If you understand this week's material to its fullest, then you already have a head start on next week's material. Over time, your efforts at understanding each week's material to its fullest snowballs as well so that nuance in the lectures soon become apparent. Then, seven or eight weeks into the semester you will be the one asking questions in class that only you, your professor, and a handful of your classmates truly understand.

Handwriting Your Notes and Post-Class Review

I mentioned earlier that handwriting your notes in class can be helpful when later reviewing your notes, and here is why. You accomplish the most during the post-class note review when you are willing to truly attack the notes. Do not be afraid to question what you wrote by crossing things out and starting from scratch if need be. Your job is to begin distilling the notes down to their essence. This will require you to remove material that, upon reflection, is superfluous or even incorrect. Your class notes are far from perfect and should be treated accordingly, which is a bit easier to do if you have handwritten notes to work from.

Handwritten notes will need to be typed into your computer, therefore you are more likely to change them and even remove material. You need to type the notes anyway, so it will not be any additional work to make changes. In addition, by typing the notes in this fashion, you will have to reconsider and review *every* aspect of what you wrote during class. In doing so, you will begin the memorization process, which is an aspect of exam preparation. If your notes are already in the computer, there will be a tendency to leave certain material untouched and therefore unreviewed. Does this mean that you cannot follow my methodology if you type your notes in class? Of course not. As I suggested earlier in the section on typing vs. handwritten notes, you can still achieve the desired affect if you print out your notes and treat them as if they were handwritten. When you are pressed for time—and all law students are— resist the temptation to leave your notes in their original form.

Step 3: Incorporating the Notes into Your Outline

Once you have finished reviewing and correcting your notes, it is time to switch gears from the "micro" to the "macro." Under the "macro" view of the course, our focus shifts away from how individual concepts operate. Instead, the goal is to incorporate these individual concepts into your course outline in the most logical way possible. In this way you will be creating a big picture of how an entire area of the law operates.

Creating a course outline will not be as simple as merely tacking this week's notes at the end where last week's notes left off. Instead, many of this week's ideas will actually contain aspects of ideas that you may have covered several weeks earlier. Similarly, this week's concepts may be incomplete without additional material that you won't cover for several more weeks. Outlining is the focus of the next chapter.

Creating Your Own Hypotheticals

One of the best ways of testing whether you truly understand a new concept is to create your own hypothetical fact patterns based on your professor's lectures and the classroom discussion. First, use one of rules discussed in class as a starting point. Then, attempt to create a variety of fact patterns to test your ability to apply this rule. If your professor used a hypothetical to illustrate the rule, then try changing the facts to see if you can still figure out how the fact pattern should be analyzed. Remember, law school exams test your analytical ability as opposed to your memorization skills, so this is good way of preparing for finals. Read the following hypothetical, and then we can work on changing it to illustrate my point.

Torts Hypothetical

Let's use the concept of negligence to illustrate how you might go about creating your own hypothetical. The tort of negligence is broken down into the elements of duty, breach of duty, causation, and damages. In determining whether an individual breached his duty of care, courts often employ the reasonable person test. Using this objective test, a jury is asked to determine whether a reasonably prudent person would have acted in that situation as did the defendant. In class, the professor illustrates this principle with the following fact pattern.

John is smoking a cigarette as he is driving down the road on his way home from work. When he is finished, he tamps the cigarette until he thinks it is out, and then throws the butt out the window. Before smoking the cigarette, John had listened to radio news report about the drought conditions in the region. Due to the dry conditions, the cigarette butt ignited the brush and caused a fire that destroyed a nearby home. A motorist who had been driving behind John reported his license plate number to the home owner who is now suing John for negligently throwing his cigarette butt out the window. Using the reasonably prudent person test, did John breach his duty of care to the homeowner? Yes he did. First, John was the one who created the risk by throwing his cigarette out the window. The facts indicate that he did try to tamp out the butt, however, he must not have done a very good job because it caused a fire. John could have simply placed the butt in his ashtray. Considering the fact that the area was suffering from a drought, a fact that John was aware of, no reasonably prudent person would have tossed a potential fire source out the window.

Now let's start changing facts to test how well we truly understand the reasonably prudent person concept. To start with, we will change only one fact in the hypothetical to test ourselves. How would the answer change if John had not been listening to the radio? If John wasn't listening to the radio, then he would not have heard about the drought. Does this mean it would be OK to throw the cigarette butt out the window? I don't think so.

First, John may have known about the dangerous conditions without the benefit of the radio report. His other senses would have told him that it was hot and dry outside. Also, keep in mind that he was traveling home from work. He wasn't magically dropped into an area that he was unfamiliar with, so he would have experienced the drought on a daily basis. While we don't have clear information regarding his awareness, he still may have known that he was engaging in risky behavior and chose to ignore the dangers. Second, even if John did not "know" about the drought, he should have known. Based on the above information—it was hot and dry outside, John lived in the area, and the conditions had persisted for a time—no reasonably prudent person would throw an ignition source like a cigarette out the window. Therefore, even if John didn't know of the risks inherent in his actions, he should have known.

Exercise 1A

Using the above torts hypothetical as a jumping off point, change the fact pattern where the outcome remains the same—John still breaches his duty of care and is negligent.

_____

_____

_____

_____

_____

_____

_____

_____

_____

_____

_____

Exercise 1B

Now, change the fact pattern enough so that John no longer breaches his duty of care. When attempting this exercise, keep the reasonably prudent person standard in mind. John will no longer be negligent once a reasonably prudent person would act in the same way.

_____

_____

_____

_____

_____

_____

_____

_____

_____

_____

_____

CHAPTER VI

Creating a Course Outline

What Is an Outline?

No later than the first week of law school, every first-year student has learned that an outline is essential if one expects to do well on exams. Students hear about them everywhere. Professors remind them that they should have already started outlining, the bookstores are full of commercial outlines, and upper class students talk knowingly about the "killer" outline that they used last year to ace contracts. Unfortunately, students receive little guidance on the "do's and don'ts" of outlining. Hopefully, I am about to change that.

So, what is an outline? An outline is an attempt to reduce the often chaotic mix of materials a student possesses for any one class into a cogent and organized study aid of reasonable length. When created correctly, an outline will become a student's primary, and possibly only, study aid for exams. While a course outline is an important study aid come exam time, the process of creating an outline is actually more important than the end product.

Students truly learn the law through the process of creating an outline. Obviously professors teach the law in class. It is while creating an outline, however, that students place the bits and pieces that they learn in class into a larger framework. For example, a student will learn about consideration over one or more contracts classes, but the student must integrate this single concept into a framework that includes topics such as offer, counter-offer, acceptance, part performance, breach, etc. Thus, a completed outline represents the "big picture" view that students crave for every class.

Outlining and Active Participation

The concept of outlining, better than anything else, illustrates the need to approach law school differently than college. Up until this point, many of my recommendations about preparing for law school classes have their corollaries in preparing for college. You read your text book and take notes in college,

85

and you read your casebook and brief cases in law school. The concept of course outlining, however, is fairly unique to law school.

When you create a course outline, you are in essence teaching yourself the intricacies of a specific course. Until you create an outline, you merely understand how individual legal concepts operate. Once you have completed your outline, you will understand how these individual concepts operate together within the context of an entire area of the law. No one will be there to tell you whether your outline is absolutely right or wrong. No one can. Your outlines are your own personal distillation of your law school classes. They are written by you, for you, and will never help anyone else understand their classes in the same way they will help you.

It's the Journey, Not the Destination

Outlining is a process that should begin fairly early in the semester and should continue until the end of the year. Classes in law school tend to build upon each other. Therefore, a thorough understanding of topics raised during the first few weeks of the semester is essential if one is to understand concepts covered later in the year. Creating your outline on a rolling basis can help. For example, reviewing and outlining a week's worth of class notes over the weekend forces you to reconsider that week's topics. In order to create the outline, you will be forced to consider how various topics fit together, and you may even need to engage in additional research regarding certain ideas. By the end of the weekend, you should have a thorough understanding of the prior week's material. As the next week's class material will likely build on the prior week's topics, you will be in a much better position to comprehend the new material on a much deeper level. In fact, as the year progresses, you may even be able to anticipate the focus for next week's classes based on what you have already covered.

When Should I Begin Outlining?

The short answer to this question is "start early." Because outlining is a process that continues throughout the year, you need to begin at some point during the first month of classes. While I cannot pick an exact date for you, keep the following points in mind. An outline is intended to be your own understanding of how the various aspects of a class fit together. It should provide context, indicating how the rules of law you learned on the first day of class might relate to the rules you learned months later. Because courses tend to move somewhat slowly during the first week or two of law school, it may be a few weeks before you have enough material to begin your formal outline.

Some of you may be planning on spending a great deal of time on your outlines near the end of the semester, completing them as exams are about to begin. This is not a plan for success. By now you are aware that law school is extremely time consuming. If you wait to work on your outlines until the end of the semester, it is unlikely that you will have enough time to complete them prior to exams. If you do complete them before exams, it means that other aspects of your studies have suffered. Also, an outline is only effective as a study aid when you have time to read it several times prior to the exams. If you wait too long, you will not have this time. As you are scrambling at the end of the semester, your goal will become completing the outline as opposed to studying from it. Not only that, but rushing to complete the outline means you are not benefiting from the process of creating it.

Should I Buy Commercial Outlines?

Should students use a commercial outline in place of their own outlines? The answer to this one is easy—NO! As I have already mentioned, students will develop a much deeper understanding of the law through the process of creating an outline. If the idea of developing a deeper understanding of the law does not convince you, then consider the following reasons for creating your own outline. Commercial outlines tend to be extremely long; 300 and 400 page outlines are not uncommon. They tend to be this long because the authors must take into account the variations in what professors from across the country cover in their courses. For the student, this means wading through dozens of pages of irrelevant material, and no one can afford to waste time in law school. Also, a 300–400 page "outline" is not helpful as a primary study aid. While you may be able to finish reading the commercial outline once by the end of the year, multiple readings are necessary in order to commit key concepts to memory.

If you still plan on using a commercial outline in place of your own outline, keep the following in mind. In your contracts class, for example, you are not learning all there is to know about contract law. Instead, your professor is emphasizing some concepts and deemphasizing or even excluding others. In a sense, you are learning the law of contracts according to your professor. Therefore, an outline geared toward how your professor taught the class is essential.

So, do commercial outlines have any role in preparing for examinations? They may. Reference material is often extremely helpful when creating an outline. It can be used to confirm your own understanding of a topic, to provide additional examples of how a rule of law might be applied, or to note how different jurisdictions might treat the same principle. While many students will use a **hornbook** for this purpose, commercial outlines can serve the same purpose. Do not, however, fall into the trap of following the commercial outline's organization when creating your own outline. First, this is only a small step away from using the commercial outline in place of your own. Second, struggling with the organization of your own outline is an important step in understanding how an area of the law operates. If you figure out a solid structure on your own, even if it differs from other sources, you will understand each of your first year courses much more completely than if you simply adopted another outline's structure.

Can I Use Someone Else's Outline?

If you are considering using a classmate's outline, I have one piece of advice for you—DON'T! This is true whether you plan on sharing outlines with members of your study group or getting your hands on the outline written by last year's valedictorian. Any time saved through using another's outline will be more than made up for by the low grades that will result. So why shouldn't you use another's outline?

- **You Learn the Law When Writing an Outline**—If you use someone else's outline, you will not understand the topic nearly as well as you would if you wrote your own outline. Remember, outlining is a part of a process that leads to a deeper understanding of your courses. Another student's outline would be fine if your exams emphasized memorizing a long list of rules, but they do not. Since exams are about identifying problems and then analyzing them, the outlining process, which requires synthesizing rules and organizing them logically, is an integral part of mastering the art of legal analysis.
- **Your Outline Must Be a Reflection of Your Professor's Class**—During their first year, most students take the same courses regardless of the law school. The content of those courses, however, differs greatly depending on who is doing the teaching. Therefore, an outline based on a different professor's property class, for example, will be useless to you when studying for your property exam.
- **Outlines Are Unique to Their Authors**—Without necessarily intending to do so, each student writes a somewhat unique outline. For ex-

ample, a student struggling with the concept of causation in a prod-
ucts liability action may spend a great deal of time in the outline laying out the concept. The student who "got" the concept immediately is
unlikely to devote much outlining time to it. Your outline will not be
helpful as a study tool unless it is written based on your own strengths
and weaknesses.

• **Another Student's Outline May Contain Mistakes**—When you consider
how expensive law school can be, why would you rely on material written by another student when preparing for exams? No first-year student,
regardless of aptitude, is an expert on any area of the law. Also, why rely
on another student's understanding of a concept when your professors
will be grading you?

Now You Are Ready to Outline

Now that the preliminaries are out of the way, you are ready to start outlining. When creating your outline, you will do the following:

• Organize your ideas around concepts and rules rather than merely list-
ing cases
• Display the proper relationship between concepts
• Classify/synthesize cases into groups
• Use cases and hypotheticals to help define concepts and illustrate rules

Organizing Your Ideas around Concepts and Rules

While organizing an outline around ideas may seem simple, this aspect of
outlining often causes students the greatest amount of difficulty. Instead, students tend to organize around cases and end up with an outline that reads like
a series of case briefs. This mistake is understandable when one considers how
much time students spend dissecting cases in class. Professors, however, rarely
expect you to memorize cases for a law school examination. Instead, they expect you to have learned the various rules of law and how those rules are applied through a discussion of cases in class. Then, it is your job to organize
these individual ideas in a way that enhances your understanding of the entire course. You are creating a logical approach to an area of the law that you
will later use to logically organize your examination answers. With these concepts in mind, the idea of organizing your outline around legal concepts,
should make more sense.

Now that you have a general idea of why you should be organizing your outline around legal concepts, your next question should be, "so where do I find these concepts?" The good news is that you already have them. They can be found in four places: your class notes; your case briefs; your case book; and your course syllabus. Start with your case book, focusing on the table of contents. The table of contents is likely broken down into topics that should be included in your outline. Once you have listed all the topics from the table of contents, move on to your syllabus. The syllabus will help you find additional concepts that the professor has focused on during the year. Next, review your class notes and case briefs. Scan them, looking for additional ideas you may have missed. For example, the review of your notes and brief on *Garratt v. Dailey* will remind you to include "knowledge to a substantial certainty" as part of your definition of intent. Now, you should have a fairly lengthy list of concepts from which to work.

Remember, your goal at this point in the process is to create a long list of ideas. Do not worry about organizing the ideas yet. That is the next step. Also, do not worry about whether a word or phrase is actually a legal concept worthy of inclusion in your outline. You will revise your outline throughout this process, so you have plenty of time to fine tune it. Below is sample list of topics that one might create based on the *first weeks* of a torts class. I have chosen the time frame based on when most students will begin writing their outlines.

Torts Topic List

intent	volitional act
reckless conduct	negligent conduct
intent to harm	assault
battery	false imprisonment
trespass to land	trespass to chattels
malice	transferred intent
mental illness/intent	transferred intent, different tort
touching	transferred intent, different person
implied consent	express consent
objective reasonable person	offensiveness
unanticipated harm	item closely associated with victim
	eggshell skull

Keep a few things in mind as you go through this list.

- This is not meant as a topic list for a year long torts class. By the end of the year, your torts outline may end up containing hundreds of topics.
- I have not tried to organize the concepts yet. That is the next step.

- I created this list of topics based on the first few weeks of *my* torts class. You may encounter some of these concepts later in the year, or not at all.
- Remember, do not worry about creating a "perfect" list. The list should be the product of your own brainstorming session, and as such will contain ideas that you may later decide to exclude.
- You will be updating your outline weekly throughout the semester, so you will have to create a new list of topics each week. Simply review your notes *since the last time you updated your outline* to find the newest topics that you will incorporate into your existing outline.

Display the Proper Relationship among Topics

Now that the list is in place, your next task is to organize it and insert the rules of law. While you should attempt to organize the material on your own, your casebook or a course syllabus can help. Be sure that your organization proceeds logically, and that you begin with the broadest ideas. For example, most torts classes begin with the intentional torts, and one might be naturally inclined to begin with the tort of battery because it is often the first intentional tort discussed. The organization for such an outline might start out looking something like this:

I. Intentional torts
  A. Battery
    1. Requires intentional contact
      a. Transferred intent

Initially, this sort of organization is a good way to begin because it moves from general to specific. The broadest level of organization is "Intentional torts," which sets up your next level of division. Thus, letter "A" will be battery, letter "B" assault, and so on through all of the intentional torts.

Digging deeper into the concept of battery, you would begin listing the elements for this intentional tort. As you can see from this example, the first element discussed is intent, and this element contains the sub-category "transferred intent." What you may not realize, however, is that the concept of transferred intent is going to cause problems if placed at this spot in the outline.

You will soon learn that the concept of transferred intent is applicable to the other intentional torts. By placing it at this point in the outline, you are indicating that its applicability is limited to the intentional tort of battery. Does that mean you would have been wrong to initially organize your outline in this fashion? The answer is no.

Course outlines are constantly evolving until the moment you incorporate the material from your last day of class. You add new ideas each time you work on the outline, and you may have to reorganize existing portions of the outline as well. Remember, an outline is intended to illustrate how the various ideas you have learned in class interact with one another. Seeing as you learn more during each of your classes, it only makes sense that your outline will evolve as does your understanding of the law. On some occasions, you may simply add new material to the end of your existing outline. On other occasions, however, you may have to fit the new material into several different locations, or even reorganize the outline entirely. While reorganizing your outline can be time consuming, do not give up! Each reorganization is enhancing your understanding of how the course operates.

Adding the Rules

Once you have completed the basic organization of your outline, the next step is to add rules of law to the topics. For example, the topic "intent" would now include the definition of this term. How detailed should your definition be? That is entirely up to you. As we have already discussed, each outline is unique to its author. Therefore, your definition of intent will depend on your understanding of the topic, how it was covered in class, and which cases were used to illustrate the concept.

Notice a few things about the organized torts topic list example on the facing page. First, I have underlined or placed in bold certain concepts. I did so because I wanted these concepts to stand out when I was reading the outline. Another person would likely highlight different parts of the outline. However, resist the urge to highlight large sections of the outline. You should highlight in order to emphasize, and when you highlight too much you are actually emphasizing less.

Next, note that I have dealt with the concept of intent independently from each intentional tort. Why? As I alluded to above, certain aspects of the concept of intent are applicable to all of the intentional torts. Therefore, it made sense to treat the concept like an introductory idea in my outline. This does not mean that the concept will not be addressed elsewhere in my outline. For example, it is possible that there is a unique aspect to intent within each of the intentional torts.

Finally, keep in mind that this is *my* outline, and certain aspects of the organization will be unique to me and my understanding of my course. It is true that your outline will bear some resemblance to the ones created by other students in your class, but do not be concerned if there are significant differences as well. And remember, do not worry if you feel the need to change the struc-

Torts Topic List, Organized and Including Rules

I. Intent—Either must desire to cause some mental or physical effect or must act with **substantial certainty** that tortious event would follow. Reckless/negligent acts generally insufficient.
   A. Volitional act—harm must result from volitional act. Movement while sleeping or involuntary body movements insufficient
   B. Malice or intent to harm unnecessary—all that is necessary is intent to affect plaintiff. Normally, party intends harm, but intent to harm not required.
   C. Transferred intent—three different types of transferred intent, all suffice
      1. **Intent to commit tort on different person**—when defendant acts with intent to commit tort on party A but commits tort on party B, intent is transferred from A to B and D still liable.
      2. **Intent to commit different tort on same person**—D still liable
      3. **Intent to commit different tort on different person**—If have intent to commit 5 most common intentional torts on party A, but act causes another tort to party B, D still liable. Torts included:
         a. Assault
         b. Battery
         c. False imprisonment
         d. Trespass to land
         e. Trespass to chattels
   D. Mental illness and intent—D with mental illness can still form intent.

ture of your outline over time. As your understanding of a topic evolves, so will your outline.

The rules to be incorporated into your outline will come from a few different sources. Primarily, you will obtain the rules from the cases you read. This does not mean, however, that you will necessarily have the rule you need once you finish reading a single case. Instead, you will need to consider the following additional sources when constructing your rules.

- **Classroom discussion**—Even after you have become proficient at reading and briefing cases, you should not rely solely on your own individual understanding of what the case stands for. You and your classmates will thoroughly discuss most of your cases in class with your professor. Allow the classroom discussion and your professor's guidance and insight help you extract the rules from the cases.

- **Conduct Additional Research Using Treatises**—Even after you have discussed a case or concept in class, you may still be confused. That is to be expected, and might even be a blessing in disguise. Actively engage the topic by conducting some independent research. Your additional research on a topic will help cement the idea in your memory, and may even disclose additional concepts that need review. Do not worry about finding a treatise that would be easily understood by a first year law student. Multiple **hornbooks** are available for every first-year course and are written with students in mind. Hornbooks are relatively expensive, so be sure to check your law school library before rushing out to purchase them for each class.

- **Read Additional Cases**—Many of your casebooks will list additional cases at the end of each chapter as suggested reading. Similarly, your professors may end class with a list of cases that can be read for those looking for additional treatment of a particular issue. If you are struggling with a concept, then these additional cases are a must read. Sometimes, a different judge's way of writing about a topic will "click" for you, making the additional reading worth your time. Even if you are not struggling with a topic, you may still want to find and read suggested cases. Not only will this additional reading enhance your understanding of the topic, the cases may be used as source material by your professors as they are writing their exams!

Adding Cases and Hypos to Illustrate the Rules

Once you have reached this point in the outlining process, you may be inclined to leave well enough alone. The concepts are well organized and the rules of law that you have derived from classroom discussion and case synthesis are all in place. If you were going to use your outline to prepare for a college examination, I might agree with you. You could simply memorize the rules, parrot them back to your college professor, and wait for your good grade to arrive in the mail. The problem is that you are no longer in college. In law school, your professors expect you to apply the rules of law to fact patterns you have never seen before. In order to do this effectively, you need to understand how the rules have been applied in the past. Multiple examples of how your professor applied the rule will help you better understand the principles involved, but do not take this idea to an extreme level. While two or three hypos might better illustrate a principle, a tenth hypo is unlikely to add much to the discussion and will lead to an extremely long outline. When done correctly, the cases and hypotheticals help define the rule. Consider the following example.

Battery Example

Rule—Unpermitted and harmful or offensive touching of another by an act intended to result in such contact is a battery.

Fact Pattern—Defendant intentionally brushes against the plaintiff subway passenger in order to get by him and to a seat on the train. The plaintiff suffers from the rare disorder ifyoutouchmeIscream, and immediately starts yelling. He later testified as to being extremely offended by the contact. A psychiatrist also testified that those suffering from this disorder detest physical contact and would suffer mental anguish if touched.

Issue—Is this a battery?

If you use only the provided rule, what would your answer to this question be? Using only this rule of law, the answer would be that this is a battery. There was a touching of another. The defendant intended to touch the plaintiff in order to get to his seat and both the plaintiff and a psychiatrist testified that the touching offended this plaintiff. Before I focused you on the rule, however, you probably answered that the defendant did not commit a battery. Why the discrepancy?

What we need is a hypo that further defines the rule. A class hypo illustrating that we judge what is offensive based on a reasonable person standard would have made things a lot clearer. It is likely that you remembered such a hypo from class and that it made this concept much easier to understand. With so much material to retain, you cannot always trust that you will remember the cases and hypos you covered in class. That is why you should add them to your outline.

Editing Your Work

Until exams begin, your outline will always be a work in progress. Therefore, do not be afraid to add, delete, and move material. This is particularly true during the early stages of the outlining process. For example, many contracts classes begin with the concept of damages. While there are many good reasons to begin teaching the course with the concept of damages, you may want to begin your outline with other topics. Remember that contract damages only become an issue when a contract has been created and then breached. So, you may want to begin your outline with contract formation as opposed to damages.

Policy Considerations

Depending on your professor, you may need to include policy considerations in your outline. In some classes, public policy plays a very important role. In others, the professors rarely mention policy issues. Policy considerations form the underpinnings of *why* certain rules of law have been created or adopted within a jurisdiction. For example, punitive damages are rarely awarded for a breach of contract. That is the rule. The underlying policy behind this rule focuses on economics. The breach of a private contract is unlikely to injure the community, and may actually benefit the community by permitting a more productive allocation of resources. Further, compensatory damages allow for the reallocation of resources while making the victim whole. If your professor discussed this concept in class, it should be in your outline because it will be fair game on an examination.

The Outline as a Study Tool

As I have noted throughout this chapter, it is the outlining process and not necessarily the final product that is valuable when trying to make sense of your classes. Still, most students intend to use their outline as their primary or only study tool, and well they should. Consider the following when viewing your outline as your primary study aid.

- **Outline length**—There is no magic length for an outline, but it should be short enough that you can read it through from beginning to end multiple times in a single day. It needs to be long enough, however, to fully explain ideas that you may not have reviewed for several months.
- **Condensing your outline**—When you first start studying from your outline, you should be reading the entire document. As you get closer to examination, however, make your outline shorter and see whether you still remember the key concepts. As a first step, remove the case references and hypotheticals. Once you have studied from this version for a day or so, remove the rules next. This should leave you with a list of topics. Once you have studied from this version, remove most of the

topics so that you are left with only the broadest organizational concepts, likely only those represented by a roman numeral.

- **Memorize a skeletal outline**—I refer to the final condensed version of an outline as a skeletal outline. Consider committing this entire version of your outline to memory. It should not be too difficult to do as this version should be no longer than 1–2 pages. Then, when you walk into your examination, write down your skeletal outline onto scrap paper (if provided), the sheet containing the question, or the inside cover of your blue book. Doing so accomplishes two things: first, it forces you to write something with which you are very familiar, thereby relieving pent up anxiety; second, this skeletal outline will act like a checklist. Consult it during your examination. If the parol evidence rule was listed on your contracts skeletal outline and you never referenced it in your answer, then you may want to go back and look at the question to see if you have missed something.

Summary

We have covered quite a bit, but when you look back on what we have discussed, the following ideas are the most important.

- An outline represents your understanding of how the various aspects of a course fit together, so you must create your own outline.
- Outlining is a process that takes place throughout the semester. Cramming to create an outline at the end of the semester does not work.
- Your outline should be built logically around legal concepts, not cases.
- Use cases and hypotheticals to illustrate those concepts.

Sample Torts Outline Structure

The following is a sample of a few pages from a torts outline. It is intended to illustrate the structure of an outline. Notice how the broadest aspects of the outline naturally lead into more specific ideas that provide further explanation. Also, notice that the hypos and cases provide further explanation, but are relatively short. I have included as much of the case as I felt necessary to illustrate the relevant point. The word "text" appears several times in parentheses. These are intended as a quick reference to the case's location in the textbook, allowing me to quickly find and reread the case if necessary. **DO NOT** use this in place of your own outline or as a substitute for anything you have discussed in your classes.

I. Intent—Defendant must desire to cause some harmful or offensive effect on plaintiff or must act with *substantial certainty* that tortious event would follow. Generally, reckless or negligent actions are not enough for intent.

   A. **Volitional act**—Tort must result from volitional act on part of Defendant. Movements while sleeping or involuntary body movements do not satisfy requirement.

   B. **Malice or an intent to hurt not necessary**—All that is required is an intent to affect the plaintiff. Normally, defendant does intend to harm, but this is not necessary.

      1. EXP—*Garratt v. Dailey* (text 10)—Child pulled chair away and plaintiff fell to ground when tried to sit. Trial court found no liability because child did not intend to hurt P. Appeals court remands and states that child liable if acted with *substantial certainty* that prohibited contact would result.

         a. Note to self—Focus of case is defining intent as knowledge to a substantial certainty. Secondarily, children may form intent and commit intentional torts.

      2. HYPO 1—D shoots gun into crowd and hopes that bullet will miss everyone. Intended battery because acted with substantial certainty that bullet would hit someone. Hope that shot would miss irrelevant.

      3. HYPO 2—D hunting and shoots at deer. Shot misses deer and hits hiker who hunter never saw. No intent. Never saw hunter, so cannot say acted with substantial certainty that harm would result. Also, no transferred intent because shooting a deer is not a battery.

   C. **Transferred intent**—Three different types of transferred intent.

      1. **Intent to commit tort on different person**—When act with intent to commit intentional tort with regard to party A, but actually commit tort on party B, intent transferred and Defendant still liable.

         a. EXP—*Talmage v. Smith* (text 15)—Defendant throws stick at boy who was with friends on roof. Stick misses intended target and hits another boy Defendant never saw. Defendant still liable because intent to hit one person in crowd transferred to actual victim.

      2. **Intent to commit different tort on same person**—Defendant still liable.

      3. **Intent to commit different tort on different person**—If have intent to commit 5 most common intentional torts on party A, but act causes another tort to party B, defendant still liable. Torts included are:

         a. assault
         b. battery

       c. false imprisonment

       d. trespass to land

       e. trespass to chattels

  D. **Mental illness and intent**—Party with mental illness can still form intent necessary for intentional torts.

    1. *McGuire v. Almy* (text 20)—Mentally ill defendant struck plaintiff with leg from piece of furniture. D guilty—Mental illness does not preclude finding of intent even if attack would not have occurred without illness. Practical solution to difficult issue. As between injured party and defendant, loss should be borne by wrongdoer.

II. Intentional torts

  A. Battery—Unpermitted and harmful or offensive touching of another by an act intended to result in such contact.

    1. Unpermitted—If party consents to touching, there can be no liability for battery.

      a. Express consent—Actual consent by plaintiff. Consent to surgery.

        i. *Mohr v. Williams* (text 22)—Defendant doctor operated on right ear, but had only obtained consent to surgery on left ear. Held: battery. Today, consent forms are written to cover additional necessary procedures.

      b. Implied consent—People must accept certain touching in society.

        i. Hypo 1—Gently nudge by someone to get on subway. Implied consent to this touching.

        ii. Hypo 2—Push someone out of the way because the person is blocking the door, and defendant pushes hard enough that plaintiff hits the ground. No implied consent to this level of touching. Goes beyond what is expected in society.

    2. Offensive touching—Courts apply **objective standard of offensiveness**. Person of peculiar sensitivity cannot recover unless touching would be offensive under societal standard.

      a. Objective standard may not apply if defendant is aware of plaintiff's sensitivity.

    3. Touching items **closely associated** with plaintiff's body—If defendant touches item that is associated with plaintiff's person, touching element satisfied.

      a. EXP—*Fisher v. Carousel Motor Hotel* (text 30)—Defendant grabs plate from plaintiff's hand while plaintiff is in buffet line because establishment doesn't serve black customers. This action satisfied touching element because plate was closely associated with person when it was grabbed. In this context, also offensive.

      b. Note to self—seems that item touched must be in contact with plaintiff's person, but that no special personal attachment to item is required.

      c. Note to self #2—Seems that this is also an example of an offensive, as opposed to harmful, touching.

    4. Unanticipated harm—As a general rule, when defendant's actions constitute a battery, then the defendant will be liable for any harm that results from the battery. Plaintiff will be compensated for unanticipated or unintended harm.

      a. HYPO—Defendant decides to play joke on friend and grabs him around the throat from behind and pretends to choke him. Startled, the friend turns his neck quickly and suffers a serious neck injury.

        i. Here, D liable for this unintended harm as long as this was a battery.

        ii. Consent—Possible, but unlikely, that plaintiff might have consented to touching if this was the kind of joke that they played on each other on a regular basis. However, facts are silent on this point.

CHAPTER VII

Legal Synthesis

You are responsible for much of the learning that takes place during the first year of law school, and that principle is most evident when students are asked to perform legal synthesis. As the term implies, legal synthesis requires you to build a rule of law from various sources. Most commonly, those sources will be cases and statutes.

In a typical class, your professor will introduce a topic for discussion. Over the course of that class, and sometimes several classes, your professor will lead you through a discussion of different cases that deal with the topic. For purposes of our discussion, we will use the torts concept of battery. As you move from one battery case to the next, you

> **Legal Definition**
>
> Legal Synthesis—The art of constructing a single principle of law from any number of cases or other legal sources.

will learn that the tort of battery is actually comprised of several different elements. Remember, elements are the various pieces of a larger rule, and the plaintiff must prove each of these elements in order to win the lawsuit. Torts are civil wrongs as opposed to crimes, so the plaintiff would have to prove each element by a preponderance of the evidence.

As you discuss the individual elements of a battery, you will notice a few things. First, the cases will not seem to say the same thing, which is strange as they are dealing with the same element of battery. Second, while your professor will encourage discussion of what these cases mean, she may not tell you what you should take from these cases. Instead, she will expect you to synthesize each element of battery from the various cases you are reading. While initially frustrating, you will be learning to perform legal synthesis.

As you become more proficient at reading cases, you will begin to realize that individual cases, while important, only give you part of the picture. No one case will illustrate all the facets of a single rule, and why should it? Remember that appellate courts attempt to limit their holdings to the facts of the cases before them. Therefore, it should come as no surprise that we need to look at multiple cases to fully flesh out any single rule of law.

Why Synthesize?

In the law school context, there are several important reasons why you must understand the concept of legal synthesis. I have already alluded to the first—your professors will not always illustrate all aspects of a rule. Therefore, you will need to perform synthesis in order to teach yourself the various facets of a single rule of law. Second, the rules you synthesize from the cases are an integral part of your outlines. Good outlines emphasize legal concepts and rules, and your synthesized rules are essential to creating a good outline. Third, your professors will expect you to use your synthesized rules on your examinations. Ultimately, you will not perform well on your examinations unless you learn to synthesize rules of law from the cases you read. There is one other important reason to learn synthesis, and it trumps even doing well on your exams.

You must learn to synthesize the law from cases if you ever expect to be a good lawyer. At the outset of your career, you will quickly learn that no one has written the giant book of answers! If you want to learn the state of the law in a particular practice area, you will need to read the relevant cases and synthesize the essential principles from them for yourself. Legal treatises are certainly available, and many can be quite detailed. Unfortunately, most cases are sufficiently unique that you will need to perform a certain amount of independent work. In addition, the synthesized rules may change as each new case becomes available.

Step by Step

Performing legal synthesis is a step by step process, and the first step is ensuring that you are working with cases that all deal with the same single element of the cause of action.[1] Otherwise, your synthesis will be inaccurate. Of course, a single case may actually stand for multiple ideas.

Let's begin our attempt at synthesis by considering the most basic aspect of the tort of battery—that it must involve some form of touching. If we pause for a moment to consider this idea, it becomes immediately apparent that we have some work to do. If every touching was a battery, then the courts would be dealing with battery cases morning, noon, and night! Obviously, some legal synthesis is in order.

---

1. Once you have synthesized each element of a cause of action, you can pull these smaller rules together to establish the entire rule.

Case 1, Smith v. Jones—*Jones, the defendant, and his friend are playing catch on a baseball field. Jones throws the ball to his friend, but it sails over his head. Jones isn't worried because the fence behind his friend will stop the ball. Unbeknownst to Jones, there is a hole in the fence. The ball goes through the hole, striking Smith and breaking his nose. Jones had no idea that Smith was even behind the fence. Smith sues Jones for the intentional tort of battery and wins at trial, but Jones appeals. The appellate court reverses the lower court decision. The court notes that a battery requires an intentional touching. Here, there was a touching with the ball, but Jones did not intend for the ball to hit Smith. In fact, he was not even aware of Smith's presence.*

Now that we have finished reading *Smith v. Jones*, we can begin our synthesis. You may be thinking to yourself that synthesis requires the creation of a rule from multiple sources, so how can we synthesize anything at this point. You would, of course, be correct. We can begin the synthesis process, however, by figuring out what this first case tells us about the touching element of battery.

The most obvious thing that we can take away from this case is that the defendant must intend to touch the victim. Here, Jones was unaware that Smith was even nearby. Even if Jones was aware that Smith was nearby, there was a fence between the injured party and the two friends playing catch. Jones did not know that the ball might pass through the fence. Therefore, we now know that the defendant must intend to touch the victim, but if you look carefully, this case teaches us something else about the kind of touching that satisfies the tort of battery.

It is the ball, and not Jones himself, who touches Smith. The court notes that there was a touching with the ball, but does not suggest that there is any problem with this. We have now added the following idea to our rule about touching—the defendant can accomplish the touching through an object. This may seem like a fairly obvious point, but even small points can add up to a much fuller understanding of any given rule. So, from *Smith v. Jones* we have learned the following:

- **The defendant must intend to touch the victim**
- **The defendant may accomplish the touching through some object**

Case 2, March v. Edwards—*Edwards decides to play a joke on his friend March. He hides outside his friend's home with a balloon full of water and waits. When March walks outside, Edwards throws the water balloon. Not wanting to hurt his friend, he aims for March's chest. Unfortunately, March ducks and the water balloon hits him squarely in the face, breaking his glasses and injuring his eyes. The injury requires surgery costing several thousand dollars. March sues for battery*

*and wins at trial. Edwards appeals, arguing that he never intended to hurt his
friend, so he cannot be liable for a battery. The appellate court upholds the decision. The court notes that a battery requires that the defendant touch the victim
and that the victim be harmed by the touching. The defendant does not, however,
have to intend the harm that results from the touching. Thus, the defendant is liable for the unintended consequences of his intentional touching.*

So, how does the *March* case further our understanding of what constitutes
a touching? We already knew that the defendant must touch the victim, but
now we know that an intent to harm is unnecessary. Therefore, when a practical joke goes awry, the defendant may still be liable for a battery. While it
was not a major issue in this case, we have also learned that the victim must
be harmed by the touching. Be sure, however, not to read too much into the
harm requirement. The court notes that the victim must be harmed by the
contact, and surgery costing several thousand dollars surely qualifies as harm.
We do not know yet whether a minor injury will satisfy the requirement that
the touching be harmful. When we add these points from *March* to what we
have already learned from *Smith*, we end up with the following:

- The defendant must intend to touch the victim
- The defendant may accomplish the touching through some object
- If the defendant intentionally makes contact with the victim, he is li-
  able for any unintended harm that may result from that contact
- The touching must cause some degree of harm, but unclear how much
  harm required

Case 3, Fisher v. Carousel Motor Hotel, Inc., 424 S.W.2d 627 (Tex. 1967)—*An
African American is in the buffet line at the Brass Ring Club, a restaurant in a
hotel. A hotel employee snatches a tray from Fisher's hands, and shouts that the
restaurant does not serve blacks. The employee never touches Fisher's person, and
Fisher is not physically injured. He is, however, extremely embarrassed. The appellate court holds that the employee's actions constitute a battery. While the employee did not touch Fisher directly, he did grab the tray that the plaintiff was holding. The intentional touching of an item that is "closely identified" with the victim,
for example the victim's clothing, may constitute a battery if that touching is offensive. Here, the plaintiff was deeply embarrassed by the employee's actions.*

Thanks to *Fisher*, a case that is covered in most torts classes, we have further refined our understanding of what constitutes a touching. In fact, *Fisher*
illustrates two new and important aspects of a battery. The first new idea may
be the most surprising—that the defendant can accomplish a battery without
ever physically touching the victim. In *Fisher*, the defendant grabs the victim's
tray, but never directly touches him. This action, of touching an item associ-

ated with the victim, still satisfies the touching element of a battery. The exact parameters of this rule are not fully clear, but we do know that contact with the victim's clothing could satisfy the touching element of the tort of battery. In addition, the court has added the idea that an offensive touching is as tortious as a harmful touching. Arguably, this enhancement is not as significant as it can be viewed as simply another type of harm. Under this view, the defendant is liable for an intentional touching that causes mental *or* physical harm. Now, our touching element looks like this:

- The defendant must intend to touch the victim
- The defendant may accomplish the touching through some object
- If the defendant intentionally makes contact with the victim, he is liable for any unintended harm that may result from that contact
- The touching must cause some degree of harm
- The defendant must touch the victim or something "closely identified" with the victim
- The touching may be harmful or offensive

Case 4, Lopez v. Zachary—*Zachary is waiting at the bus stop. When the bus arrives he gets on and notices an empty seat a few rows back, but he needs to get past Lopez, who is standing between him and the seat. He asks if she is going to use the seat, to which she responds "No." Zachary moves past Lopez, but can't help but brush against her in order to get to the seat. Ms. Lopez immediately starts yelling that Zachary has touched her and invaded her personal space. Ms. Lopez sues Mr. Zachary for the tort of battery but loses at trial. At trial, a doctor testified that Ms. Lopez suffered from an extremely rare condition that causes her to detest any physical contact. Ms. Lopez appeals and the appellate court upholds the lower court decision. The court agrees that the defendant did intentionally touch the plaintiff, but that the touching was neither harmful nor offensive. The appellate court believed that Ms. Lopez had been terribly offended by the touching but noted that her condition was not relevant in this instance. The court reasoned that offensiveness must be judged by a more objective standard. Therefore, the issue is not whether Ms. Lopez was offended, but whether an ordinary reasonable person would be offended by this touching. The court holds that no reasonable person would have been offended by this touching.*

Our last case helps explain why every touching does not amount to a battery. We must use an objective rather than subjective standard when determining whether a touching is offensive. Keep in mind that the court is not questioning whether Lopez was offended by this touching. In fact, the court accepts that the plaintiff was offended by this contact. Her subjective feelings are not relevant. Instead, we have to ask whether an objective, reasonable person would have been offended. When we add all the aspects of our rule together we end up with the following:

- The defendant must intend to touch the victim
- The defendant may accomplish the touching through some object
- If the defendant intentionally makes contact with the victim, he is liable for any unintended harm that may result from that contact
- The touching must cause some degree of harm
- The defendant must touch the victim or something "closely identified" with the victim
- The touching may be harmful or offensive
- We must use an objective standard when determining whether a touching was offensive

At this point, we have completed our synthesis of the touching element of the tort of battery. We can leave the bulleted points alone, treating them as sub-concepts that must be considered when determining whether a touching has occurred, or we can attempt to integrate these ideas into a single statement. The integration of these ideas into a single concept is what most lawyers would refer to as synthesis. If you integrate the ideas into a single statement, your synthesis should look something like this:

> The defendant must intentionally make a harmful or objectively offensive contact with the victim or with something "closely identified" with the victim, and the defendant will be liable for any unintended consequences of the harmful or offensive contact.

The above is correct, but quite a mouthful. For purposes of creating an outline or studying for final examinations, it may be easier to group the bulleted points into categories. In this example, you may divide the touching element of a battery into the categories of contact and harm, and the resulting synthesis would look like this:

- The defendant must intentionally make contact with the victim or with something "closely identified" with the victim
- The touching itself must be harmful or objectively offensive, and the defendant will be liable for any unintended consequences of said touching

This synthesis of the touching element of battery may be a bit easier to remember come exam time.

Synthesis Exercise

Below you will find summaries of three actual Massachusetts cases. Read the case summaries and try to synthesize a rule of law from the facts, holdings, and reasoning of each opinion. The cases involved multiple issues, but I have edited out a great deal of material for purposes of this exercise. Remember, first try to determine what each case means individually. Once you understand what each case stands for, you can then attempt to synthesize a broader rule combining the rulings from all the cases.

Case #1 — *Commonwealth v. Delgado*, 367 Mass. 432 (1975).

The defendant appeals from his conviction for robbery by means of dangerous weapon with the weapon in question being a gun. The defendant entered a store with several accomplices. During the course of the robbery, one of the accomplices was holding onto the struggling victim. The defendant said, "Hold him or I'm going to shoot him." The prosecution did not introduce any other evidence of a gun, and the defendant was convicted of robbery while "being armed with a dangerous weapon, to wit: a handgun."

On appeal, the defendant argued that, as a matter of law, his statement standing alone was insufficient evidence that he was armed. The appeals court upheld the conviction, and stated the following:

> "It is true, of course, that as a general rule words are not sufficient to constitute an assault ... and would therefore not usually be sufficient to meet the robbery requirement. However, a distinction is to be drawn between words that are merely threatening and those that are also informational.... The words spoken by the defendant in this encounter were clearly informational, warning the victim store manager that the defendant would and could shoot and thus impliedly informing the victim of the presence and possession of a weapon. In our opinion this was clearly sufficient, particularly in the circumstances of an ongoing robbery, to cause the victim reasonable apprehension with respect to his physical security. Hence the crime as charged was robbery 'with a dangerous weapon, to wit: a gun,' and the jury could reasonably conclude that the defendant should be taken at his word."

What principle, or principles, of law does this case stand for?

_____

_____

_____

_____

Case #2—*Commonwealth v. Tarrant*, 14 Mass. App. Ct. 1022 (1982).

After a jury trial, the defendant was convicted of armed robbery with a gun. On appeal, the defendant challenged the sufficiency of the evidence, arguing that the prosecutor failed to establish beyond a reasonable doubt that he was armed. The appellate court stated that the jury could have found the following facts:

> "[T]he defendant, wearing a wraparound coat with deep front pockets and carrying a travel bag, entered the Longwood Hospital where Joan Carey, a receptionist, and John Dadman, a security guard, were on duty. The defendant put the robbery in motion by handing Dadman a note which read: 'This is a holdup, put all the money in a bag or I will shoot, hurry.' Dadman took the defendant at his word and handed the note to Carey. In allowing Carey to answer a call on the switchboard, the defendant warned her not to say or do anything or he would 'shoot to kill.' His hand was inside the travel bag, and he was pointing the bag at Carey....
>
> As Carey watched the defendant, she began to suspect that, in fact, he did not have a gun, and she thought about grabbing for the bag. She reasoned that if her suspicions proved wrong and she should get hurt, she was in a hospital and aid would be available. With more courage than wisdom, she lunged for the travel bag, hitting and raising the defendant's arm, and the travel bag along with it.... The defendant fled, leaving his travel bag behind, with Dadman and another hospital employee in pursuit. They were unable to catch the defendant, nor could they find a gun after a search of the premises. The defendant was arrested about two weeks later, but no gun was ever recovered."

The court upheld the defendant's conviction. The court reasoned that the victim's suspicions that the defendant was unarmed were just that, suspicions. She did not possess actual knowledge that the defendant was, in fact, unarmed. While it was true that the defendant left his travel bag behind, the court noted that the defendant could have concealed the weapon in his pants pocket. In addition, although the defendant was unarmed when apprehended, he had ample time to dispose of the gun prior to arrest. Therefore, the jury was entitled to believe the defendant's informational statement that he would "shoot."

What additional principle, or principles, of law does this case stand for?

_____
_____
_____
_____

Case #3—*Commonwealth v. Howard*, 386 Mass. 607 (1982).

The defendant was convicted of armed robbery based on the following evidence: The defendant approached the victim and had his right hand in his pocket and said, "Walk straight, look down, and don't try anything foolish or I'll pull the trigger." In order to avoid being seen by passersby, the defendant forced the victim down an alleyway. As the victim was giving her money to the defendant, two police cruisers arrived on the scene with one cruiser positioned on each side of the alley. The officers arrested the defendant, but did not find a gun on his person or in the immediate vicinity. In overturning the defendant's conviction for armed robbery, the court distinguished this case from *Delgado* and *Tarrant*.

In those cases, the facts allowed the jury to infer beyond a reasonable doubt that the defendant possessed a weapon. Although investigators failed to discover a weapon, both Delgado and Tarrant were arrested long after their crimes took place, thus giving them ample opportunity to dispose of the weapon. In contrast, police arrested the defendant in *Howard* during the commission of the crime. Based on these facts, the *Howard* court reasoned as follows.

> "We do not construe the Delgado case as eliminating the statutory requirement that a defendant have a dangerous weapon but only as holding that the jury were warranted in inferring beyond a reasonable doubt that, in the circumstances, Delgado had a gun. In the case before us, the defendant's statement alone, implying that he had a gun, where no gun was seen or found and he had not opportunity or reason to dispose of it, cannot be sufficient to warrant a conviction of robbery while 'armed with a dangerous weapon.'"

What additional principle, or principles, of law does this case stand for?

_____
_____
_____
_____
_____

Now, try to synthesize a single rule from the holdings of *Delgado, Tarrant,* and *Howard.*

_____

_____

_____

_____

_____

CHAPTER VIII

Legal Analysis and Answering the Question "Why?"

The ability to perform thorough legal analysis is the hallmark of a good law student, and ultimately a good attorney. As a law student, your grades in all of your classes will rise or fall based on the strength of your legal analysis. You may not notice it, but your professors are helping you to refine this skill through the class dialogue.

Every time your criminal law professor asks you to answer a hypothetical problem, she is testing your analytical ability. Every time your contracts professor changes the facts from a case and asks you to determine how to resolve this new problem, he is testing your analytical ability. When your legal writing professor asks you to write out the resolution to a thorny problem she has created, she is testing whether you can perform analysis in its written form. Finally, when you read through the fact patterns that form the basis for your first set of law school examinations, every professor is testing whether you can perform legal analysis. Unfortunately, most students come to law school with little idea of what legal analysis means.

Legal analysis is the art of using the past and the present to prudently predict the future.[1] The past in this definition is the law, and it does not matter whether the law originated in cases, statutes, or the United States Constitution. The law represents established

> **Legal Analysis**
>
> The art of using the past and the present to prudently predict the future.

principles that we must work with in predicting a future outcome. Ignore the current state of the law, and your analysis will not be accurate.

The present in our definition is the new set of facts. As an attorney, your clients will present you with new facts every time they come into your office

---

1. I am paraphrasing Professor Bernadette Feeley, Clinical Faculty, Suffolk University Law School.

to tell you their story. The story is usually in the form of a problem they want you to resolve. During law school, you will receive these new facts in class and on your examinations. Every time your professor discusses a new hypothetical in class, she is giving you a new set of facts to analyze and work through. As for examinations, most are in the form of fact patterns that you will read through looking for legal issues or problems. In class and on your examinations, your professor will expect you to apply the laws you have memorized to these new facts. This application process requires you to sift through a variety of outcomes, laying out the pros and cons as to each possibility, before finally predicting the future.

That final prediction, or your conclusion, is often the least important part of your analysis. This comes as quite a surprise to students, which is understandable considering our conclusion driven society. In most aspects of our daily lives, the final answer to a question is more important than the process taken in arriving at that answer. In law school, the opposite is true. The path you take in arriving at an answer is more important than the answer itself. In good legal analysis, the writer explains "why" she has come to a particular conclusion. In addition, answering the question "why" requires you to explain "why not" as to other possibilities. If you fail to consider all reasonable possibilities, then you are not acting prudently. Instead, you'll be conclusion driven, and will allow the answer to drive your analysis instead of the other way around. Once you have finished addressing all reasonable possibilities, you will have completed your legal analysis.

Learning to write out your analysis in a logical and understandable way takes time, but you already have more of a head start than you realize. Every one of us performs analysis every day of our lives. It is not legal analysis, and we may not recognize that we are even doing it, but our minds are analyzing the pros and cons of every decision we make.

The human brain is an unbelievably fast processor of information. It constantly takes in the information around us, sifting through what is irrelevant and relevant, and then spits out a conclusion. This all happens so fast, that we are often only aware of the conclusion. Behind the scenes, however, our minds are crunching through an enormous amount of data to give us the answers we need.

Consider something as simple as driving to a destination that is about 10 miles from your home—a friend's house will suffice. When we take this kind of trip, most of us simply get into the car, turn the ignition, and drive using the best route. When we arrive, we sometimes barely remember the trip at all. It is almost like we are on autopilot. We have our brains to thank for making these trips seem so easy.

Now, let's replay that 10 mile trip in slow motion. As you do, start noticing all the alternatives you had to choose from when taking the trip. How many different routes could you have taken? Would your route depend on the time of day and would it change if it was a weekday as opposed to a weekend? Are some routes better in summer than in winter? Was there any construction to consider? Was school in session? If so, would you take a different route to avoid the busses and reduced speed zones? Did you want to stop for a cup of coffee or maybe a quick bite to eat on the way to your friend's house? If so, how much does this change your route? And so on, and so on....

If you can successfully analyze all of the decisions you make in a given day without truly thinking about them, then you can perform legal analysis. The trick is to make sure the reader understands all of the options and why certain choices are better than others. Unlike when you are driving to your friend's house, you cannot analyze the route to your answers in your head. Your complete analysis has to appear on the page so the reader does not get lost. Do not worry, because I have more good news for you.

You already have experience in writing out your analysis. Using our car trip example again, have you ever given someone directions to your home? If you give good directions, then you probably consider most of the questions I raised a few paragraphs ago. If you give great directions, you probably anticipate problems before they occur and explain what to do. For example, let's say that people often miss the turn onto Maple Street because of a large tree that blocks the street sign. Anticipating this problem, you will take the time to warn visitors to be on the lookout for the problem tree and intersection. Even better, you may give an alternative way of finding Maple St. Instead of simply saying "take a right on Maple and watch out because a tree blocks the sign," a better set of directions might add "and Maple will be third right after the stop sign." The best directions will go even a step further and tell visitors what to do if they still miss the intersection—"if you miss Maple, don't worry. Take the next right and then another right to bring you back to Maple St." Directions like these may seem excessive, or even anal, but your visitors will never get lost!

Legal analysis is a lot like giving a great set of directions. While the final destination is important, getting there is the key. In both: you have a starting point; you provide simple, easy to understand directions; you consider alternatives depending on the facts; and you address potential problems in your directions so that the reader does not get lost.

While you do have experience in writing out your analysis, it still isn't easy to do well. We have all received a bad set of directions, and ended up miles from our destination. Below is a short exercise illustrating that it takes a little time and patience to give good directions. The same is true when performing legal analysis.

Exercise 1A

In this exercise, you will be measuring your ability to write out a complete set of directions. Remember, your ability to thoroughly explain an idea is the hallmark of good analysis. If you do a good job, you will take into consideration every reasonable challenge that will be faced by your reader. If you do a poor job, the reader will get lost.

First, pick a destination at least several miles from your home that is not particularly easy to get to. Now, write out a set of directions that takes every reasonable variable into consideration. Don't worry about unreasonable variables. For example, you don't need to take snow and ice into consideration if you are performing this exercise in a warm climate or in the summer. Pick any mode of transportation that is reasonable under your personal circumstances — car, bike, public transportation, etc. Next, find a friend and give him the directions. Now, have your friend try to make it from your home to the destination in question using your directions and nothing else. If you are good friend, you will take part in the odyssey to ensure that no one gets lost!

Exercise 1B

Instead of writing out a set of travel directions, this time the topic will be cooking. Pick a favorite recipe and try to write out a description of how to cook the dish in question. Assume that your reader has never cooked a meal before and has a reputation for burning water! Again, be sure to take all reasonable variables into account. Now, have a friend try to cook the meal. You can also try to follow your own directions as long as you don't read between the lines and add information that was not written out. Be sure to define any "terms of art" that might be unfamiliar to your reader, just as you would in a legal memorandum. For example, terms like dice, fold, and sauté may be unfamiliar to the neophyte cook.

Legal Analysis

Now we are ready to move onto legal analysis, which will require us to add a few more ideas to the ones we have already discussed. Those ideas are:

- **Use the C-R-A-C or I-R-A-C formula** — The letters in the IRAC formula stand for Issue, Rule, Analyze (or Apply), and Conclude. In the CRAC formula, the first C stands for Conclusion, and the rest of the letters remain the same as in IRAC. By themselves, these formulae are not legal analysis. Instead, they are merely a suggested way of ordering the most important aspects of your analysis. Every time you perform legal analysis, the reader needs to know what issue you are seeking to resolve, the rule of law applicable to resolving the issue, your analysis of how the new set of facts fits within established legal principles, and your conclusion.

- **Do not be conclusion driven**—Let your analysis bring you to your conclusion as opposed to allowing your conclusion to drive your analysis. For this reason, many students and professors prefer the IRAC to the CRAC formula. If you start your analysis with a conclusion, you may be tempted to write toward that conclusion.
- **Always consider the alternatives**—In good legal analysis, the writer considers alternative points of view. By the end of your analysis, you will have considered all reasonable alternatives and addressed why your position is the correct one. Be sure, however, to differentiate between reasonable alternatives and alternatives that are merely possible. If you address every possible argument you will run out of time on your exams.

To start us off, we will use one of the laws you will discuss in your torts class—the intentional tort of assault. Most torts professors define an assault as an "intentional act that places another in apprehension of an imminent battery." Do not be fooled by the seeming simplicity of this definition because it actually contains several independent elements that a plaintiff must prove to establish the tort of assault. They are:

- Intent—An individual acts intentionally if he wants to cause some effect to the individual or knows to a substantial certainty that his actions will produce the effect.
- Placement of another—You can only assault other people.
- Apprehension—This element is one of the trickier aspects of an assault, and is often highlighted on torts examinations. It *does not* mean that the victim must be afraid. Instead, the victim must apprehend, or be aware of, the defendant's actions. If the defendant takes a swing at the plaintiff but the plaintiff's eyes are closed, then an assault is extremely unlikely.
- Imminence—The word imminent seems clear enough on its face, but an important question should come to you if you pause and truly consider the term for a moment. How close in time must the impending battery be before it is considered imminent? Essentially, imminent means that there will be little or no time for an intervening act between the defendant's actions and the battery. Typically, verbal threats are insufficient to satisfy the imminence element of an assault. Often, verbal threats merely suggest the possibility of contact. So, if a defendant yells

"[L]eave or you will get a beating," these words standing alone will not satisfy the imminence element of an assault. Words accompanied by physical movement on the part of the defendant, however, can make contact with the plaintiff "imminent."

- Battery—This is a tort unto itself, and is defined as the intentional, unpermitted, and harmful or offensive touching of another.

In your torts class, you will likely spend days working through the case law that helps to illustrate these concepts. Here, I've already extracted the principles from the cases. Now we have the past, or the law, that we need to perform our analysis. Next we need the present, or a set of facts to work with:

The Heavyweight Champ

Henry, the heavyweight boxing champion of the world, was sitting outside on his front stoop enjoying a lovely spring day. Not only was Henry the heavyweight champ, but in his neighborhood he was known as "the man without fear."

Fred, the neighborhood's resident 98 pound weakling, rounded the corner and saw Henry sitting there. Fred was upset because he had just broken up with his girlfriend. She left his apartment saying, "I can't stand being seen with someone who is such a wimp. Why can't you be tough like Henry?" When Fred saw Henry sitting there, an idea came to him. If he walked over and punched Henry, then people would stop thinking of him as a wimp.

Fred walked over to Henry and pulled back his arm to throw a punch. At that moment, Henry looked over and noticed Fred standing there with his arm drawn back. Henry realized that Fred was going to punch him, but was more surprised than alarmed. Henry didn't want to be hit, but he knew that the neighborhood weakling was unlikely to hurt him. Fred, with Henry staring at him, threw the punch. Unnerved by Henry's staring, Fred stumbled and completely missed Henry.

Question: Can Henry make out a claim for the intentional tort of assault? Use the above rule of law when answering this question, and be sure to explain your reasoning. While this fact pattern may raise additional issues, confine your answer to the issue of Fred assaulting Henry.

Now that we have the past and the present, we are ready to predict the future. Before we move on to an example of good analysis, however, it will be helpful to review a few examples of weak legal analysis. I have based each of the following examples on actual answers I have received from law school students.

First Sample Answer

Fred did not assault Henry.

This answer is "wrong" on several levels. First of all, it is a bare conclusion and nothing more. The law of assault is missing, as is any reason to agree with the writer's conclusion. Additionally, the conclusion itself may or may not be correct, but the writer has failed to give us any support for the conclusion and has not discussed any opposing points of view. Remember, the support for your conclusion is the "answer" your professor is looking for.

Second Sample Answer

Our issue is whether Fred assaulted Henry. Here, Fred didn't assault Henry because Henry was never intentionally placed in apprehension of an imminent battery. Fred did try to batter Henry, but he never placed Henry in fear or apprehension of his battery.

This sample answer does get a few things right, but still has several basic problems. The writer does start off the discussion by correctly framing the issue—did Fred assault Henry. Next, the writer does provide us with the basic rule of assault. These preliminary steps are not analysis, but analysis precursors. The reader needs your statement of the issue and the rule of law in order to follow the analysis to come. What comes next in this example, however, is not analysis.

First, the writer has misunderstood the apprehension element of battery, confusing awareness with fear. While your analysis is more important than your conclusion on law school examinations and papers, you must base that analysis on correctly stated legal principles. The writer does give us the basic rule of assault, but fails to discuss the individual elements of this definition any further. If he had done so, he may have remembered that apprehension means awareness in the context of an assault.

Assuming for the sake of argument that the writer correctly stated the rule of apprehension, what follows still is not legal analysis. The writer does note that Fred failed to place Henry in fear of an assault, but the "why," or the explanation of this conclusion is missing. For example, is the problem that Henry isn't afraid or that Fred failed to make him afraid? Also, why doesn't the reader believe that Henry is afraid? Wouldn't fear be a normal reaction to an impending battery? If so, why isn't Henry's reaction "normal" and should that make a difference? There are facts in the hypothetical that address each of these questions, but the writer has failed to use them in arriving at the conclusion. If you do not reference the facts, then you are not performing legal analysis.

Third Sample Answer

The issue here is whether Fred assaulted Henry. An assault occurs when one is placed in apprehension of an imminent battery. Because Henry was aware of Fred's imminent battery, Fred is liable for the tort of assault.

Here, the writer correctly states the issue and correctly states the law, but the analysis is still missing. When the writer states that Henry was aware of Fred's imminent battery, it is clear that he understands that apprehension in the assault context does not mean fear. Unfortunately, the writer does not go on to explain his position. Once again, the facts from the hypothetical are missing.

Fourth Sample Answer

The issue here is whether Fred assaulted Henry. An assault occurs when one is placed in apprehension of an imminent battery. In the context of an assault, apprehension means awareness of the impending battery and not fear. Here, Fred walked over to Henry thinking that if he hit him, people would stop thinking he was a wimp. Henry looked up when Fred pulled back his arm to throw the punch, but Fred tripped and never actually hit Henry. Therefore, Fred assaulted Henry.

Our fourth answer contains several of the elements required of good legal analysis, but it still misses the mark. The writer does start off with a statement of the issue and then goes on to provide the basic rule of assault. The writer goes even further by refining our basic rule and explaining the difference between fear and awareness in the assault context. Then, the writer lists the material facts, the facts on which the resolution of this issue will turn. Together, we have the law (the past), the facts (the present), and a prediction of an outcome (the future), so what is missing?

The writer has failed to answer the most important question—*why* these facts lead to a particular conclusion. Instead of explaining the importance of these facts, the writer has simply placed them in the answer. While you must place the material facts into your answer in order to perform legal analysis, listing facts by itself does not get the job done. A list of facts forces the reader to do the hard work of figuring out why the facts are relevant to the conclusion.

Do not make the mistake of assuming that the answer is so obvious that it does not require further explanation. Your professors will not make this assumption and they won't be able to read your mind as they review your answer.

Fifth Sample Answer

The issue here is whether Fred assaulted Henry. For Fred to be liable for an assault he must have intentionally placed Henry in apprehension of an imminent battery. Importantly, apprehension in this context does not mean fear. The victim does not have to be afraid of the battery or batterer. Instead, the victim must be aware of the imminent battery.

First, Fred did act intentionally toward another. As Fred approached Henry, he was thinking about striking the heavyweight champ in order to impress his girlfriend. Therefore, he did not accidentally attempt to punch Henry. In addition, while Fred did stumble, the timing is important. He stumbled as he was attempting to strike Henry, meaning that he was trying to commit a battery but failed.

Second, Henry was placed in apprehension. Henry saw Fred approaching with his arm pulled back and the facts state that he realized that Fred was about to throw a punch. This realization or awareness that Fred was about to throw a punch satisfies the apprehension element of an assault. Importantly, it doesn't make any difference that Henry was not afraid of Fred. While Henry is the heavyweight champ and the "man without fear," these facts are irrelevant when considering whether an assault has been committed. Similarly, the fact that Fred is a "98 pound weakling" has no bearing on whether these actions amount to an assault because the weakest person in the world can assault the largest person.

Finally, Fred's actions satisfy the imminent battery element of an assault. To satisfy this element, the plaintiff must believe that he is about to be struck. Fred pulled his arm back and actually took a swing at Henry. There can be no more imminent battery than watching someone take a swing at you.

Our fifth and final sample answer is structured a little bit differently than the first four. Notice that the writer opens with an introductory paragraph in which he lays out the issue and relevant legal principles. As for the legal principles, the writer spends additional sentences expanding upon the apprehension element of battery, and notes that this aspect of rule is of particular importance. By doing so, the writer is indicating the aspect of this issue that will require the most in depth analysis.

Next, the writer divides the discussion of the assault into several distinct paragraphs. Seeing as an assault is divided into several elements, it only makes sense to address each element separately. In essence, each element of an assault becomes a separate issue requiring analysis.

The analysis, or discussion of the facts, is not limited to the most vexing issues. For example, the writer spends time explaining that Fred acted intentionally toward another person. It is quite obvious that this element has been satisfied, so the discussion is brief and straightforward. By taking the time to explain even the obvious, the writer ensures that his analysis is on the page and not in his head. Just as important, on occasion a seemingly obvious point will turn out to be much more complicated. By forcing yourself to analyze each element, you won't make the mistake of treating an issue dismissively when it actually requires a great deal of attention.

The writer spends the greatest amount of time discussing the element of apprehension. On the surface, the analysis should be quite clear. Apprehension means awareness, and the facts clearly indicate that Henry was aware of Fred's actions. That being the case, why does the writer spend time noting that Henry's lack of fear is irrelevant? The fact pattern contained several references to Henry's lack of fear. From these references, it is apparent that the professor is testing whether folks understand that an assault requires awareness of an imminent battery. Therefore, the writer uses these facts to demonstrate his understanding of the difference between fear and awareness in the assault context. By doing so, the writer has anticipated the strongest counterargument to his position.

Finally, notice that every aspect of the answer is there for a reason. The writer has not merely dumped all of his knowledge onto the page. Instead, the referenced legal principles are all relevant to the resolution of the issue being discussing. Also, the facts are all there to support some aspect of the analysis.

Analysis Exercise

Fact Pattern

John and Ed, two good friends, were playing basketball together when John pushed Ed to prevent him from making an easy basket. Ed took offense and threw the ball at John. The ball missed, but John's back was turned away so he didn't realize what had happened. He thought that Ed simply threw the ball because he was angry at himself for missing the basket. Play resumed, but Ed kept getting angrier and angrier as he fell further behind. Eventually, Ed grabbed the ball, turned to John and yelled—"I'm tired of your rough play. You almost took my head off a few plays back and if you don't watch yourself I'm going to do the same to you." John thought that his friend was just blowing off some steam, and retorted "Stop being such a baby and let's play some ball." Ed was incensed. Still holding the basketball, he reared back as if he was going throw it at John. John ducked trying to avoid the ball, but Ed never threw it. Ed laughed, dropped the ball to the ground and said "Who's the baby now?"

This is the kind of fact pattern that you might see on a law school exam, although the examination version would be a great deal longer. At the end, your professor will ask you to discuss the rights and liabilities of all the parties. This kind of broad question gives you sufficient latitude to address both the obvious, and not so obvious, torts and defenses. This particular fact pattern creates several different issues that you would address on an examination. For purposes of this exercise, focus on a single issue—whether Ed assaulted John when he yelled "[y]ou almost took my head off a few plays back and if you don't watch yourself I'm going to do the same to you." As you write out your answer, be sure to discuss all relevant facts and address counter arguments when necessary.

CHAPTER IX

"However, ..." Constructing Your Counterarguments

An essential part of the analysis of any legal issue involves the discussion of all reasonable alternatives, or counterarguments, to your conclusion. If you fail to address the reasonable alternatives to your conclusions, your answers on your examinations, and ultimately as a practicing lawyer, will be incomplete. Despite this fact, many students have difficulty with the notion of constructing counterarguments because the idea, at least on the surface, can seem counterintuitive. One student put it to me this way—"I'm supposed to be an advocate for my client's position. It doesn't make sense to be writing about the other side's position. If I did, I would be doing their work!"

While this point of view has some surface appeal, it reveals two important misconceptions about legal analysis and the role of a lawyer. First, lawyers are often called upon to analyze a legal problem objectively and they are not acting as advocates in these circumstances. At its heart, objective legal analysis requires the writer to come to a conclusion that is based on the assessment of all reasonable possibilities. Second, a thorough discussion of the alternative points of view actually strengthens the analysis that supports your conclusion regardless of whether you are writing from an objective or persuasive standpoint.

How does considering the alternatives strengthen your primary analysis? For one thing, it demonstrates to the reader or listener that your answer was the product of thoughtful deliberation. In addition, when you consciously consider and address the alternatives, you are forcing yourself to address one of the most troubling aspects of legal

> **Herb's Hints**
>
> Lawyers are rarely 100% certain as to their conclusions, which is why they tend to avoid using words like clearly, always, and never.

analysis—you will rarely be 100% certain of your conclusion. As a lawyer, coming to a conclusion does not necessarily mean that there is only one possible answer to a problem. When performed correctly, your analysis merely identifies the best answer to a problem, not the only answer, and lets the reader know about the weaknesses in that best answer.

Before we dig into the role of the counterargument any further, we need a good definition of the term that we can refer back to when necessary. The Oxford English Dictionary defines the word counterargument as "[a]n argument on the opposite side, or against anything."[1] While this is an accurate definition of the term, it is not particularly helpful to us. The definition that I use with my first year students is as follows:

> **A counterargument is the legal, factual, and logical support for *an* answer to a problem, just not the answer you adopted.**

Implicit within my definition of the word counterarguement is the notion that there may be more than one answer to a legal problem. Even further, these other answers will have their own legal, factual, and logical support. As long as there are other reasonable approaches to solving a problem, part of your job as a law student is to address these possibilities. Of course, there may not be any reasonable alternatives to a solution, but the default position of good lawyers is that there is always a counterargument. In fact, you will spend a lot of your time as a first-year law student learning to see the alternatives to your answers and then learning how to address them properly.

Back to IRAC

The best way to continue our conversation of counterarguments is to review the I-R-A-C formula that we touched on in Chapter VIII, *Legal Analysis and Answering the Question "Why?"* In that chapter we learned that the acronym I-R-A-C stands for the words Issue, Rule, Analyze (or Apply) and Conclude. Remember, the formula itself is not legal analysis. It is merely an organizational tool that you can use in order to be sure that you are answering legal questions in a logical order.

The first two parts of the formula—the Issue and the Rule—are the simplest. Stating the Issue is merely informing the reader of the question that you are about to address and, hopefully, resolve. Providing the reader with the Issue at the outset also orients the reader, which is relevant when the writer is addressing multiple issues in a document as is the case on a law school examination. The Rule is the legal authority that you are relying on to perform your analysis and may originate in statutes, case law, constitutions or any other

---

1. *The Oxford English Dictionary*, Vol. III, 1022 (2d ed. 1989).

source that you feel is relevant to resolving the Issue. Your explanation of the Rule can be accomplished in a single sentence, but in other instances you may have to discuss multiple cases in detail in order to accurately convey the Rule to your reader.

The "A" in I-R-A-C stands for Analyze or Apply, and this is the most important aspect of the formula. Up until now, your answer has consisted of material that originated elsewhere. Your examinations, for example, will contain the facts that form the basis of the Issue you are seeking to resolve. Similarly, the Rule will originate in statutes, cases and other legal authority that you have researched and read during the course of the year. In contrast, the Analysis section contains *your explanation* as to how the facts in the problem, coupled with the legal principles already discussed (the Rule), lead to a Conclusion. This explanation is the only part of the answer to a legal problem that is completely unique to you, and is part of the reason that professors value it so highly when grading your exams. To fully understand the concept of a counterargument, however, we need to dig more deeply into the concept of legal analysis.

Recurring Patterns in Legal Analysis

When performed correctly, two major patterns tend to appear over and over again in the Analysis section of the I-R-A-C formula. In the first of these patterns, the writer provides the reader with a piece of factual information that originated in the problem and then explains its significance. This explanation of a fact's significance is at the heart of legal analysis, and is the answer to the question "Why" that is the title of the preceding chapter. If there are multiple pieces of factual information that are relevant to resolving the issue, then each of these facts will be placed into the Analysis section of our formula and explained in turn. So our first pattern looks like this—**fact/explain its relevance**.

This means that the facts from the question must reappear in your answer. Some students believe that this is repetitive because (1) the professor already knows the facts of the problem and (2) they already appeared in the question itself. There is a simple answer to both of these concerns. While your professors will certainly remember the facts from their exams, they will not assume that you understand how to use these facts. Examination hypotheticals will contain dozens of facts that are relevant to several different issues, each of which requires its own resolution. The professor needs to see that you can identify the facts that are relevant to each separate issue.

In addition, your examinations will contain, at times, factual information that is irrelevant to the resolution of the various issues. Unless you thoughtfully discuss the facts, your professors will not know whether you can differentiate between the relevant and the irrelevant. In other words, your professors need to know *what you know.*

Our second pattern involves a further refinement to the "A" or Analysis section of the I-R-A-C formula. As we have been discussing, good legal analysis requires the writer to address all reasonable counterarguments. So, our "A" in the I-R-A-C formula usually contains the analysis of both sides of any legal argument. Therefore, if we shine a spotlight on the "A" of our formula, it actually looks something like this: A1-A2-Resolve. This simply means that you are analyzing the problem from one perspective (A1), then you are addressing any reasonable alternatives to that argument (A2), and then finally determining which of the two positions is the strongest (Resolve).

In the abstract, all these patterns and formulae can seem quite confusing. When applied to a legal problem, however, they become much easier to understand and apply.

I Want to Ride My Bicycle

Steven, a 15-year-old young man, contracted with a "Bikes-A-Lot" to purchase a $2,000 bicycle. His parents, Mr. and Mrs. Schwinn, want their son to void the purchase, but the toy store wants to hold the young man to the contract. Steven, while an intelligent young man, is a little immature for his age. Remembering your contracts course from your first year of law school, you decide to research whether a 15-year old person may be forced to abide by any contracts he or she signs. Quickly, you find a statute that reads, "[n]o child under the age of 14 may be held to any oral or written contractual agreement. Such a contract is voidable by the minor." The statute seems fairly clear on its face, but you perform additional research to determine whether any cases have applied the statute based on a young person's emotional, as opposed to chronological, age. The relevant cases consistently use a young person's chronological age when applying the statute, however, it seems that a case like Steven's has never come up before.

The Schwinn's request your advice as to the likelihood of succeeding in a lawsuit seeking to void their son's purchase of the bicycle.

Based on the above fact pattern, the Schwinns are unlikely to prevail in a lawsuit against the bike store. While this is the likely answer, there are other possibilities that must be explored. The trick is to give the reader a well-reasoned and organized answer that addresses the various possibilities fairly and accurately. Such a letter to the Schwinns would look something like this:

A Letter to the Schwinns

Mr. and Mrs. Schwinn,

You asked me to determine whether your son, Steven, would be able to void the contract he signed with "Bikes-A-Lot" for the purchase of a new bicycle. During my research, I discovered a statute that states in relevant part "[n]o child under the age of 14 may be held to any oral or written contractual agreement. Such a contract is voidable by the minor." To date, courts interpreting this statute have applied it based on a person's chronological, not emotional, age.

Your son is 15 years old, but the statute only allows children less than 14 years of age to void their contracts. This fact, at least on the surface, indicates that your son may not use the statute to void his contract with "Bikes-A-Lot." You did mention, however, that your son, although intelligent, is a little immature for his age. Assuming for the moment that your son's emotional age is under 14 years, we can argue to the court that the statute should apply because it was likely intended to protect immature individuals from entering into agreements that they did not fully comprehend. Despite the fact that your child is 15, his emotional age make may make him similar to the younger children the statute was likely meant to protect. If a court agrees with this position, your son could void the contract and return the bike.

To date, the courts have consistently used chronological age when interpreting this statute; although a scenario exactly like your son's has never come up before. Still, it would be an uphill battle arguing for a different interpretation of the statute, and one that could be quite expensive in the end. This is particularly true when one considers that the bike is only worth $2,000 and the cost of litigating this dispute would far exceed that amount. While I do believe we can make a strong argument to a court in favor of voiding the contract, I estimate our chances of prevailing before a judge at less than 50%.

Therefore, I recommend against filing a lawsuit. Instead, we should contact "Bikes-A-Lot" and try to negotiate a mutually acceptable settlement. Please contact me at your earliest convenience and let me know how you would like to proceed.

Sincerely,

Herbert N. Ramy

The above letter answering the Schwinns inquiry is relatively short. Despite its brevity, the letter conveys a great deal of information to the Schwinns. In addition to answering the Schwinns question regarding a lawsuit against Bikes-A-Lot—they will probably lose—the letter provides the basis for the answer, considers a reasonable counterargument, compares the two possibilities, and does so using the modified I-R-A-C format we have been discussing. To make these aspects of the letter easier to see, I have reproduced the letter below and identified the various parts in **bold**. The words in bold are not, of course, part of the actual answer. As you review the below answer, note that both of our analysis patterns are evident. First, when facts are mentioned, their relevance is explained and discussed. Second, the writer provides analysis to both points of view (A1 and A2) and then explains which of these possibilities is the more likely to prevail.

Issue—Mr. and Mrs. Schwinn, you asked me to determine whether your son, Steven, would be able to void the contract he signed with "Bikes-A-Lot" for the purchase of a new bicycle.

Rule—During my research, I discovered a statute that states in relevant part "[n]o child under the age of 14 may be held to any oral or written contractual agreement. Such a contract is voidable by the minor." To date, courts interpreting this statute have applied it based on a person's chronological, not emotional, age.

Analysis, including a discussion of a possible counterargument—Your son is 15 years old (Fact), but the statute only allows children under 14 years of age to void their contracts. This fact, at least on the surface, indicates that your son may not use the statute to void his contract with "Bikes-A-Lot." (Explanation of the Relevance of this fact. Together, the fact and explanation are the analysis to A1.)

You did mention, however, that your son, although intelligent, is a little immature for his age. (Fact supporting the counterargument). Assuming for the moment that your son's emotional age is less than 14 years, we can argue to the court that the statute should apply because it was likely intended to protect immature individuals from entering into agreements that they did not fully comprehend. Despite the fact that your child is 15, his emotional age may make him similar to the younger children the statute was likely meant to protect. If a court agrees with this position, your son could void the contract and return the bike. (Explanation of the relevance of this fact. Together, the fact and this explanation are the analysis to A2)

To date, the courts have consistently used chronological age when interpreting this statute; although a scenario exactly like your son's has never come up before. Still, it would be an uphill battle arguing for a different interpretation of the statute, and one that could be quite expensive in the end. This is particularly true when one considers that the bike is only worth $2,000 and the cost of litigating this dispute would far exceed that amount. While I do believe we can make a strong ar-

*gument to a court in favor of voiding the contract, I estimate our chances of pre-vailing before a judge at less than 50%. (**Integrating the two possibilities and re-solving the analysis in favor of A1**).*

Conclusion—Therefore, I recommend against filing a lawsuit. Instead, we should contact "Bikes-A-Lot" and try to negotiate a mutually acceptable settlement. Please contact me at your earliest convenience and let me know how you would like to proceed.

Focusing on the analysis portion of the letter for a moment, did it seem that the answer went on for a little longer than you expected? The relevant statute only applies to children "under the age of 14" and the Schwinn's son is 15 years old. So why did I bother discussing a possibility that I did not adopt? The facts from the hypothetical created a reasonable counterargument that I

> **Herb's Hints**
>
> You cannot perform legal analysis without discussing the facts. So, make sure that the facts from the problem always reappear in your answer.

felt compelled to address. If you disagree, try the following. Reread the letter to the Schwinns, but this time remove any reference to the counterargument regarding their son's emotional maturity. The final answer to the problem does not change, but it is a harder answer to agree with absent the additional analysis and explanation.

Just as importantly, the facts regarding the son's intelligence and emotional maturity raise the possibility of a reasonable counterargument. On its face, the statute is concerned with a child's chronological age, but one could reasonably argue that the legislature created this statute to protect immature children from entering into bad agreements, not just children of a certain age. Importantly, those reading the analysis will have the same thought. Therefore, your answer will appear incomplete unless you address this reasonable possibility. Applying the statute based on emotional maturity may be something of a stretch, particularly where cases applying the statute have only used chronological age. How will your reader know this, however, unless you explain it on the page?

Different Roles Equals Different Analysis

While it is essential to address all reasonable counterarguments when dealing with a legal problem, your analysis will differ depending on the role you are in when asked to tackle a problem. There are 3 primary roles you will find yourself playing as a law student and lawyer. Those roles are the **researcher**, the **objective lawyer**, and the **persuasive lawyer**.

The Researcher

In the initial stages of the analysis process, you will be a researcher. As a researcher, your primary job is to find the law that is applicable to the facts and problem before you. An important part of finding the answer, however, is to avoid any preconceived notions as to what the answer should be. Therefore, the researcher must be both objective and creative when considering how a problem might be resolved. The easiest way to see how this works is to consider another short hypothetical.

Driving Difficulties

Danielle, a 16-year old young woman, is eager to obtain her driver's license and constantly asks her father to give her lessons. Her father declines because he thinks driving is far too dangerous for such a young person. Danielle decides to take matters into her own hands and takes the keys to the family car from their customary place on a hook next to the front door. She then goes outside and enters the car, which is parked on the street in front of her home. She starts the car, but then remembers some of the instructions she received during her first driver's education class. Danielle puts on her seat belt, adjusts the seat so that she can reach the pedals comfortably, and adjusts her rearview mirror. The passenger side mirror cannot be moved from the driver's seat, however, so she unbuckles her seat belt and reaches across to adjust the mirror. As she does so, she accidentally puts the car into gear. The car lurches forward and hits the car in front of her, causing over $1,000 in damage to her neighbor's automobile and $3,000 in damage to her family's car. Danielle also suffered a broken arm in the accident.

Your firm is hired by Danielle's parents. Perform legal research into the rights and liabilities of the parties in the above problem.

The end of the problem indicates that Danielle's parents hire your law firm, but your researching instructions are very broad. This is not uncommon during the early stages of a new case when a lawyer wants to make sure that all reasonable possibilities are considered.

The first step in the analytical process is a brainstorming session. Your goal is to consider all possible problems or issues created by Danielle's accident. At this stage in the process it is important that you list *every* potential cause of action and avoid discarding problems before giving them sufficient consideration. This brainstorming session is quite similar to the issue spotting that goes on at the beginning of a law school exam. The analysis that occurs at this stage of the process is about the possibilities produced by the fact pattern, so do not be afraid to list ideas that you will ultimately discard after more thoughtful consideration.

The most obvious issue created by this problem involves the damage to the neighbor's car and who is going to pay for it. While this is certainly an important issue in this fact pattern, too often students view it as the only problem requiring attention. Remember, you must be both objective and creative during this researching phase of your analysis. List all potential problems so that you can consider them more fully before addressing or disposing of them on the page as opposed to in your head. This process will help you avoid missing important issues that need to be addressed, and will ensure that you have answers to every potential problem that your supervising attorney sees.

Exercise 1

Analyze the above fact pattern carefully, and create a list of issues that you will address during your research. In some instances, these issues will be in the form of questions that require additional factual information to resolve. As you create your list of issues, notice how the consideration of one potential problem will often generate ideas regarding other issues that may require attention. Feel free to provide any additional thoughts you have regarding any listed issue.

Driving Difficulties — List of Issues

1. _____	11. _____
2. _____	12. _____
3. _____	13. _____
4. _____	14. _____
5. _____	15. _____
6. _____	16. _____
7. _____	17. _____
8. _____	18. _____
9. _____	19. _____
10. _____	20. _____

When you first viewed the space provided for completion of the exercise, I will bet that you were surprised to see places for 20 separate issues. Take a look at the answer key and you will see that I have come up more than 20 issues, and the list could have been even longer! If your list was significantly shorter than mine, then one of two things likely occurred. First, you saw some of the issues I included, but decided to exclude them from your list because they were not all that important. Remember, this was supposed to be a brainstorming session where you listed *every* problem created by the fact pattern. The cardinal sin that the researcher can commit is to dispose of a potential issue or point of view without fully considering it.

The second possibility is that you became an advocate for Danielle and excluded issues that were against her interests. If this is what happened, then you likely failed to mention the possibility that Danielle committed a crime when she took the keys, when she started the car, or when she took off her seatbelt. Remember, the best way to be an advocate for your client is to consider all problems. You cannot effectively advise your client or advocate for her if you disregard arguments that work against her. Instead, consider the negative points of view very carefully so that you can come up with a course of action that works to the benefit of your client. During the next phase of the analytical process, you can better assess which arguments work best.

The Objective Lawyer

As the objective attorney, your job is to take the potential issues you discovered during the research phase and analyze the pros and cons of each position from an objective viewpoint. Based on the instructions from your supervising attorney and your own more careful consideration of the list you generated, you may not end up addressing all of the issues you discovered as a researcher. For example, you may learn that the district attorney's office will not be bringing any criminal charges against Danielle or her family based on the accident. If this is the case, then your objective analysis will likely focus on who should be liable for the damage to the neighbor's car.

The counterargument plays a very important role in objective analysis, and acts something like a devil's advocate. For every argument in favor of a point of view, the devil's advocate is there to lay out the reasons why that point of view might not prevail. The counterargument is not, however, argument for argument's sake. Instead, the counterargument is there to help you and your client determine an appropriate course of action. To illustrate, consider the following scenario:

Just Being Neighborly

Keith and Luke are neighbors and friends. One day, Keith decides to plant a small tree on his property. When Keith finishes his work he stands there admiring his new tree and is visited by his neighbor Luke. Luke has always been a pleasant neighbor, but he is upset because he believes that Keith's tree is on his property. Keith greets his neighbor with a pleasant "good morning," but Luke immediately begins shouting about the location of the tree. Eventually Luke brings his face to within inches of Keith's and says, "Dig up the tree right now or you will be sorry." Keith, frightened due to the threat, punches Luke in the face, runs into his home, and locks the door. Luke, more surprised than physically hurt, calls the police who arrest Keith and charge him with battery. Keith hires your law firm to defend him. You are assigned Keith's case and immediately realize that he has, under the law of your jurisdiction, battered his neighbor. You also realize that Keith may be able to argue that he was acting in self defense. You begin researching the law of self defense in your jurisdiction and tell Keith that you will get back to him. During the course of your research you learn that an individual may strike another person in self defense, but only if that person reasonably believes he is under physical attack.

How do you advise your client?

Even though Keith is your client and you have a duty to "zealously advocate" on his behalf, a good lawyer remains in an objective posture when assessing the best course of action.[2] Considering the above scenario, the central issue will be whether Keith "reasonably believed he was under physical attack" when he punched Luke in the face. Considering the issue objectively, there are several facts in your client's favor. For example, the parties were arguing, Luke warned Keith that he would be sorry if he failed to dig up the tree, and he issued this warning as he brought himself to within inches of Keith's face. Telling Keith that he "will be sorry" could be construed as a threat, which seems to be how Keith interpreted these words. The fact that Keith threw the punch *after* Luke used the threatening words strongly suggests that Keith's actions were in response to the perceived threat. In addition, Keith ran inside and locked his door after striking his neighbor, and he did not continue punching Luke. Again, this suggests that Keith was reacting to a threat and was doing what he believed was necessary to get away. At this point, you may be tempted to tell Keith not to worry because it is very likely that he was acting in self de-

---

2. ABA Model Rules of Professional Conduct, Rule 1.3.

fense when he struck Luke. This conclusion, however, is based on looking at the facts from only one point of view.

The easiest way to make sure that you are objectively analyzing a given scenario is to pretend that you are counsel for the opposing side. In this instance, that would mean pretending that Luke had hired you to sue Keith for battery. Initially, you would perform the same research and would come to the same preliminary conclusion — that Keith's actions constitute a battery unless Keith was acting in self defense. After this initial assessment, however, Luke's lawyer is likely to view the same facts in a very different light.

Under the law, self defense is an option only where an individual **reasonably** believes that he or she is under **physical** attack. This means that Keith's belief that he was in danger is only relevant if: (1) that perception was reasonable; and (2) that perception was of a physical attack. It seems apparent that Keith's punch was precipitated by Luke saying "dig up that tree right now or you will be sorry." Further, the facts state that Keith was "frightened due to the threat." The lawyers for the two sides are in agreement up to this point, but now the analysis takes a different tack depending on who you represent. While the language could be construed as a threat, it is not at all clear what Luke was threatening. Was he threatening a physical attack? Was he planning on suing Keith for the removal of the tree? Was he going to tell the neighborhood that Keith was being a jerk? All of these possibilities, as well as many others, are potential interpretations of Luke's words. In addition, the facts do not indicate that Luke raised his hand towards Keith or made physical contact with him. Without more information, how can we say that Keith's actions were based on a reasonable belief that he was under physical attack? Well, we do have more information, but it does not help Keith's argument. The facts also state that Luke had always been a pleasant neighbor. Suddenly, Keith's belief that he was under physical attack seems decidedly unreasonable!

While I often advise students to use the above methodology — first pretend you are the plaintiff's lawyer and then pretend you work for the defendant — when performing legal analysis, it does have one potential drawback. Although I looked at the argument from both sides, I was not being truly objective. Although I did view both sides of the issue, I adopted something of a persuasive posture in both instances. At the end of my pro-plaintiff analysis, I came to the conclusion that Keith has a good chance of prevailing using a self defense argument. Not surprisingly, I come to the opposite conclusion in my pro-defendant analysis. Do not misunderstand me; the above methodology is a good way of forcing yourself to consider both sides of a legal argument. In its current form, however, the reader will be left wondering which conclusion is stronger. I have not finished my work if the reader is left to choose between these two conclusions without any guidance.

The final step in the process is to integrate my counterargument into my analysis, thus creating a multi-facetted explanation of my single conclusion. I no longer have the luxury of looking at the problem from the defendant's or plaintiff's viewpoint. Instead, I must objectively look at the relative strengths and weaknesses of both positions, thus allowing the conclusion to flow freely from the analysis. The strength of Keith's position lies in the fact that he was provoked. He did not simply punch Luke as part of some drunken bar fight. Instead, the facts support the argument that Keith believed he was in danger of being harmed. The strength of Luke's position is that Keith's belief that he was about to be harmed, while arguably sincere, was based on insufficient information. Luke never struck Keith, never raised his hand against his neighbor, and did not even say that he was going to do so. With the strengths, and by extension the weaknesses, of these arguments in place, we can create a single objective answer to the issue that would look something like this:

Was Keith Just Defending Himself?

Keith may have committed a battery when he punched Luke, but self defense is a possible justification for his actions. In our jurisdiction, this defense is available to individuals who strike others based on the reasonable belief that they are under physical attack. Here, it appears that Keith believed he was under attack from Luke.

Luke initiated the confrontation by yelling at Keith and he did seem to threaten Keith when he stated that Keith would be "sorry" if he did not dig up the tree the two men were arguing over. In addition, Luke brought himself to within inches of Keith's face when he made this statement, an action that may have been intended to intimidate his neighbor. The fact that Keith's punch and subsequent flight from the scene took place after this verbal threat support the contention that Keith believed he was going to be harmed. Unfortunately, self defense is an option only when an individual acts "reasonably."

Keith's subjective fear is not enough, and we must assess his actions from a more objective perspective. The law requires that the individual fear that he is "under physical attack," but Luke never struck Keith or even raised his hand against him, although he did bring himself to within inches of Keith's face. Further, the phrase "under physical attack" suggests that words alone will never be enough provocation to support a self defense argument. It seems more likely that an individual must be struck first in order to assert that they are "under physical attack." Even assuming that some words could be so inflammatory as to amount to a physical attack, it is difficult to view Luke's words in this fashion. Luke's threat that Keith would be "sorry" certainly suggests that negative consequences will arise unless Keith moves the tree. While this could mean that Luke was about to strike Keith, the words could also mean a lawsuit or a further verbal confrontation between the neighbors. When you add the fact that Luke had always been a pleasant neighbor up until this point, it was probably unreasonable for Keith to believe that he was under physical attack. Therefore, a self defense argument will likely fail, and we should consider coming to financial settlement with the plaintiff, Luke.

The Persuasive Lawyer

Although students are rarely called upon to perform persuasive legal analysis during the first year of law school, the topic still deserves some attention. As the persuasive lawyer, your role changes quite dramatically from that of the objective lawyer, but there are some similarities. The law and the facts do not change, and you still perform legal analysis as the persuasive lawyer. Further, you still address the reasonable alternatives to your conclusion. So what is the difference? As the objective lawyer, you are searching for the best answer to a problem. As the persuasive lawyer, you are a paid advocate so you know the answer prior to beginning the process. Your goal is to present the information in a way that highlights the strengths and deemphasizes the weaknesses of your client's position. To do this, keep the following factors in mind when analyzing problems from a persuasive standpoint.

Tips for Artful Persuasion

- **Typically, begin your analysis with a strongly worded conclusion that emphasizes the positive aspects of your client's position.** While you may choose to begin your objective analysis with a strongly worded conclusion, it is an essential part of persuasive analysis. In addition, this first sentence is where you will often establish the central theme of your analysis, a factor discussed more fully below.
- **Avoid equivocating.** When performing persuasive analysis, you are usually in the role of a paid advocate who is trying to convince another party—often a judge—that your side should prevail. If you, a paid advocate, express serious doubts as to the correctness of your client's position, then why should anyone else agree with your ultimate conclusion?

- **Do not forget the counterargument.** Performing persuasive analysis does not mean that you ignore the counterarguments. When you ignore the counterargument, the reader will have only opposing counsel's version of that argument to consider. Therefore, address the opposing side's argument, but be sure to make your position the more compelling of the two!
- **Strive for the appearance of objectivity.** In an effort to be persuasive, many lawyers end up insulting their reader's intelligence. They will pepper their analysis with words like "obviously" and "clearly," even when the conclusion is far from obvious or clear. These same lawyers will also avoid touching on any weaknesses in their client's position. Instead, avoid the rhetorical flourishes and tackle the weaknesses in your argument head on, letting the reader know that some aspect of the law or the facts addresses the perceived weakness in your position. In doing so, you will appear to be objective, thus gaining credibility with your reader.
- **Tell a compelling story.** Writing legal analysis is not the same thing as writing fiction, but there is one important similarity. In both instances, the writer's goal is for the audience to keep reading. The more compelling your narrative, the more likely it is that your reader will read your entire story.
- **When possible, build your story around a central theme or idea.** Building your analysis around a strong central theme can help with the previous tip—telling a compelling story. In addition, all good writers know that their readers can lose focus. If your readers lose focus, they may miss an essential aspect of your analysis. A central theme will help you, and your reader, maintain focus throughout your analysis.

With the above tips in mind, the next step in performing persuasive legal analysis is to look at the problem from an objective viewpoint. The above answer to the "Just Being Neighborly" fact pattern—*Was Keith Just Defending Himself?*—is an example of objective analysis. Looking at a problem objectively allows you to see how opposing counsel will likely view the case. Once you have an objective understanding of any weaknesses in your client's case, you can perform persuasive legal analysis that addresses and minimizes these weaknesses.

To illustrate, consider the objective analysis to the "Just Being Neighborly" problem. Assume that your law firm's senior partner, impressed with your work on the objective memorandum, asks you to write a document that now advocates on Keith's behalf. Using the objective memorandum as a starting point, the following factors are in Keith's favor: (1) Luke was the one who threatened Keith in the first instance, saying "dig up the tree or you will be sorry"; (2) Keith seemed to believe that Luke was going to strike him; (3) Keith only struck Luke once, which supports the contention that Keith was merely defending himself from an anticipated attack; (4) Luke brought his face to within inches of Keith when he issued his "threat"; and (5) one reasonable interpretation of Luke's words "you will be sorry" is that a physical attack is imminent. On the opposing side, the following factor work against Keith's claim of self defense: (1) Keith's subjective belief that he was under attack is not enough, his belief must have been objectively reasonable; (2) in this jurisdiction, self defense requires that the individual be "under physical attack," but Luke never struck Keith; and (3) the words "you will be sorry" are subject to interpretation and do not mean that a physical attack was necessarily forthcoming.

When you are in the role of an advocate, persuasiveness should permeate every part of your analysis. In fact, the very first sentence of a persuasive document often looks different from what you might see in an objective memorandum on the very same topic. As we have discussed, legal writers often begin writing their objective analysis with the statement of an issue or question to be resolved. In addition, good writers frequently use words like "if," "possibly," and "may" in objective analysis to soften their conclusions and to let the reader know that other answers are possible.

For example, consider the first sentence from the objective analysis to the *Just Being Neighborly* problem—"Keith may have committed a battery when he punched Luke, but self defense is a possible justification for his actions." Grammatically, I have not written this sentence in the form of a question. As a practical matter, however, the words "may" and "possible" have softened this conclusion to the point that it may as well be a question. Interestingly, it does not take very much to change an objectively worded conclusion into the beginning of your persuasive analysis. Compare the same objective first sentence from *Was Keith Just Defending Himself* with the more strongly worded versions of the sentence that follow.

Version 1—Keith may have committed a battery when he punched Luke, but self defense is a possible justification for his actions.

Version 2—Keith committed a battery when he punched Luke, and self defense is not a reasonable justification for his actions.

Version 3—Keith overreacted and escalated the verbal confrontation with his neighbor into a physical one when he punched Luke in the face, thus precluding his use of self defense as a justification for his actions.

As you can see, the three sentences are extremely similar in content, with only a few words separating one sentence from the next. Despite their surface similarities, the three sentences convey different messages. In Version 1 of the sentence, the writer is conveying that there is some degree of doubt as to the final conclusion through the use of the words "may" and "possible." In Version 2, all doubt has disappeared and the writer is conveying a high degree of certitude. Despite the strong wording, Version 2 could be used at the beginning of either objective or persuasive analysis, as long as the writer is trying to convey that the conclusion is not in doubt.

Version 3 of the sentence also conveys that the writer is certain as to the conclusion, but the conclusion was written with persuasion in mind. In Version 3, the writer has begun developing a theme that Keith, not Luke, was the problem. For example, the word "overreacted" is not necessary to convey the conclusion that Keith committed a battery, but the writer chose it to paint Keith in a negative light. The word "escalated," a more legally significant term, conveys a similar message. Finally, it is no coincidence that the writer notes that Keith "punched Luke in the face." A fact like this one portrays Keith as the aggressor and helps engender sympathy for Luke.

Objectively, the best answer to the *Just Being Neighborly* problem is that Keith committed a battery and is not entitled to the justification of self defense. Below, I have taken the opposite position and written out persuasive analysis in support of Keith and the argument that he was merely defending himself from attack. In doing so, I have employed many of the *Tips for Artful Persuasion* listed above.

Blame It on Luke

Keith had no choice but to defend himself when his neighbor, Luke, initiated a screaming match between the two men and threatened to make his neighbor "sorry" if he did not remove a small tree from his property. Under the law of this jurisdiction, an individual may use force to defend himself when he: (1) *reasonably* believes (2) he is under *physical attack*.

In these circumstances, Keith's belief that Luke was about to harm him was certainly reasonable. Keith had just finished planting a tree when he was approached by Luke, and the difference in their actions was apparent from the start. While Keith greeted his neighbor with a pleasant "good morning," Luke immediately began shouting at Keith regarding the location of the recently planted tree. Because Luke is normally a pleasant neighbor, his over the top reaction to the recently planted small tree frightened Keith, as it would any reasonable person in the circumstances. While Keith was frightened by Luke's initial reaction, he maintained his composure and refused to use force to defend himself.

Unfortunately, Luke continued his tirade against Keith and escalated the confrontation to the point where Keith believed he was under physical attack. First, Luke invaded Keith's physical space, bringing himself to within a few inches of his neighbor's face. Despite the threat implicit in this action, Keith held his ground but still refused to engage in a physical altercation. Luke, apparently upset at his inability to intimidate his neighbor, escalated the confrontation a final time when he uttered the ominous words — "Dig up that tree right now or you will be sorry." While it is true that the phrase "you will be sorry" could allude to any number of actions on the part of Luke, the words must be viewed in context. Keith had just witnessed a normally pleasant neighbor start screaming at him for no apparent reason. Then, while Keith remained calm, Luke invaded his physical space and told him that he would be sorry. Importantly, when Luke used the word "will," he was telling Keith that an attack was imminent.

Under these circumstances — screams, the invasion of one's physical space, and a threat of harm — any reasonable person would believe they were under physical attack. It was only at this point that Keith defended himself with a single punch. Keith could have struck Luke more than once, but his measured response gave him the time to escape the situation and return to his home. Keith's reasonable response to Luke's unreasonable conduct ended the confrontation immediately before either individual suffered serious harm.

Although the answer to the *Just Being Neighborly* problem has changed, the two major analysis patterns discussed throughout this chapter are still present. The facts from the original problem are present in *Blame it on Luke,* and the importance of each fact is discussed and explained — **fact/explain its relevance.** Just as importantly, a relevant counterargument is presented and compared with the primary argument. This time, however, the argument is resolved in favor of Keith — **A1, A2, Resolve.** No matter your role when performing legal analysis, these patterns will always be present.

Exercise 2

Review the above persuasive analysis, and answer the following question. How many different things can you identify that transformed the objective analysis contained in "Was Keith Just Defending Himself" into persuasive advocacy on Keith's behalf?

What Makes "Blame It on Luke" Persuasive Analysis?

_____

_____

_____

_____

_____

_____

_____

_____

_____

_____

_____

Wrap Up

Chapters 8 and 9 contain a great deal of information on the topic of legal analysis. Like many aspects of law school, your understanding of this topic will evolve over time. Therefore, you should read these chapters multiple times during your first year of law school. As your understanding of legal analysis evolves, the ideas contained within these chapters will speak to you on a deeper level. For the time being, these are the key ideas to hold onto to:

- Using the IRAC formula is an excellent way to ensure that you are including the various aspects of legal analysis into your answer, but the formula itself is not legal analysis.
- Legal analysis is merely the explanation of *why* you have chosen an answer to a legal problem.

- The two major components that should support your belief as to why you have chosen a particular answer are the current state of law and the facts of your problem.
- Legal analysis requires a discussion of the facts, so be sure that the facts from your problem reappear in your answer.
- When performing legal analysis, your default position is that there is a reasonable counterargument to the main argument.
- A counterargument is the legal, factual, and logical support of an answer to the problem, just not the answer you have chosen.
- In objective analysis, the counterargument helps explain to the reader why you have chosen a particular answer to a problem.
- You must still address reasonable counterarguments when performing persuasive analysis.

CHAPTER X

Legal Writing

The ability to write clearly and analytically is extremely important to your success during the first year of law school. It is so important, that I am dedicating an entire chapter of this book to the topic even though I do not treat any of your other first year courses in a similar fashion. This is because the ability to write well is a prerequisite to performing well in all of your classes. If you cannot effectively communicate your knowledge of a given topic to your professor, your grades will not reflect all of the time and effort you spent during the school year reading, reviewing, and outlining.

While we will cover a great deal, there is no way that I can teach you all you need to know about legal writing in a single chapter. This is a topic that is the subject of dozens of excellent books. Still, by the time you finish reading this chapter, you will be ready to explore the topic more fully in your legal writing class.

The Basics

Your legal writing class is quite a bit different than your other first-year classes. First of all, it will likely be the only class where you receive regular, graded feedback. In most first-year classes, your grade will depend on how well you perform on one or two examinations. This type of grading can make it difficult to gauge how well you understand the subject matter during the semester. In contrast, most legal writing professors will base your final grade on several papers and possibly homework assignments that you will be given throughout the course of the entire school year. Before we move onto some specific aspects of legal writing, there are a few basic things to keep in mind.

- **Do not underestimate your writing assignments.** Most students have had the experience of writing a 6–7 page paper the day before it is due and still getting a very good grade in return. This will not happen in your legal writing class. To do well, you will spend more time writing a 4 page legal memorandum than you spent on your 25 page college papers.

- **The skills you learn in your writing class are applicable across the first-year curriculum.** In your writing class, you will learn to perform legal analysis in its written form. The ability to analyze an issue thoroughly and explain potential outcomes is just as important on your criminal law final as it is on your legal writing assignments. Do not leave your legal writing skills behind when you take your exams.

- **Even if you are a good writer, you will find your legal writing class extremely challenging.** Many first-year students have solid writing skills. In fact, anyone with a degree in the liberal arts is accustomed to writing fairly long and detailed papers. While your good writing skills helped you get into law school, we will be teaching you legal writing. Even experienced legal writers, including folks like me who teach legal writing, receive documents back from our colleagues covered with suggested changes. Remember, you are learning to write in a new language, so do not be surprised if it takes the better part of the school year to become fluent.

- **Avoid spending too much time on your legal writing assignments.** Most law students are hungry for feedback, and some will spend a great deal of time writing their legal memoranda hoping to receive positive feedback from their professor. While you should strive to do your best on every assignment, do not let yourself get behind in your other classes.

The Memorandum of Law

The memorandum is the most common document lawyers write, and learning to properly organize and write these memos will be the focus of your first year writing class. Legal memoranda are written in one of two different styles, persuasive or objective, and you will likely learn both forms.

Most students enter law school ready to be advocates. They expect to be assigned to one side of a dispute, and then to argue passionately for their client's position. While all lawyers must learn to write persuasively, lawyers actually spend much of their time viewing issues in a much more objective fashion. During law school, the ability to write objectively is much more important than being able to advocate for one side. For example, your first year professors will likely expect you to write your examinations in an objective fashion, emphasizing your analyses of the issues involved. So, what are the main differences between the two styles?

Objective writing requires you to view an issue dispassionately and from multiple perspectives. You will inform the reader as to how you expect the issue to be resolved, but you will also discuss opposing points of view. If you fail to discuss the opposing points of view objectively, you are giving the reader a misimpression as to the strengths and weaknesses of a particular legal argument. In essence, the writer of an objective document must be a teacher.

The best teachers explain an idea fully, without assuming too much knowledge on the part of the reader. In addition, good teachers anticipate potential problem areas because they have completely thought through the concept being taught. Did you ever notice that good teachers often answer the questions you were thinking about before you even ask them? You have the same responsibility when writing an objective legal memorandum. If you have done your job correctly, the reader will not have any questions after reading your objective memo.

I am not suggesting that you should be wishy-washy. The reader needs to know what you have decided. In objective legal writing, however, the path you took in arriving at your conclusion is more important than the answer itself.

In the practice of law, objective legal memoranda are used internally in state, federal, and private law offices. The most typical scenario involves a senior lawyer asking an associate to perform some legal research on a specific topic or topics, with the assignment based on a new client's[1] problem. The associate would then perform legal research on the topic and report her conclusions in the form of an objective memorandum. Based on these conclusions, the senior attorney will decide on the appropriate course of action. This may include whether or not to take the case, file a lawsuit, or settle the case prior to trial. For the memo to truly assist the senior lawyer, the associate must allow the facts and law to lead her to an unbiased conclusion as opposed to the conclusion driving the analysis.

In a persuasive memorandum, the author knows her conclusion before she ever begins writing. Unlike an objective memorandum that is intended to help the reader decide on a course of action, in a persuasive document the writer has already decided what to do. The goal is to convince another, usually a judge, of the correctness of your position. The persuasive writer must still point out weaknesses in her argument. Failure to do so would leave the court with only the opponent's argument on a potentially critical matter. In the best

---

1. I am using the term client here quite broadly. For example, if you were working in a district attorney's office your clients are the people of your state and you would be researching an individual's alleged criminal conduct.

persuasive memos, the author emphasizes the strengths and minimizes the weaknesses in her arguments, but does so while *appearing* to be objective.

Grammar, Punctuation, and Proofreading

Too often, a student's well thought out and organized paper receives a low grade because of the details: proofreading, punctuation, and grammar. These "details" are an important part of the message that you send to the reader about your argument and yourself. If the memorandum has several proofing errors and mistakes in punctuation, then the message you are sending is that you could not be bothered to make the corrections. If readers cannot trust you to get the details right, then why should they trust that your conclusions are based on thorough research and accurate analysis? While it is impossible in a short chapter to address every potential proofreading pitfall, here are a few ideas to get you started.

- **Give yourself enough time to proofread.** This may seem obvious, but remember that legal writing is new to you and your assignments will often take longer to complete than anticipated. Try mentally moving up the due date for your assignment. For example, if the memo is due on a Wednesday, treat it as if it is due on Tuesday instead. This will give you an additional day to clean up your text.
- **Always proofread from a hardcopy of your document, not from a computer screen.** Computers have been an enormous boon to writers in that they have greatly simplified the editing and proofreading process. Unfortunately, computers have also created some unique problems. For example, programs that check your spelling and grammar, while helpful, often lull writers into a false sense of security. In addition, text always looks clean and correct on a computer screen. You will be astonished at how many more mistakes you will find by proofing your documents from a paper copy.
- **Proofread multiple times, looking for different things during each pass through the document.** Proofing your own work is never easy, and this difficult task is magnified when you try to look for multiple problems all at once. Instead, try to proof your documents multiple times. For example, concentrate on spelling mistakes during the first read and nothing else. Next, look for grammar problems like subject/verb agreement and the passive voice, and so forth. By slowing down the proofing process, you will catch more errors before passing in your assignments.

- **Beware of the passive voice!** In general, write your documents in the active voice as opposed to the passive voice. In the active voice, the subject of the sentence is acting while in the passive voice the subject is being acted upon. Active voice—The police arrested John. Passive voice—John was arrested by the police. Passive voice sentences tend to be a bit longer and may even hide an important party. For example—"The victim was attacked and murdered." Here, we have no idea who attacked the victim. In some instances you may intentionally use the passive voice in order to downplay a party's role in the events, particularly if that party is your client. In general, however, write in the active voice to keep your sentences short, concise, and clear.

> ### *Herb's Hints*
> ———
> A quick way of finding the passive voice is to look for uses of the verb "to be," which includes is, are, was, and were. While not perfect, forms of the verb "to be" often indicate the presence of the passive voice.

- **Give your brain a rest between writing and proofreading.** Proofread a document with fresh eyes. If you proofread too soon after you have written a document, your mind will correct your mistakes without you being aware of it. A good practice is to give yourself at least 24 hours between writing and proofreading a document.
- *When possible* **have another person proof your work.** The freshest proofreading eyes that you can find will belong to someone else. We all tend to be proprietary about our writing, often becoming quite stubborn as to whether it needs revision. Another proofreader can provide an objective assessment as to the quality of your work, but be sure to follow all of your writing professor's instructions. Your completed writing assignments must be the product of your effort and no one else's, and this includes proofreading in many schools.
- **Try reading your papers out loud.** As previously noted, sometimes our mind plays tricks on us when we proofread and corrects mistakes that are present in our work. A good counter to this phenomenon is to read your work out loud and slowly. This is a great way to find errors in grammar and sentence structure. Oftentimes our ears will pick up an error in grammar that our eyes may miss.
- **Read your memos from beginning to end without pausing**—With all the detailed aspects to proofreading, we sometimes miss the big picture. In the case of a legal memorandum, this means asking whether the document accurately communicates your point. One of the best ways to answer this question is to read your memos without pausing to change sentences or

make corrections. A big picture proofread like this one will disclose gaps in your logic, overused phrases, and unaddressed points of view.

Common Proofreading Mistakes

Example	Problem	Solution
And John as well. But not Mary.	Beginning sentences with conjunctions (and, but, or) can create sentence fragments.	The simplest solution is to avoid using conjunctions at the beginning of your sentences.
Irregardless Supposebly	These examples are not words! Try irrespective and supposedly.	Use a dictionary whenever you are in doubt.
The Court of Appeals *found* that the trial court misapplied the hearsay rule.	Words like "find," "hold," and "reason" have specific legal meanings and must be used correctly. Use the word "found" when referencing a judge's or jury's findings of fact.	Consult a legal dictionary whenever you encounter a legal term of art for the first time. Do not rely on your ability to ascertain the word's meaning from the context of the sentence.
Its and It's	*It's* is a contraction that means "it is" while *its* indicates possession.	Learn the most common exceptions to the rules of grammar and punctuation.
Once *a* student completes a document, *they* loathe changing it.	Incorrect pronoun usage. The word "they" indicates the plural, but the sentence is referencing a single student.	Rewrite your sentences to avoid awkward pronoun usage. This sentence could be rewritten using "he" or "she," but a better option would be to rewrite the entire sentence to avoid gender specific pronoun usage.
This United States Supreme *court* should follow the precedent established in *Smith v. Jones.*	Knowing when you should and should not capitalize the word court.	Capitalize court when naming a court in full, when referring to the United States Supreme Court, and when referring to the court that will be receiving the document in question.

E-mail Etiquette

Although I have touched on proper e-mail etiquette in a few different places in this book, the topic deserves a more thorough discussion. E-mail has become the preferred mode of communication for many of us, in part, because of its immediacy and informality. These same factors, however, can make it a dangerous mode of corresponding in a more professional environment. If you follow these simple suggestions, you will never be undone by an unprofessional e-mail.

Rule 1 — Treat e-mails like any other form of professional writing. This can be the most difficult of my rules to follow because one of the most appealing aspects of e-mail is its informality. Regardless, you must strive for the highest degree of formality when e-mailing anyone in a professional situation. A professional context includes e-mails to professors, potential employers or their staff, colleagues (including your classmates!), and existing or potential clients.

To begin with, use the subject line in your e-mail as opposed to leaving it blank. If the recipient fails to recognize your name, a subjectless e-mail may be treated like an unwanted solicitation. At home, unwanted solicitations end up in the trash, which is where your e-mail might end up.

Next, use a salutation as opposed to jumping into your topic. For example, my students should begin their e-mails to me with "Professor Ramy." The inclusion of my name in the body of the e-mail is not only more professional, but allows the recipient to confirm that the correspondence is not part of a mass e-mail solicitation.

Once you reach the main body of the e-mail, spend a few moments explaining any relevant background that might make your correspondence easier to understand. At the very least, identify yourself by name! Do not assume that the e-mail recipient will know who you are based solely on your question. In addition, the answer to your question may be different based on who you are. For example, if you are e-mailing a follow-up question to an employer with whom you have had already had an interview, remind them of who you are, when you met, and why you are asking a question. Consider the following examples, and whether one is more likely to elicit the response you are looking for.

First Sample E-mail

Please send me any available information regarding insurance options at your law firm.

Second Sample E-mail

Mr. Ramy,

My name is Mary Smith, and I had the pleasure of meeting you on No-
vember 12, 2010, when I interviewed with your law firm. At that time,
you graciously offered to answer my questions regarding the benefits
package offered to new employees and I would like to take you up on
that offer.

During the interview, you noted that the law firm pays the full amount
for employee health insurance. As I am married, I was wondering what
the costs would be to insure my spouse as well. Also, are life insurance
and disability insurance offered as part of your firm's benefits package?
Thank you for taking the time to review my request, and please let me
know if I should be addressing these questions to someone in your
human resources office. I may be reached at this e-mail address—
msmith@mail.com—or by phone at 123-456-7890.

Sincerely,

Mary Smith

In the first e-mail, it is not even clear that the sender and recipient of the
e-mail have met before. While it is possible that the recipient will recognize
your name if it is part of the e-mail address, do you truly want to rely on
this when trying obtain important information? Because the sender's iden-
tity is unclear in the first e-mail, it is doubtful that the recipient of the e-
mail will even respond. As for the second sample, it is more professionally
written and is more likely to produce the information the sender is seeking
without the necessity of additional e-mails. Although professionally written
e-mails take a few more minutes to write, they ultimately save time because
of their clarity,

Rule 2—Be sure that your e-mail is going to the intended recipient—By now,
most of us have made the mistake of sending an e-mail to a group instead of
an individual. This is the classic "Reply" vs. "Reply all" error. Thankfully, the
problem is easily corrected. ALWAYS check the "To" line in your e-mails before hitting send.

Rule 3—Assume your e-mail will be read by an unintended recipient—
E-mail communications have a bad habit of ending up in the wrong hands.
They are forwarded to others, posted to the internet, or printed out and tacked
to a bulletin board. At best, the sender ends up being embarrassed. At worst,
the sender may lose a job or end up as the defendant in a lawsuit. Many businesses have learned the hard way that all those deleted e-mails can still be re-

covered and used as evidence in a trial. Assume your e-mails will be read by others and you will not be embarrassed by a misdirected e-mail. As for confidential communications, do not use e-mails for this purpose.

Rule 4—E-mails cannot convey the subtler aspects of communication—Have you ever sent an e-mail that unintentionally angered or offended another person? For most of us, the answer to this question is "yes." The reason? We tend to forget how much non-verbal information we communicate to each other when we are face to face. Your body language or a smile can tell the listener that your seemingly harsh words were intended as a joke, but these aspects of non-verbal communication are not present in e-mails. The best way to address this problem is to reread your e-mails before you hit send, and try to place yourself in the recipient's shoes.

Rule 5—Never send an e-mail when you are angry—The real issues here are the immediacy of e-mail communication coupled with its remoteness. In regard to immediacy, e-mail lets you vent your anger before you have a chance to calm down and look at the situation more dispassionately. Over the years, I have received a few angry e-mails from students to whom I have given a low grade. Typically these e-mails are sent shortly after the student becomes aware of the grade, which inevitably leads to embarrassment and an apology the next morning. In addition, the remote nature of e-mail communication also promotes poor etiquette. Many of us will "say" things in an e-mail that we would never say face to face or over the telephone. Once again, the solution is simple. Never e-mail your employer, colleagues, or professors when you are angry. The satisfaction you might feel will last only a few moments but the embarrassment will last for much longer.

Rule 6—Allow the e-mail to demonstrate how much work you have already done—Law students and new lawyers ask a lot of questions and this is only natural. The questions themselves are not a problem. If improperly formulated, however, questions can suggest that the asker has done little independent work. For example, do not ask a supervising attorney for sample interrogatories relevant to a slip and fall case without providing a list of the questions you have already come up with and the sources you have consulted. Similarly, do not e-mail your professor for an explanation of the rule against perpetuities without noting the sources you have already researched or a precise explanation of which aspects of the rule are giving you the most difficulty. In addition to portraying you in a more positive light, the additional information will help the e-mail recipient provide you with a more focused response to your inquiry.

Legal Citation

Legal citation is the way lawyers attribute ideas to another source. In legal documents, writers often reference cases, statutes, or legal treatises in support of their ideas. Each time the writer references another person's ideas, that source must be attributed using legal citation. Legal citation tells the reader that the ideas originated somewhere else, and more importantly provides the information needed to find the source material.

There are two main sources that provide the rules for legal citation. The older of the two sources is *The Bluebook, A Uniform System of Citation,* which is compiled by the law review editors at Columbia, Harvard, University of Pennsylvania, and Yale law schools. The other commonly used citation source is the *ALWD Citation Manual,* which was created by the Association of Legal Writing Directors, The Legal Writing Institute, and Darby Dickerson of Stetson University College of Law. *The Bluebook* has been the standard for many years, but the *ALWD Citation Manual* is gaining acceptance due to its ease of use. The rules for citing to the most commonly used sources — cases and statutes — are essentially the same regardless of which manual your professor uses. The important thing to keep in mind is that your reader must be able to find the source material based on your citation. If your citation is incorrect and the reader has difficulty finding your sources, the best case scenario is that you will be viewed as lazy or incompetent. At worst, the reader will believe that you are trying to be misleading and that your sources do not actually support your assertions.

Both the *Bluebook* and the *ALWD Citation Manual* are hundreds of pages long in order to provide guidance when citing to even the most esoteric source material. Therefore, I will not provide you with citation examples because even the simplest citations will generate questions that will generate additional examples and so on. Instead, my only recommendations regarding citation are as follows:

- **Pay close attention to the details.** A misplaced comma or space can make your citation incorrect.
- **Be sure to cite in every instance where your sentences represent an idea that originated elsewhere.** For example, when you discuss case law in a legal memorandum, every sentence about the case will require a citation. Even paraphrases require legal citation because the idea contained within the paraphrased words originated somewhere else.
- **Do not forget to pinpoint cite.** Pinpoint citation refers to the practice of providing the reader with the exact page where the referenced idea or language appears. Too often, writers give the reader the first page of the

source, but not the pinpoint cite. When you consider that some cases are over 50 pages long, the need for pinpoint citation becomes apparent.

- **When in doubt, go back to the basics.** There are hundreds of rules regarding legal citation, and they can become quite confusing. Whenever in doubt as to how you should cite, remember that the purpose of citation is to allow the reader to find the original source. Let this rule be your guide.

To Quote or Not to Quote

In general, there are two distinct writing reasons to quote as opposed to paraphrase another's work. First, you should quote source material where failing to do so might change the original author's intended meaning. Typically, this is why most lawyers use quotes in their writing. As we have previously discussed, the law is its own unique language. Legal terms of art are often necessary to convey a specific legal concept, and failure to use these terms of art might confuse the reader. Similarly, legal writers will often quote the language from a statute or the holding from a judicial opinion to accurately convey the law. This rationale for quoting, while valid, is overused. Accurately conveying the law is certainly a laudable goal, but too often writers will quote ordinary language that they could easily paraphrase. Not every word in a statute or a judicial opinion is a legal term of art that requires quotation. More importantly, your own words may better serve your ultimate goal—clearly communicating the law using an economy of language. In addition, keep in mind that your professor is assessing *your* writing ability, which is difficult to do if you quote excessively.

The second reason for quoting, and in my opinion the more important reason, is for emphasis. When you use quotation marks, you are telling the reader to pay careful attention. The quoted language must be read exactly as presented to best communicate an essential idea. A writer who is trying to emphasize through quotation may quote the same word or term numerous times in a single document to drive home an important point. Similarly, the writer might quote a phrase when laying out the law, and then use that same quotation again later when analyzing the facts. By doing so, the author is driving home the law's applicability to this new set of circumstances. Unfortunately, this rationale for quoting is also overused. The power of a quotation to emphasize language is lessened each time the author decides to quote another word or phrase. Eventually, the reader will no longer believe your unstated assertion, that these words, in this exact form, must be remembered. The reader will begin paying less and less attention to your quotes, which is the opposite of your intent! Therefore, regardless of your reason, quote judiciously.

When you do use another's words, you must use quotation marks. Failure to do so is plagiarism, and can lead to disciplinary action. In many schools, an individual's intent to plagiarize another's work may be considered in assigning punishment, but may not be an absolute defense to a charge of plagiarism. A student may still be punished for plagiarism if they accidentally leave off necessary quotation marks. Plagiarism policies are not unique to law schools, but the nature of legal writing is such that students must be extra vigilant when writing their papers.

The Legal Writing Formula

Good legal writing is very well organized and, initially at least, can seem somewhat formulaic. The reason is that most writing professors actually use an organizational formula when teaching students the basics of legal writing. This formula goes by different acronyms—IRAC, CREAC, CRAC. These formulae should look familiar because I briefly discussed them in my chapter on legal analysis.

Regardless of the acronym used, the ideas behind these formulae remain the same. There are certain points that you must always address when performing legal analysis and these formulae help ensure that you address all of these points in the most logical way possible. The formulae are quite simple, almost rudimentary in nature. However, do not let their simplicity fool you. Through a few simple modifications, you may employ these formulae to analyze even the most complex legal issues. In addition, keep in mind that these formulae are only a single aspect of good legal writing.

For purposes of our discussion, we will be using the CREAC formula. The letters in CREAC stand for the following ideas:

C—**Conclusion**. Legal writing is extremely practical. By starting with your conclusion, you let the reader know your position immediately. Also, it will make it easier for the reader to follow your discussion of the issue if you start off with your destination.

R—**Rule**. After you state your conclusion, the next logical step is to provide the reader with the rule upon which you are basing that conclusion. The rule can originate in cases, statutes, the Constitution, rules of procedure, regulations, legal treatises and periodicals or some combination of these sources. Sometimes, finding the rule of law is quite simple. For example, a court may come right out and say "we are following the rule announced in Terry v. Ohio[2] in determining whether the police officer's search of the suspect's vehicle was warranted." In other instances, you will create the rule through legal synthesis.

E—Explanation. Standing alone, a rule may be subject to multiple interpretations. To help the reader better understand the rule, an explanation of how this rule has been used in the past may be necessary. Commonly, a rule is explained through a discussion of relevant case law. Through a discussion of how judges previously applied the rule, the reader will have a better understanding of how it may be applied to the facts of the case at hand. Cases are not, however, the only source that you may use to explain a rule of law. In addition to cases, other rules, commentaries by legal scholars, and even notes regarding legislative sessions, individually or taken together, can help the reader better understand the rule. When using these sources, keep in mind that some will carry more weight with the reader than others. Always try to explain your rule by using sources of primary authority. A discussion of the rule by a legal commentator, while potentially persuasive, cannot bind another court's actions.

A—Analysis/Application. When you write a memo, everything is leading up to the moment when you begin your analysis. Your conclusion, the statement of the rule, and your explanation of the rule are all there to support your analysis. This is the spot in the memo when you as the writer have a chance to shine. Using the rule you have just laid out as support, you will explain to the reader the likely outcome of the case. In the end, you will explain to the reader "why" a court will rule in a particular way. If you do your job well, this explanation will include why the court is unlikely come to a conclusion that is different than yours. When writing an objective document, you must address any weaknesses in your analysis in a forthright fashion without downplaying their significance. In contrast, a persuasive document requires you to address the weaknesses in a given position, but to downplay them.

C—Conclusion. This is the final wrap up. Your legal analysis will seem incomplete unless you end it with a statement that wraps up your conclusion.

Thesis Sentences

Thesis sentences are similar to topic sentences. Most writers understand that they should begin their paragraphs with a topic sentence, or a sentence

---

2. 392 U.S. 1 (1968).

that sets out the main point of the paragraph. Similarly, thesis sentences appear at the beginning of the paragraph and are also what the paragraph is about. There is, however, one additional aspect to a thesis sentence. A thesis sentence is also an assertion that the writer intends to prove by the end of the paragraph. It is the difference between saying "[M]ost families in the U.S. own more than one car" and "[T]he automobile has completely changed the way that Americans live their lives."

When appropriate, begin your paragraphs with a thesis sentence. Typically, this applies to your paragraphs of explanation and analysis. By beginning with a thesis sentence, you are letting the reader know the key to understanding the remainder of the paragraph. It is a way of grabbing the reader's attention and shouting "REMEMBER THIS IDEA."

In addition, the thesis sentence is a valuable tool when writing a persuasive document. A good thesis sentence helps you guide the reader to your point of view. That is because you can emphasize a particular way of understanding the law through a carefully worded thesis sentence.

Finally, consider for a moment how most people read lengthy documents. When pressed for time, most of us tend to quickly scan through a document. Commonly, this means carefully reading the first sentence of each paragraph to see what it contains before moving on to the next paragraph. Using a thesis sentence ensures that the reader understands the key elements of the points you are trying to make.

Writing Your First Legal Memorandum

Most legal writing classes require you to become proficient at writing the legal memorandum. Typically, these assignments are constructed around a memo from a senior partner asking you for assistance in resolving the legal issues generated by a fictional fact pattern. Your professor will give you a set of facts that will form the basis of the issue you will address. In some instances you will receive these facts in a packet of information furnished by your writing professor. Some professors, however, prefer to provide these facts through a series of mock client interviews or depositions.

Once you have the facts and know the issues, you must find the law. Early in the year, your professor may provide you with the law you will use in writing the memo. As the year progresses, however, the professor will expect you to conduct your own legal research to find the legal authority needed to complete the assignment.

The assignment will be difficult to complete if you focus on your conclusion as opposed to your analysis of the issues. Students are often surprised when the law they find fails to neatly resolve the issues generated by the memo. Get used to it! Lawyers are often expected to predict an outcome based on incomplete information. To help you hone this skill, legal writing problems are often constructed so that there is no easy answer. The cases you use to settle the issues generated by the fact pattern will be both similar to and different from your facts. Based on the existing law and facts as provided by your professor, it is your job to decide whether the differences or the similarities are more important.

Sample Memo

To better understand the memo writing process, I have created the following fact pattern, cases, and memorandum. We will walk through each aspect of this problem together to better understand what your professor will expect when you write your own legal memos. Text appearing in *italics* will be my explanation of what you are seeing, and would not appear in a problem created by your writing professor. As you read through the problem, please be aware that the facts, cases, statute, and state of Acadia are all fictional.

MEMORANDUM

To: Assistant DA Michael Smith
From: DA Elizabeth Jones
RE: State v. Baxter

A memo like the one below is a common device used by writing professors to get the ball rolling. Through these memos, you may be given a few basic facts, a statement of the issues in need of resolution, and a brief explanation of what is expected of you. In this instance, you are being asked to determine the likelihood of the government prevailing on the defendant's appeal of his criminal conviction. This means that there has already been a trial and the defendant has lost. Unhappy with the outcome, the defendant is asking an appellate court to review the matter because certain mistakes led to an unfair conviction.

Note that you are being asked to perform an objective evaluation of the strengths and weaknesses of the defendant's arguments. Therefore, you will not advocate for the government despite the fact that you are playing the role of an assistant district attorney.

I need you to perform some research for me regarding the following situation. In State v. Baxter, this office successfully prosecuted the defendant for assault and battery by means of a dangerous weapon. The weapon in question was alleged to be the defendant's shoes.

After trial, Baxter's lawyer filed the required **notice of appeal** in order to challenge the verdict. In his appellate brief, which was submitted to the Acadia Court of Appeals and the DA's Office, Baxter's attorney argues that the District Attorney did not submit sufficient evidence to the jury to support their verdict. First, he argues that the description of the defendant's shoes was too vague for the jury to find that the victim's injuries were the result of the shoes Baxter was wearing, as opposed to simply the blows themselves. She also argues that the jury could not base their finding of a weapon on Baxter's injuries because they were not significant enough to indicate the presence of a weapon.

After you have completed your research, please write me a memorandum discussing the likelihood of this office prevailing on appeal. I need to determine whether I should assign valuable office resources to this appeal, and your objective assessment of the situation is essential to my decision.

I have attached the relevant portions of the trial transcript to this memorandum. In addition, I have attached a summary of the facts that was based on witness interviews conducted during trial. This should provide you with the factual background necessary to write your memo.

Summary of the Facts

These facts create the "world" for this problem. Once you receive the facts from your professor, read them very carefully. You may also take some notes regarding facts that appear to be important. I used the phrase "appear to be important" because you cannot be sure which facts are truly important until you find the law. As you begin to find cases and relevant statutes, review these facts again and again. If you don't, you are likely to miss some crucial details that seemed unimportant at first blush. Also, resist the temptation to embellish upon the facts. As I noted, these facts are your "world" for this problem, so do not change the world to make the issues easier to resolve.

On October 27th, Murray was having a beer at the local bar and enjoying himself immensely. His baseball team was about to clinch the World Series after 86 years of frustration. Murray's team was ahead with two outs in the bottom of the ninth when the final batter swung and tapped the ball back to the pitcher. As the first baseman closed his mitt on the baseball for the final out, Murray jumped out of his seat in jubilation. Unfortunately, Murray didn't realize that Mary was standing directly behind him. As Murray jumped to his feet, he jostled Mary and her beer spilled all over her clothes.

Trying to be as chivalrous as possible under the circumstances, Murray grabbed some napkins to help clean the beer from Mary's clothing. Although she wasn't all that happy to be soaked with beer, Mary decided to be a good sport and accept Mark's apology and offer of a fresh beer. Mary's boyfriend, however, wasn't a good sport.

Mary's boyfriend, Ted, was returning from the bathroom and arrived just in time to see some strange guy touching his girlfriend and offering to buy her a beer. Ted had recently finished drinking his sixth beer and didn't seem to notice that Murray was just trying to clean up the beer and apologize for his clumsiness. In Ted's mind, some creep was touching his girlfriend inappropriately, and that creep was going to pay.

Ted tried to make his way back to the bar but his way was blocked by dozens of cheering patrons. By the time he got back to his seat, Murray had already paid his bill and left the bar. Ted asked Mary where the creep who'd been touching her had gone. Sensing Ted's anger, Mary tried to explain what had happened, but he ignored her explanation about a spilt beer and an apology. Instead, Ted ran outside to see if he could catch up with Murray.

As soon as he stepped outside, Ted saw Murray walking away from the bar. He confronted Murray about the incident inside the bar and pushed him to the ground before Murray could offer any explanation. Murray was never able to get off a single punch during the course of the fight. During the melee, Ted punched and kicked Murray until a good Samaritan pulled Ted away. A few minutes later an officer arrived on the scene and arrested Ted. The officer tried to take a statement from any witnesses to the beating, but the Samaritan had already left. Murray went to the hospital to get checked out, but fortunately his injuries consisted mainly of deep bruises over much of his body. He left the hospital later that evening, but experienced soreness for over a week.

Ted was indicted for assault and battery by means of a dangerous a weapon "to wit, the defendant's shoes."

I have provided the remaining facts through excerpts of the trial transcript. During a trial, a stenographer takes down everything said in the courtroom. Here, you have the relevant portion of the District Attorney's direct examination of the victim, Murray Slaughter. The questioning of a witness can take hours, or even days, to complete. To save space, I have given you only a portion of the witness' testimony. When an attorney calls a witness to testify, the questioning is referred to as a direct examination. After the attorney finishes questioning the witness, opposing counsel will ask her own questions. Lawyers refer to this as "cross examination" of the witness.

Excerpt of Direct Examination of Murray Slaughter

DA: After your attacker, Ted Baxter, knocked you to the
         ground, what happened next?

Murray: He kept punching and kicking me.

DA: Can you be more specific?

Murray: He kicked me in my arms, my legs, my ribs ... really
         all over my body.

DA: Was your attacker barefoot or was he wearing shoes?

Murray: Are you kidding? It was late October and it was about
         55 degrees outside. Of course he was wearing shoes.

DA: Did you see the shoes?

Murray: No, I was too busy covering up so that I wouldn't take
         a kick to the face. But, I could feel the shoes as he
         was kicking me, and I know he wasn't kicking with his
         bare feet.

Excerpt of Cross Examination of Murray Slaughter

Defense: Mr. Murray Slaughter—you claim that your assailant was
         wearing shoes during the incident in question, is that
         correct?

Murray: I'm not claiming anything. He was wearing shoes and I've
         got the bruises to prove it.

Defense: But you didn't see your attacker's feet, so how can you
         be so sure?

Murray: Like I've already said, I could feel his feet as he was
         kicking me and he sure wasn't barefoot.

Defense: Mr. Slaughter, you used the term "shoes" when describ-
         ing the defendant's footwear ... isn't that correct?

Murray: Yes.

Defense: But you have no idea whether he was actually wearing
         shoes as opposed to sneakers, do you?

Murray: Well ... when I said shoes, I was just using another
         word for footwear. I just meant that he wasn't barefoot.

Defense: Thank you for that clarification. So is it possible that
         he was wearing sneakers?

Murray: I guess so, but you can still do a lot of damage kick-
         ing someone with sneakers.

Defense: Mr. Slaughter, I'm not trying to minimize your injuries,
         but you didn't suffer from any broken bones did you?

Murray: No.

Defense: How about broken ribs?

Murray: No.

Defense: Were you even scratched?

Murray: I was covered with bruises! Of course I was scratched!

Defense: Let me be more specific ... were you bleeding after the assault?

Murray: Bleeding? No, I wasn't.

Defense: Mr. Slaughter, just a few more questions and we'll be finished. Earlier you admitted that the attacker may have been wearing sneakers. Isn't it possible that he was wearing something even softer than sneakers, like slippers?

Murray: Slippers! Who the heck wears slippers when they go to a bar?

Defense: Mr. Slaughter, can you say definitively that your assailant was not wearing soft slippers?

Murray: It definitely didn't feel like slippers.

Defense: But you can't describe in any way what the defendant was wearing on his feet, can you?

Murray: Like I've already said, I know he wasn't barefoot.

Defense: But other than not being barefoot, you really can't say what he was wearing can you?

Murray: No, I guess I can't.

After Murray completed his testimony, the prosecution called Doctor Louis Grant to the stand. The doctor worked in Acadia Hospital's emergency room, and he treated Murray when he was brought to the hospital for his injuries.

Excerpt of Direct Examination of Dr. Louis Grant

DA: Doctor Grant, now that we've finished discussing your qualifications, let's move on to the night in question. You were in Acadia Hospital's emergency room on October 27th, weren't you?

Doctor: Yes I was.

DA: And do you recall that the victim, Mr. Slaughter, was brought into the hospital on that date.

Doctor: I do remember Mr. Slaughter, and I was the doctor who treated his injuries.

DA: Could you please describe those injuries for us?

Doctor: He had contusions over much of his body. His back, arms, and shoulders in particular, were covered with bruises. There were also several contusions on his legs and buttocks.

DA: Did Mr. Slaughter indicate whether he was in any pain?

Doctor: Due to the pain, it was difficult for him to takeoff his clothing in order for me to perform the examination. He winced several times when I touched the contusions.

DA: Doctor, in your medical opinion, what could cause these injuries.

Doctor: Really any number of things. Most commonly, a car ac-
            cident, a fall down a flight of stairs, or a beating.
DA: Are you familiar with what the results of a beating
            would look like?
Doctor: Unfortunately, I am. As an emergency room doctor, I see
            several patients a week who have been beaten, usually
            by their spouses.
DA: Did you admit Mr. Slaughter that evening?
Doctor: No—I suggested that he stay overnight for observation.
            I was concerned about the possibility of kidney damage.
            He decided not to stay, and left for home.
DA: Did you prescribe any medication for the patient.
Doctor: Tylenol with codeine.
DA: Is Tylenol with codeine a medication that he could have
            obtained over the counter?
Doctor: No, it requires a doctor's prescription

*Once the District Attorney finished his questions, defense counsel cross examined
the doctor. The relevant parts of the cross examination appear below.*

Defense: Doctor, when the prosecutor asked you to describe Mr.
            Slaughter's injuries, I heard you say that he had con-
            tusions, is that right?
Doctor: Yes it is.
Defense: And aren't contusions just a fancy way of saying that
            you saw bruises?
Doctor: Contusions is the medical term for bruises, and there
            was a great deal of bruising on Mr. Slaughter's body.
Defense: Thank you doctor. Now, if I recall correctly, you did-
            n't describe any other injuries, or did I miss something?
Doctor: No, my examination revealed serious bruising, but noth-
            ing more.
Defense: No broken bones?
Doctor: No.
Defense: No cracked skull?
Doctor: No
Defense: Any deep gashes?
Doctor: No.
Defense: Was he bleeding from anywhere?
Doctor: No he was not.
Defense: Doctor, earlier you compared Mr. Slaughter's injuries
            to those that might be sustained by a victim of spousal
            abuse, did you not?
Doctor: Not exactly. I said that I had a great deal of experi-
            ence treating the victims of spousal abuse, so I have

a good idea of what a beating looks like, and this man was beaten.

Defense: Thank you for the clarification doctor. Did you ever examine a victim of spousal abuse who had been beaten with some item, a stick or rock for example.

Doctor: Yes I did. I even examined a victim who'd been kicked, just like Mr. Slaughter.

Defense: This person who had been kicked just like Mr. Slaughter, how serious were his or her injuries?

Doctor: Well, if I remember correctly, that victim had several broken ribs, a broken arm, and a punctured lung.

Defense: So those injuries were quite a bit more serious than Mr. Slaughter's?

DA: Objection

Judge: Sustained

Defense: Let me rephrase that question. Did this particular victim end up going home on the same day, like Mr. Slaughter, or did you admit her?

Doctor: We admitted her.

Defense: For how long?

Doctor: About a week.

Defense: Did she require surgery?

Doctor: We performed a minor surgical procedure to set her arm.

Defense: Did this victim happen to mention what her attacker was wearing on his feet while he was kicking her?

Doctor: She said that he was wearing workboots.

Defense: So, to be clear, when this victim was kicked by an attacker wearing workboots, she ended up in the hospital for a week, she suffered from broken ribs, a punctured lung, and a broken arm that required surgical treatment, is that right?

Doctor: Yes, that is correct.

Defense: I guess I'm unclear as to how this was just like Mr. Slaughter's situation.

DA: Objection

Defense: Withdrawn. No further questions.

After the doctor's testimony, the district attorney rested, as did defense counsel. The defendant moved for a "__judgment as a matter of law.__" The judge denied defense counsel's motion. Once closing arguments were completed, the judge instructed the jury on the crimes of assault and battery and assault and battery with a weapon. After two days of deliberation, the jury returned a verdict of guilty of assault and battery with a weapon, with the weapon in question being the defendant's shoes. Defendant then moved for a judgment notwithstanding the ver-

dict (J.N.O.V.),[3] *which the trial court judge also denied. The judge sentenced Ted Baxter to one year in the Acadia House of Corrections.*

Legal Research

Legal research is an integral part of the writing process. You cannot accurately provide the reader with your conclusions without first determining the state of the law in your jurisdiction. Initially, research is about educating yourself regarding a particular area of law. Typically, this will require you to start with relatively broad concepts before moving on to the more specific laws governing your situation. Starting off with broad concepts helps ensure that you fully understand the guiding principles behind each specific rule and may provide you with key phrases and terminology fundamental to your research. Once you have mastered the background concepts, it is time to move onto the specifics.

Once you are ready to start looking for specific principles of law, you must start with the governing statute. If there is a relevant statute, the courts in the jurisdiction must follow its language when ruling. Statutory compilations are divided into official and unofficial versions. The text of the statute is the same in both the official and unofficial compilations, but the unofficial versions also contain annotations. The annotated statutes, or codes, contain lists of cases and other source material commenting on various aspects of the statute. These annotations are organized within each statute by topic, and are extremely helpful when conducting legal research. In the state of Acadia, the assault and battery with a weapon statute reads as follows:

> Any person convicted of using a weapon during the commission of an assault and battery will be placed in the house of corrections for a term not to exceed 5 years.
>
> (A) A weapon is defined as an item designed specifically to cause harm. Such items include, but are not limited to, guns, bayonets, blackjacks, saps, brass knuckles, throwing stars and nunchucks.
>
> (B) An item that has not been designed to cause harm may still be a weapon under this statute if it is used with an intent to cause harm. Under this subsection, in addition to an intent to cause harm, it must be shown that it was the item in question, rather

---

3. *See* Chapter I—The First Days—for a brief description of a judgment as a matter of law and a JNOV motion.

than just the blow itself, that had the capability of causing serious bodily harm. 30 Acad. Stat. Annot. §17 (1947).

After finding the relevant statute, the next step in most research projects is to find case law interpreting the statute. It is not uncommon to find hundreds of cases that reference a particular statute, so you must find the cases that most closely mirror your facts. Remember, the cases you find will often be different than your facts, sometimes drastically so. I have provided you with three fictional cases—State v. Georgette, State v. Carlton and State v. Morgenstern—that we will use in writing our memo.

State v. Georgette
199 Acadia 216 (1995)

The defendant argues that the trial court incorrectly denied his motions for a directed verdict and for a judgment notwithstanding the verdict. *See* Acadia Rules of Crim. Proc. 50. More specifically, the defendant contends that the jury did not hear sufficient evidence to determine that he did indeed possess a dangerous weapon, a necessary element of a conviction for assault and battery by means of a dangerous weapon. 30 Acad. Stat. Annot. §17. The weapons in question were, allegedly, the defendant's shoes which he used to kick the victim.

> **Legal Definition— De Novo Review**
>
> An appellate court must apply one of several different standards of review when addressing an appeal. Under the *de novo* standard, the appellate court will review the legal question as if the matter had never been addressed before by the lower court.

When addressing the denial of a defendant's motion for a directed verdict, this court reviews the matter on a *de novo* basis to determine whether the prosecution presented sufficient evidence from which any reasonable jury could find all elements of the crime beyond a reasonable doubt. Based on the appellant's brief to this court, we will limit our review to the evidence supporting the existence of a weapon. From the evidence presented at trial, the jury was entitled to find the following.

On October 10th, the defendant was attending a party. It was a rainy day, and the defendant arrived at the party by way of the Acadia subway system. For reasons not relevant to the issue before us, he engaged in an altercation with another attendee at the party. During the course of this altercation, the victim fell to the ground where the defendant proceeded to kick him. The victim testified that he was kicked once in the arm, but that his injuries did not require any medical attention. He did note, however, that the kick did leave a small bruise.

A careful review of the record indicates that the jury did not hear any evidence, testimonial or otherwise, regarding the kind of shoes the defendant was wearing. The victim did testify that he was kicked, but at no time did he discuss whether the defendant was even wearing shoes, much less what kind of shoes he was wearing.

It is a settled point of Acadia law that an assailant's shoes may be, under the appropriate circumstances, a dangerous weapon in satisfaction of our assault and battery by means of a weapon statute. *See State v. Morgenstern,* 98 Acadia 17, 22 (1950); 30 Acad. Stat. Annot. §17. Obviously shoes are not designed to cause harm, therefore defendant must intentionally use the shoes intending to cause harm. In addition, where, as here, the weapon in question is not dangerous per se, the prosecution must establish that the item is capable of causing "serious bodily harm." 30 Acad. Stat. Annot. §17(B). The prosecution may establish an item's capability of causing harm in two ways: through a description of the item in question; or through a description of the victim's injuries.

First, a jury may infer that an item is capable of causing serious bodily harm if it is provided with sufficient details about the item in question. For example, in *State v. Morgenstern* the victim described the lady's high heeled shoes worn by her assailant. *State v. Morgenstern,* 98 Acadia at 22–23. Both the tips of the shoes and the heels were described as being "very pointy and sharp." *Id.* From this description, the jury could infer that the shoes were capable of causing serious bodily harm. Importantly, the jury could make this finding even though the defendant had not been seriously injured during the confrontation. *Id.* at 24. Under Acadia's assault and battery statute, an item must be "capable" of causing serious bodily. 30 Acad. Stat. Annot. §17(B). Whether the item actually causes serious harm is irrelevant where the item is sufficiently described during the course of the trial.

In this instance, the defendant's shoes were not described in sufficient detail in order for the jury to find them capable of causing serious bodily harm. In fact, the defendant's footwear was not described at all. At no time did the victim or any witness even mention that the defendant was wearing anything on his feet. The jury might be allowed to infer that the defendant arrived at the party wearing something on his feet, particularly where he had used public transportation as his means of transportation. In Acadia, public transportation riders are required to use some type of footgear as a condition of use. Two further inferences, however, are necessary to support defendant's conviction. First, that he was still wearing the footgear at the outset of the altercation, and second, that the shoes were capable of causing serious bodily harm. Such piling of inference upon inference is tantamount to guesswork on the part of the jury and cannot support a finding of a weapon beyond a reasonable doubt.

Even without a sufficient description, the jury may still find the existence of a weapon based on the injuries sustained by the victim. *See State v. Carlton,* 88 Acadia 77, 79 (1952). As previously noted, it is the item's capability to cause serious harm that is required under the statute. However, where a description of the item in question is lacking, the jury may infer from the victim's injuries that the defendant employed a dangerous weapon during the altercation. Here, the victim testified that the defendant's kick resulted in a small bruise to his arm that did not require medical attention. The victim's minor injuries cannot establish that the defendant's footwear was "capable" of causing "serious bodily harm." *See* 30 Acad. Stat. Annot. § 17(B). Therefore, the trial court was in error when it denied defendant's motion for judgment as a matter of law.

Reversed and remanded for further action consistent with this opinion.

Now that you have finished reading the case, we need to brief it in order to determine how much of it might be useful when writing the memo. To save space for this exercise, we won't go through the procedural history or facts. Instead, we will focus on the issue, holding, rule, and court's reasoning.

Issue: The issue here is whether the jury heard sufficient evidence to find that the defendant's shoes were a weapon, but this statement of the issue is a bit broad for our purposes. As you begin to incorporate more facts into the issue to make it more specific, you will probably notice that there are really two separate but related issues. First, could the jury find that the defendant's footwear was a weapon capable of causing serious bodily harm where they received no description of the footwear? Second, could the jury find that the defendant's footwear was a weapon based on a single small bruise that the victim sustained in the attack? Is it mandatory that I divide the issue in this fashion? It is not, but I am doing so to assist me later when writing my memo. As I read my cases, I am trying to extract principles that I will later need to address in the memo. State v. Georgette *seems to allow the prosecution to prove the existence of a weapon directly (through a description of the item) or indirectly (through a description of the victim's injuries). This may be important to us when we write our memo.*

Holding/Rule: The answer to issue #1 is that a jury cannot find that the defendant's footwear was a weapon based solely on the inference that he wore something on his feet. As for Issue #2, a jury may not find that a defendant's footwear was a weapon capable of causing serious bodily harm based solely on relatively minor injuries to the victim. Notice that my holding/rule is written specifically enough to answer my issues, but broadly enough to be useful when applied to future cases.

Reasoning: The reasoning is extremely important to us, because it will inform our later conclusions in our memo. Knowing why the court ruled as it did is essential if we are to predict how it will rule in the future. In this instance, the reasoning regarding both issues is related. To find that an object is a weapon, the jury must be able to determine that it could cause "serious bodily harm." Believing that the defendant was wearing something on his feet is not enough to make this determination. Similarly, the victim's injuries can provide a basis for finding that the defendant's shoes were a weapon, but only if the injuries established that the shoes were capable of causing serious bodily harm. A single small bruise is not evidence to establish an ability to cause serious harm.

State v. Carlton
88 Acadia 77 (1952)

This case comes before us based on the trial court's denial of defendant's motion for a JNOV. The district attorney's office sought and received an indictment against the defendant for assault and battery by means of a dangerous weapon, to wit: the defendant's shoes. After a two day jury trial, a jury found the defendant guilty of the crime charged, at which time the defendant made his motion for a JNOV. Defendant argued below, as he does here, that the jury did not hear sufficient evidence to find that the defendant was wearing shoes, much less that his shoes were capable of causing serious bodily injury. *See* 30 Acad. Stat. Annot. §17(B). The trial court denied defendant's motion.

When reviewing the denial of a motion for a JNOV, an appellate court must be careful not to substitute its opinion for the jury's. Under Acadia's rules of procedure, a court may grant a motion for a JNOV only where the evidence is such that no reasonable jury could have found sufficient evidence establishing all elements of the crime in question beyond a reasonable doubt. *See* Acadia Rules of Crim. Proc. 50. In this instance, our inquiry is confined to a *de novo* review of whether the jury heard sufficient evidence regarding the existence of a weapon. From our review of the record, it is clear that a reasonable jury could have found the following.

On March 2, the defendant, Carlton, and the victim were on a hiking trail in Twin Cities Park in Acadia. The two had been drinking for much of the day, and as often happens when too much alcohol is consumed, the former friends began fighting for reasons that neither could remember during trial. During the course of the 10 minute fight, both men punched and scratched each other.

The defendant, however, also kicked the victim in the chest and shoulder. Both individuals were scratched and bruised during the altercation, but the victim had to be rushed to the hospital after complaining of having some difficulty breathing.

The treating physician testified that the victim's injuries included two broken ribs and a dislocated shoulder. The prosecution asked the doctor to describe the likely cause of the injuries, specifically the victim's broken bones. Over the defendant's objection, the doctor testified that the broken bones were likely caused by the defendant's kick and because of the "shoes" he was wearing. Importantly, the doctor did have the opportunity to see the defendant in the hospital's waiting room shortly after examining the victim. Inexplicably, the prosecution failed to introduce any additional evidence regarding the defendant's shoes. Therefore, the jury must have found the presence of a weapon based solely on the doctor's testimony.

Acadia's assault and battery with a weapon statute actually contains two separate definitions of a weapon. First, a weapon is any item "designed specifically to cause harm." 30 Acad. Stat. Annot. §17(A). Obviously, this aspect of the statute is inapplicable to the case currently before us. However, the statute also defines any item as a weapon if the "item in question, rather than just the blow itself, that had the capability of causing serious bodily harm." 30 Acad. Stat. Annot. §17(B). Under this definition, the jury was entitled to find that the defendant used a weapon during the altercation in question.

Only two years ago, this court concluded that an individual's shoes may be a weapon for purposes of Acadia's assault and battery with a weapon statute. *See State v. Morgenstern*, 98 Acadia 17, 22 (1950). In this instance, however, we are faced with a different inquiry. May a jury find that the defendant used a weapon without being presented with a description of the item in question?

As we noted above, the prosecution inexplicably failed to introduce any description of the defendant's footgear. Normally, this would prove fatal to the prosecution's case. While an individual's footgear *may* be a weapon, not every pair of shoes has the "capability of causing serious bodily harm," as is required by Acadia Statute. 30 Acad. State. Annot. §17(B). In *State v. Morgenstern* the victim described the defendant's high heeled shoes as "very pointy and sharp." *Morgenstern*, 98 Acadia at 22–23. From this description, the *Morgenstern* jury could conclude that the defendant's shoes were weapons. Not every pair of shoes may be described as "sharp and pointy." For example, an attacker's soft bedroom slippers are unlikely to cause any more harm to a victim than would the kick itself, and, therefore, would not be a weapon under Acadia law.

In this instance, there are two pieces of evidence that do help establish that the defendant used a weapon during the altercation. First, the treating physician did refer to the defendant's footgear as "shoes." Standing alone, this description is helpful to the prosecution's case, but alone cannot establish that the shoes were weapons. Without additional information from the testifying physician, it is unclear what was meant by the term "shoes." The jury did, however, hear additional information from which they could determine that these shoes were used as dangerous weapons.

In addition to this brief description of the defendant's shoes, the jury also heard evidence regarding the severity of the victim's injuries. The victim suffered from two broken ribs and a dislocated shoulder. The victim also testified that the defendant kicked him in the chest and shoulder. In comparison, the defendant, who had not been kicked, sustained merely some bruising and a few scratches. From this evidence, the jury could conclude that it was the defendant's shoes that caused the victim harm, and that this harm was more than would have been sustained based solely on the blows themselves.

Appeal denied.

Exercise 1

Try to write a mini-brief of this case. As you brief, be sure to think about the memo you will be writing. Try to extract information that will be useful to you later.

Issue: _____

_____

_____

_____

Holding/Rule:_____

_____

_____

_____

_____

Reasoning: _____

_____

_____

_____

_____

State v. Morgenstern
98 Acadia 17 (1950)

The appellant, Lydia Morgenstern, is appealing her conviction for assault and battery by means of a weapon. On appeal, the defendant argues that the prosecution did not submit sufficient information for any reasonable jury to determine that she used a weapon. More specifically, she argues that shoes, regardless of style or type, may not be a weapon under Acadia law. This is an issue of first impression in Acadia, and the Court will review the matter using the *de novo* standard of review.

Based on the evidence the prosecution submitted at trial, a reasonable jury could have found the following. The victim testified that she was looking for a parking place near Marie's Shoes, an establishment where she planned to shop. She found a spot immediately in front of the store and pulled in, but as she was leaving her car the defendant Morgenstern approached her and began screaming obscenities. Apparently the defendant had also been waiting for a parking spot to open and yelled that the victim had "stolen" this spot from her. A shouting match between the victim and the defendant ensued, but it was Morgenstern who escalated the verbal confrontation into a physical one. She grabbed the victim by the hair and pulled her to the ground, at which point she ground the heel of her shoe into the victim's hand. The victim began to bleed from the wound, and it was later determined that the attack had broken two bones in her hand. The prosecution presented the victim as a witness, and she described the defendant's shoes as "sharp and pointy." Further questioning revealed that she was referring to both the tips of the shoes and to the heels. The Appellant argues that this court has never held that shoes may be dangerous weapons under Acadia law. Further, she contends that allowing a jury to find that shoes may be weapons would contravene the legislature's intent as expressed through the language of our assault and battery with a weapon statute. See 30 Acad. State. Annot. § 17. Finally, appellant argues that ruling for the state in this matter would result in every article of clothing becoming a weapon in future prosecutions and would transform every ordinary fight into an assault and battery with a weapon.

The only one of defendant's contentions that has any merit is her first—that this court has never held that shoes may be a weapon. This court has never held the converse, however, making the issue one of first impression and ripe for resolution.

Next, the defendant's argument that we would be contravening the legislature's intent as expressed through the state's A&B with a weapon has no basis whatsoever. While the statute does not explicitly include shoes as weapons, it need not do so. See 30 Acad. State. Annot. § 17. The legislature drafted subsection B of the statute quite broadly, allowing for any item to be a weapon if: (1) the defendant intends to use the item as a weapon; and (2) the item, rather than just the blow, has the *capability* of causing serious bodily harm. 30 Acad. State. Annot. § 17(B) (emphasis added). A reasonable jury could conclude from the testimony that the defendant intended to use her shoe as a weapon based on the ncture the victim's hand and break a number of bones. As ~oint, the description of the shoes as "sharp and pointy" coupled ictim's injuries was more than sufficient for the jury to determine that nad the *capability* to cause serious harm. During oral argument, defense counsel opined that the victim's injuries would have been the same regardless of the shoes worn by the defendant. Even if this Court agreed with defendant's point (we do not), it still would not change our ruling. The statute requires that the item be capable of causing more harm than would the blow alone, and the jury was entitled to find this based on the evidence at trial.

Defendant's final argument contemplates a world where every article of clothing has become a dangerous weapon, and every simple assault has become a felony. But, defendant fails to consider the language of the statute in making this assertion. As noted above, the statute requires that the defendant intend to use the item as a weapon. Therefore incidental touching with one's clothing would not be indictable under our A&B with a weapon statute. Finally, it is possible that our ruling will lead to increased prosecutions under our A&B with a weapon statute. However, if defendants use articles of clothing as weapons, then their conviction under the statute is wholly consistent with the intent of the legislature as expressed through Chapter 30, §17 of Acadia's statutory laws.

For the above stated reasons, the defendant's conviction is upheld.

Exercise 2: Write a Mini Brief of *State v. Morgenstern*

Issue: _____

_____

_____

_____

Holding/Rule: _____

_____

_____

_____

_____

Reasoning: _____

_____

_____

_____

_____

Outlining Your Memo

Once you have finished reading the relevant statute and caselaw, it is time to begin writing your memo. You must resist the temptation, however, to dive right into the memo itself. Instead, spend time working through an outline of what you intend to write. Use the facts of your situation and the relevant law to construct the basic form of your document. Time spent here will ultimately save you time when writing the document.

There is no absolute rule as to how detailed your memo outline should be. Some folks spend a great deal of time working on their outline to the point where it is really a first draft of their memo. Others write a fairly skeletal list of concepts that must be addressed. I recommend a middle of the road approach. List the concepts that must be addressed, but also include some additional information in the form of a description of the idea or a reference to relevant facts from your situation. Once again, you will use your facts, the cases, and any relevant statutes to help determine which ideas deserve further attention. This is a very early step in the memo writing process, so do not be concerned with creating a perfect outline. Not only are you free to add or subtract concepts from your outline, you are encouraged to do so as your understanding of the issues increases.

Based on a review of the law and our facts, it seems that the following concepts deserve at least some attention in our memo.

- **The standard of review**—Whenever an appellate court decides a case, it employs one of several different standards of review to assess the merits of the appellant's arguments. Law and legal procedure dictate which standard of review a court will employ. In some instances, the standard of review requires the appellate court to be extremely deferential to the trial court's decision. In other instances, such as we have here, the appellate court will review the matter on a *de novo* basis.
- **The statute**—In Acadia, there is a statute that defines a dangerous weapon. This must be included in the memo, although the cases interpreting the statute will likely be discussed in more detail than the statute.
- **An item designed to cause harm**—Acadia's statute actually contains two separate definitions of a weapon. Under one of these definitions, an item is a weapon when it has been designed to cause harm. This definition of a weapon is not particularly relevant to our situation, but it is part of the statute and we may want to at least mention it.
- **Items used with an intent to cause harm**—The statute's alternative definition of a weapon is much broader. Anything may be a weapon *if* the defendant uses the item intending to cause harm.

- **Item must be "capable" of causing serious harm**—As long as the item can cause serious harm, it may be a weapon even if the victim's injuries were minimal. Also, you must show that the item, and not just the blow to the victim had the capability of causing harm.
- **The prosecution may establish an item's capability of causing serious harm may in two different ways**—It seems that much of our memo will be devoted to this topic. Our central question will be whether or not the jury heard enough evidence to determine that the defendant's shoes were a weapon capable of causing harm.
  - **A sufficient description of the item**—Under this test, the jury must hear a sufficiently detailed description of alleged weapon from which they could assess its ability to cause harm. In *Morgenstern*, the court upheld a conviction where the defendant's shoes were described as "sharp and pointy." In contrast, the court in *Georgette* overturned a conviction where, at best, the jury could infer that the defendant was wearing something on his feet. A jury could find that our defendant was wearing "shoes," however, the victim also admitted that defendant could have been wearing sneakers.
  - **Severity of victim's injuries**—In *Carlton*, the treating physician testified that the defendant was wearing "shoes." Alone, this description was not enough to find the "shoes" capable of causing serious harm. The doctor also testified, however, that the victim suffered from broken ribs and a dislocated shoulder. Together, this was enough evidence for a jury to conclude defendant's shoes were a weapon. Our victim did require medical attention, but he did not spend very much time in the hospital.

Did you notice anything about the structure of my outline? At the outset, I deal with relatively broad ideas and concepts and then I get more specific as I move along. This inverted pyramid style—starting off broadly and getting progressively narrow—is the hallmark of any effective outline. This form also is the hallmark of a well-written memo because it allows the reader to follow along as you develop each concept fully.

The Memo Format

There are several distinct sections to every memo. The ordering of these sections varies from office to office (and school to school), and some offices may not require that every section appear in your memos. Once you have the basic format down, however, it is easy to modify it to fit the requirements of any office in which you work.

The Facts

The facts section is fairly self explanatory. You must list every fact that you will later analyze in the memo. In an objective document, it is relatively easy to write a statement of the facts. Simply describe the facts in a straightforward fashion, without embellishment, and your job is done. In most instances it is best to relate the facts in chronological order, but this won't always be true. Writing the facts section for a persuasive document is a little trickier. In a persuasive document, the facts section is your first chance to advocate for your client and you should not let this opportunity go to waste. It may be hard to imagine writing a persuasive set of facts without lying or leaving out certain details, but it is simply a matter of emphasis and embellishment. For example, in an objective memo where the topic involves a murder, I might write the following:

> Mark Smith, a 15-year-old minor, was on his way to school on October 13th when he was stopped by the defendant, John Doe. Doe produced a gun and told Smith "give up your money, and you won't get hurt." Smith refused and tried to push past the defendant, at which time the defendant's gun discharged killing the victim.

While the story is still a sad one, the writer is relating the details in a dispassionate fashion. This same set of facts will read quite differently in a persuasive document written by a prosecutor seeking to keep the defendant in jail.

> Mark Smith, a 15-year-old sophomore at Anytown High School, was on his way to school on a beautiful October morning. A star athlete and honors student, Mark was excited to get to school to participate in a planned pep rally. He was stopped by the defendant, John Doe, who screamed "give up your money and you won't get hurt." Startled, Mark tried to run past his attacker, but he was not allowed to get away. They bumped each other, and the defendant's gun discharged. The defendant ran, and Mark slowly bled to death on the sidewalk less than a block from the safety of his high school.

The main facts are the same in both, but notice the level of detail in this version. I have tried to paint a much more vibrant picture of the victim in an attempt to remind the reader that this was a real person with a future. In addition, I refer to the victim as "Mark" and John Doe as the "defendant" as often as possible. In doing so, I am subtly creating a more intimate picture of one individual while dehumanizing another.

The Question Presented

The question presented is quite similar to the issue section of your case briefs. In a case brief, your statement of the issue is the question, or questions, the court was seeking to resolve. Similarly, in your question presented you are articulating the question that will be resolved in the document. An accurately framed question presented contains the key facts, the law, and your question. Consider the following example:

> Will an individual be guilty of Acadia's larceny statute where he took a rake from his neighbor's yard based on the reasonable, but mistaken, belief that it was the same rake he lent his neighbor two weeks earlier?

In the above example, I have clearly identified the law in question, Acadia's larceny statute. The key facts—the item taken, the fact that a similar item was lent by the defendant, and the reasonableness of the defendant's mistake—are also present. As for the question, it is whether this defendant is guilty based on this law and these facts.

Another way of writing a question presented is to follow the *under, does, when* formula. In this formula, *under* refers to the law, *does* is a reference to your question, and *when* alludes to the facts. Using the under, does, when formula, our question presented would look like this:

Under Acadia law, *does* an individual commit larceny *when* he takes a rake from his neighbor's yard on the reasonable, but mistaken, belief that it was the same rake he lent out two weeks earlier?

As you can see, the two examples are quite similar. The only real advantage to using the *under, does, when* formula is that it reminds you to address the three aspects of all good questions presented.

The Brief Answer

Lawyers tend to be quite busy people, and sometimes you only have time to read a quick summary as opposed to an entire document. The brief answer section of a memo serves this purpose. Here, you will provide the reader with your overall conclusion and a brief explanation of the law and material facts. Typically, the brief answer is only a paragraph long, but do not worry that you won't be able to lay out the entire rationale for your conclusion; that is what the rest of the memo is for.

The Discussion or Argument

This is the main body of the memo. It is often referred to as the discussion section in an objective document and the argument section in a persuasive memo. Your overall conclusion, as well as every sub conclusion that was necessary to arrive at your conclusion, must be laid out, addressed, and supported. At the end of this section, your reader will have a thorough understanding of the issue, and why you believe it should be resolved in a particular fashion.

Conclusion

This is the final wrap up of your memo. Depending on the format followed, this section may be as simple as a single sentence in which you restate your overall conclusion. In some formats, this section would be up to a paragraph long, allowing the writer to reiterate all sub conclusions that lead to the final conclusion.

Bringing the various sections together, the district attorney's objective memorndum regarding *State v. Baxter* would look something like this:

MEMORANDUM

To: DA Elizabeth Jones
From: Assistant DA Michael Smith
RE: State v. Baxter

I. Facts

On October 27th, Ted Baxter ("defendant") was drinking at a local bar when he encountered the victim, Murray Slaughter ("Slaughter"). The defendant apparently believed that the victim had made an unwanted advance on his girlfriend, and followed Mr. Slaughter as he left the bar. Once outside, the defendant confronted Slaughter and attacked him before he could offer any explanation. The defendant kicked and punched Slaughter until a bystander pulled him away.

Initially, Slaughter testified that the defendant was wearing shoes during the attack, but later admitted he was using the term generically. On cross examination he admitted that the defendant could have been wearing "sneakers." The jury received no further description of defendant's footwear.

At the conclusion of the fight, an ambulance brought Slaughter to a local hospital for treatment of his injuries. Slaughter testified that he was covered with "bruises," but that he did not suffer any broken bones or cuts. The treating physician, Dr. Louis Grant ("Dr. Grant"), corroborated Slaughter's testimony and added that the victim's "back, arms, and shoulders in particular, were covered with bruises." Dr. Grant also noted that Slaughter had a great deal of difficulty disrobing for his physical examination due to the pain caused by the bruising. Additionally, Dr. Grant recommended that Slaughter remain at the hospital overnight for observation. Slaughter chose to leave that evening, but did receive a prescription for Tylenol with Codeine to alleviate his discomfort. Based on these facts, the prosecution sought and obtained an indictment against the defendant for assault and battery by means of a dangerous weapon ("ABDW"), and he was brought to trial in Acadia Superior Court.

At the conclusion of the evidence, the jury returned a verdict of guilty of ABDW, with the weapon in question being the defendant's shoes. Defense counsel sought to have the verdict set aside and made a motion for a judgment notwithstanding the verdict ("JNOV"). The trial court judge denied the motion. The defendant filed a notice of appeal arguing that the trial court should have allowed his motion for a JNOV because the jury did not hear sufficient evidence to conclude that his footwear was a weapon capable of causing serious bodily harm. The likelihood of defendant prevailing on his appeal is the subject of this memorandum.

Notice the objective tone used by ADA Smith in writing these facts. Although he is an advocate, an Assistant District Attorney for the State of Acadia, he is not in an advocacy posture while writing this memo. His supervisor has asked for an objective assessment of the likelihood of his office winning this case on appeal, so even the facts must be stated objectively.

On several occasions I have written out a phrase, and then provided a parenthetical abbreviation of the term. I have done so in order to avoid writing out the same lengthy phrase or name throughout the brief. You are free to abbreviate terms in any way you like, but over time you will learn the common abbreviations to certain phrases. For example, the term judgment notwithstanding the verdict is invariably abbreviated to JNOV. Just be sure to maintain consistency throughout the document.

At the end of the facts, Smith briefly lays out the procedural history leading up to this moment. Some writers prefer to begin the facts section with this information, and others may even choose to exclude it entirely. I have placed it at the end of the facts to create a smooth transition from the facts to the rest of the memo.

II. Question Presented

Under Acadia's assault and battery with a weapon statute, may a jury find that the defendant's footwear was a weapon based on testimony describing the footwear as shoes or sneakers and based on evidence of severe bruising over much of the victim's body that was caused by the attack?

Although the sentence is a little on the long side, our question presented does present the reader with an accurate summary of the issue in need of resolution.

III. Brief Answer

No reasonable jury should have found that the defendant was armed. Otherwise innocent items may be weapons under Acadia law, but the jury must hear evidence establishing the item's ability to cause serious bodily harm. *See* 30 Acad. Stat. Annot. §17; State v. Carlton, 88 Acadia 77 (1952); State v. Morgenstern, 98 Acadia 17 (1950). Here, the jury heard enough evidence to find that the defendant wore something on his feet during the attack, but nothing more. In addition, defendant's bruising was sufficient for a finding that a fight occurred, but not that the defendant's footwear had the capability of causing serious bodily harm.

The brief answer section can be difficult to write because it is not all that easy to be brief and accurate. For example, I have tried to summarize Acadia's multipart A & B with a weapon statute by focusing on the item's ability to cause serious bodily harm. While I am leaving out some information, I have the rest of the memo to explain each concept more thoroughly.

IV. Discussion

Baxter is likely to prevail on his appeal of the trial court's denial of his motions for a directed verdict and judgment notwithstanding the verdict. The Acadia Court of Appeals will apply the *de novo* standard of review in determining whether our office presented sufficient evidence at trial for the jury to find the existence of a weapon beyond a reasonable doubt. See State v. Georgette, 199 Acadia 216 (1995). Acadia's ABDW statute actually contains two separate definitions of a weapon. First, an item is a weapon if it is specifically designed to cause harm. 30 Acad. Stat. Annot. §17(A). Obviously, shoes are not designed to cause harm, making §17(A) of the statute inapplicable to this case. Under, §17(B) of the statute, however, any item may be a weapon if it is intentionally used to cause harm and it has the "capability of causing serious bodily harm." See 30 Acad. Stat. Annot. §17(B). Importantly, the item, and not just the blow to the victim, must be capable of causing the requisite harm. Id. The state may establish an item's ability to cause "serious bodily harm" either through a sufficient description of the item or based on the severity of the victim's injuries. <u>State v. Carlton</u>, 88 Acadia 77 (1952); <u>State v. Morgen-stern</u>, 98 Acadia 17 (1950). In this instance, the description of the defendant's footwear as "shoes" or "sneakers" is insufficient to establish their ability to cause serious bodily harm. The bruising over much of the victim's body was serious, but still not sufficient evidence to establish that the defendant's footwear was a weapon.

The first paragraph of your memo is often referred to as a thesis paragraph and it acts as a road map for the remainder of the document. First, start off with your broadest conclusion, which in this instance is that the defendant is likely to prevail on his appeal. By broadest conclusion, I mean the answer to your question presented. Next, introduce the reader to the legal concepts that you will discuss more fully later in your memo. Through this introduction you are creating the road map, or outline, that the reader can use to follow the remainder of the memo. In this instance, I have introduced several distinct legal principles. First, I have started off with the standard of review. The standard of review is the law governing how much deference the appellate court will apply to the trial court's ruling.

After the standard, I reference Acadia's A & B with a weapon statute. Because courts must follow all constitutionally valid statutes, statutory references should appear before court cases that have interpreted the statute. Note that I have cited to both sections of Acadia's A & B with a weapon statute even though the section regarding items designed to cause harm is not relevant to our fact pattern. I have done so in order to provide the reader with as complete a picture as possible concerning this area of the law, but I have not belabored the obvious. I dispose of the concept almost immediately after mentioning it. Such an abrupt treatment of the issue is warranted where the answer is obvious, but the trick is to be sure the answer is obvious to the reader and not just to you. Many of the answers in your memo will seem obvious to you because you will have spent days researching the issues.

Next, I move on to the statute's second definition of a weapon, and I began emphasizing the idea that the weapon must have the "capability of causing serious bodily harm." Notice that I have taken this language directly from the statute, making quotation marks necessary. In this instance, however, I could have paraphrased the language. I chose not to because this is an essential concept that I want to emphasize, and the quotation marks tell the reader to pay attention to these words. Later in the document, I continue to quote this same language in order to draw parallels between the law and our facts. After the statute, I introduce the reader to the relevant case law, which forms the basis for later sections of this memo. These two ideas, that you may establish an item's capability of causing harm through a description of the item or of the victim's injuries, are sub-rules. They are principles of law that derive from our primary principle. For the remainder of this memo, you will notice that these sub-rules form the backbone of our discussion.

After laying out our the legal principles, I briefly analyze these principles for the reader. Remember, legal analysis is an application of relevant and established legal principles to a new set of facts. My analysis is not complete because this is only my introductory paragraph, but I am again setting the stage for the remainder of the document.

Once completed, thesis paragraphs often follow a conclusion, rule, analysis (C-R-A) pattern. This formula, like the C-R-E-A-C formula I use in the rest of the memo, is a simple way of assuring that you address all necessary points in the most logical fashion. In the hands of skilled legal writer, this formula can be modified and manipulated to fit any legal scenario.

Description of Defendant's Shoes Insufficient

The jury did not hear a sufficiently detailed description of Baxter's shoes to find that they were a weapon. Under Acadia's ABDW statute, an item may be a weapon only if it is capable of "causing serious bodily harm." It is difficult for a jury to make this finding without an adequate description of the item in question. 30 Acad. Stat. Annot. § 17(B); see State v. Carlton, 88 Acadia 77 (1952); State v. Morgenstern, 98 Acadia 17 (1950).

If the jury receives a relatively detailed description of the item in question, they may be entitled to find that it was used as a weapon. In State v. Morgenstern, a jury convicted the defendant of using her shoes as a weapon. Morgenstern, 98 Acadia at 19. During trial, a witness described the shoes as "sharp and pointy." Id. at 18. In addition, the defendant's shoes punctured and broke two bones in the defendant's hand. Id. From this evidence, the court concluded that a reasonable jury could find that the shoes in question had the "capability of causing serious bodily harm." Id. at 19. The Morgenstern Court went on to reason that it was irrelevant whether the injuries were more severe than could have been accomplished without a weapon. Id. The key was whether the weapon, in this case the defendant's shoes, could cause more harm than could the blow by itself. Id. In contrast, the Court in Georgette held that the jury had not received a sufficient description of the defendant's weapon, again a pair of shoes, to determine that they were capable of causing serious harm. State v. Georgette, 199 Acadia 216 (1995). In Georgette, the state failed to introduce any description of the defendant's shoes. Id. at 218. From the evidence at trial, the jury could have inferred that the defendant was wearing some type of footwear. Id. Yet, the court reasoned that any additional inference as to the type of footwear would be "tantamount to guesswork" and impermissible. Id.

These two paragraphs are the beginning of the first C-R-E-A-C in our memo. I start off by providing the reader with the conclusion to this sub-argument. Notice that the conclusion is only to whether the jury heard a sufficient description of the shoes, making it narrower than the conclusion that began the memo. Next, I move directly to our rule. The language that I use in describing this rule tracks the language at the end of the introductory paragraph—this is intentional. I want the reader to see that I am continuing the conversation that we began in the first paragraph.

Once I have set out the rule, I begin my next paragraph with a thesis sentence that introduces a key principle from Morgenstern *and* Georgette. *This explanation is the "E" in our C-R-E-A-C. These cases are illustrations of how the court has applied this rule in two instances, and will provide guidance as to how a court may resolve our situation. I have incorporated the discussion of both cases into a single paragraph because they both deal with the same issue. Even though the courts in* Morgenstern *and* Georgette *come to different conclusions, they do so for the same reason. Namely, that the jury must know enough about the weapon to determine that it could cause serious bodily harm.*

In both instances, the case descriptions are quite narrow and focused because the reader does not need a case brief. Instead, the reader needs a focused discussion of what these cases have to say about the specific issue being addressed. In most instances, the case description will include the key facts, the court's holding, and the court's reasoning. If done well, this paragraph will set up the analysis to come.

In the instant case, the prosecution failed to introduce a sufficient description of the defendant's shoes to warrant the jury finding they were a weapon. Initially, the victim testified that the defendant was wearing "shoes" during the attack, but later modified his testimony on cross examination. On cross, he admitted that he had used the term "shoes" as another word for footwear, explaining that he "just meant that [the defendant] wasn't barefoot." Reviewing the evidence in a light most favorable to the prosecution, the district attorney established that the defendant was wearing shoes, but this description is little more than what was presented in State v. Georgette. 199 Acadia at 218. In both instances, the evidence required the jury to infer that the term "shoes" described an item capable of causing serious bodily harm. The drawing of such an attenuated inference amounts to the kind of guesswork proscribed by the Georgette court.

Further, the term "shoes" is extremely general as compared to the description of the weapon in <u>State v. Morgenstern</u>. 98 Acadia at 18. In <u>Morgenstern</u>, the Court emphasized the specific description of the shoes as "sharp and pointy" in upholding the defendant's conviction. <u>Id.</u> When one considers the broad range of footwear that could be described as shoes, this description standing alone cannot establish their capability of causing serious bodily harm. However, the jury is allowed to review evidence beyond the description of the shoes in determining whether they were used as a weapon.

In the analysis or "A" section of your C-R-E-A-C, you will apply the facts of your situation to the facts and principles of law you established in the "E" portion of your memo. The first sentence of the paragraph is a thesis sentence, informing the reader of the paragraph's focus. Here, the thesis sentence tells the reader that the paragraph will focus on the insufficient description of the defendant's shoes. Also, notice how this thesis sentence is a mirror image of the thesis to my paragraph of explanation. The thesis sentence to my paragraph of "E" told the reader that this was an important idea. It only makes sense that I follow through on my assertion and address how to resolve this important idea in the context of our facts.

The key to a strong analysis paragraph is the weaving together of the law and the facts. Notice that each time I discuss a fact, I bring the law back into the conversation. Once you have spent time laying out the law, it only makes sense to use it to strengthen your analysis. If you fail to weave the law into your analysis, then you are forcing the reader to do your job for you. Don't assume that the reader will see the same connections between the law and facts that you see.

The final sentence of the paragraph is not really part of the analysis. Instead, it works as a transition between the conclusion of the first point and the beginning of the second point.

Severity of Defendant's Injuries

The jury may use the severity of the victim's injuries as some basis for establishing that the defendant used an otherwise innocent item as a weapon. In <u>State v. Carlton</u>, the court looked to a general description of the defendant's footwear as well as the extent of the victim's injuries in upholding the defendant's conviction. <u>State v. Carlton</u>, 88 Acadia 77, 78 (1952). The jury heard sufficient testimony for a finding that the defendant was wearing "shoes," but the Court reasoned that, without more, this description was insufficient to uphold the conviction. <u>Id.</u> The jury did hear more, however, in the form of testimony that the victim suffered from broken ribs and a dislocated shoulder as a result of the defendant's kicks. <u>Id.</u> In contrast, another victim, who had not been kicked with shod feet, sustained a few bruises. Id. The Carlton Court held that the severity of these injuries allowed for a jury finding that the defendant was armed with a weapon that was capable of causing serious bodily harm.

This second paragraph of Explanation focuses on using the victim's injuries as some evidence that the defendant used a weapon. Once again, I give the reader just enough detail about the case law to follow my thesis. There are details about the Carlton case that go unstated, but these details are unnecessary if they don't enhance the reader's understanding of the issue being discussed.

Slaughter's injuries were not sufficiently severe to establish that the defendant's shoes were a weapon. Unlike the broken bones sustained by the victim in Carlton, our victim merely sustained severe bruising over his entire body. While these injuries are not to be minimized, it is doubtful that they support a finding that the shoes were used as a weapon. Our office needed to prove that the shoes had the capability of causing more harm than would the kicks alone. Without some additional details regarding the extent of the victim's injuries, no reasonable jury should have found that these bruises established the presence and use of a weapon.

Once again, our paragraph of analysis attempts to weave together the legal principles and the facts on this issue. After the opening sentence, I immediately contrast our situation with the facts in Carlton. Comparing your situation to the case law is an important step in legal analysis, but is only the first step. Importantly, I go on to explain why I think our situation is distinguishable from the existing case law.

V. Conclusion

The court is likely to agree with the defendant's contention that the jury did not hear sufficient evidence to find that he was armed with a weapon. While the jury could have inferred that the defendant was wearing shoes during the attack, they did not receive enough of a description of the shoes to determine they were capable of causing "serious bodily harm." Similarly, the defendant's injuries were not sufficiently severe to warrant a finding that they could only have been caused by a weapon, defendant's shoes, as opposed to the blows themselves.

This final section of the memo is intended as a wrap up. Some instructors require a single sentence where you simply restate your overall conclusion. I feel that the conclusion section of a memo is more useful if it is also used to restate the subsidiary conclusions that lead to the overall answer.

CHAPTER XI

Study Groups, Study Aids, and Study Schedules

Study Groups Are Not for Studying

Study groups are one of the most misunderstood aspects of law school life. Most students envision a study group as quite a few students getting together daily throughout the year to study. Together, these students will study every facet of the topics covered in their classes, and membership in the most desirable study groups is a guarantee of success. This description is flawed in several important ways.

To begin with, the term "study group" is something of a misnomer. Study groups are most effective when all members of the group have studied on their own and then come together to test each other's knowledge. For this reason, I prefer the term "review group" to "study group."

Most students are surprised to hear that they should not study extensively with their review group, but there are some extremely good reasons why you should not. First, studying is both time consuming and stress producing. As I discussed in earlier chapters, students must study approximately 3 hours for every hour of class time to succeed in law school. There are not many people with whom you can work closely for 8–10 hours a day, 6–7 days a week without driving each other crazy. In addition, it is very difficult for several people to regularly find large blocks of time where their schedules coincide.

Second, people study in very different ways. Some students need absolute silence, while others cannot imagine studying without their favorite music blaring. Similarly, there are a variety of locations where people prefer to study. The library, your home, and the local coffee house are all legitimate, but very different, study locations. There are also some personal habits that should be taken into account. For example, can you imagine a smoker and an anti-smoker effectively studying together?

Be sure to take human nature into account when creating a review group. There is a strong tendency among all of us to procrastinate when we are in a group setting. Study time can quickly become a social hour, particularly when a lengthy and complicated case needs to be read for the next day's class. You will get a lot more done, and in turn perform better on your exams, if you study on your own.

So, if you aren't studying as a group, then what is the point of a joining a review group? Review groups are an outstanding way of testing your knowledge. These groups are most effective when students study on their own, and then meet weekly to discuss everyone's impressions of the week's topics. Students should then test each other on how well they understood the week's topics. An easy way to do this is to have members take turns teaching the group the material covered during the preceding week's classes. If you understand a topic well enough to teach it to others, then you know it well enough to perform well on an exam. Also, members of the group should feel free to correct the "teacher" when they disagree. If you are the "teacher," do not be upset when others correct you. A mistake corrected during a review session is one less mistake on an examination. Another easy way to test each other is through the use of hypotheticals. You can use hypotheticals from class, from outside study aids, or from practice exams. Just be sure to write out the answers to the hypos before attending a review session. It is good practice for exams, and it is clear indication of whether you are fully communicating your understanding of a given issue.

Review groups are also an excellent way of addressing the more troubling topics covered in class. When confronted with a particularly difficult legal concept, come to your review group session with a list of questions that need answering. Just be sure that you have done your best to resolve the questions on your own before bringing them to the group's attention. Members of your group will not appreciate it if you waste their valuable time with questions that you could have easily handled on your own. Now that we have laid out some of the basic ideas behind review groups, there are a number of practical concerns that need attention.

Do I have to join a review group? No, but most students do join review groups. In addition to helping with the mastery of your first-year subjects, these groups can help you assimilate into the culture of your law school. Law school can be much easier to handle if you feel that you aren't going through it alone. That being said, review groups are not for everyone. To determine if a review group is for you, make an honest assessment of how effectively you work in a group setting but keep in mind that this is very different from an ability to socialize in a group setting. Students often meet informally early in the school year to discuss their classes, and you may attend these sessions to assess whether a review group is for you.

You should not make the decision to join a review group lightly. Once you join, the other members of your group will quickly come to rely on your expertise and insight. Therefore, leaving a review group is no small matter. If you join a review group, you should expect to remain with that group for the entire year.

How many people should be in a review group? There are no hard and fast rules, but review groups of between three and five people seem to work best. Larger groups tend to become somewhat unwieldy to manage. Scheduling becomes more difficult and the chance that any two members just won't get along increases dramatically.

How do I choose the other members of my review group? Be sure to choose people that you like well enough to work with on a regular basis. It is a good idea, however, to avoid working with your best friends. When working with good friends, the temptation to socialize is too great. Also, try to find students who take law school as seriously as you do. You will quickly become annoyed with members of the group who come ill prepared to discuss that days topics and contribute little of their own knowledge. Resist the temptation, however, to join up with carbon copies of yourself! Some differences between members can lead to a more well rounded group, and may expose you to subtleties in the law that a more homogeneous group might miss.

Where should we meet? Meet in a location with few distractions, and avoid places, like your school's library, where group discussions might disturb others. Empty classrooms can work well and have the added benefit of chalkboards where you can diagram and create flow charts for complicated issues. Also, check with your library to see if they have small study rooms you can reserve. Any quiet location can work, but try to keep one thing in mind. Select a single location that works well for all members of the group, and then use that location throughout the academic year. Simplifying the logistics of meeting in this fashion will help ensure that everyone arrives at the same place, on time, and ready to work.

When should I join a review group? Give yourself at least two weeks to get into the flow of your classes and to firm up your study schedule before joining a review group. You will be tempted to create a study group almost immediately, but resist this urge. The first days of class are an extremely hectic time, so give yourself the opportunity to get acclimated before taking on anything new. You will spend a great deal of time with the members of your review group, so choose them carefully. A decision made in haste during the first day or two in class can come back to haunt you throughout the semester.

How often should my review group meet and for how long? Review groups should meet between once and twice per week. Meeting less often means that you won't have time to address all the group's questions, and more often means that you are taking too much time away from your individual studies. If you decide to join a group, you need to spend enough time reviewing material to make the sessions worthwhile. Early in the semester, 2–3 hours per review session should be enough to cover everyone's questions. As the year progresses and you begin to cover more complicated material, 3–5 hour sessions may be necessary. This may seem like a long time to work together, but it isn't if you consider the number of classes you are taking and the number of students in your group.

Should the members of my review group share their outlines? Sharing outlines is a terrible idea for a very simple reason. Creating an outline forces you to turn the seeming chaos of individual classes into an ordered and logical explanation of how various areas of the law operate. A large part of the learning process takes place as you are creating an outline, and you will not understand your courses nearly as well if you rely on someone else's understanding of them. For the same reason, avoid the temptation of "assigning" one class to each member of your review group. Students who fall into this trap may end up with an "A" in the course they were assigned, but the remainder of their transcript will be covered with "Cs" and "Ds."

Using another's outline in place of your own, however, should be distinguished from simply reviewing another's outline. As long as you have done your own work, evaluating another's outline during a review session can be an extremely effective way of clearing up mistakes or incomplete ideas and testing your own knowledge. Evaluating outlines in this fashion is just another way of utilizing the collective knowledge of the members of your study group.

How do we set the agenda for out meetings? At the end of every review session, spend a few minutes scheduling your next meeting and establishing the topic to be discussed. Otherwise, you will waste precious time at the beginning of each session figuring out the topics to review. Be as specific as possible when setting your agenda so that everyone is on the same page from the moment the review session starts.

Study Aids

When you enter the law school bookstore, one of the first things you will notice is the vast array of study aids available for purchase. It is quite common for first-year students to purchase multiple study aids at the outset of the semester, and then to later regret their decision. While these study aids can be helpful, they are also quite expensive. I recommend that students avoid purchasing any study aids, at least at the beginning of the academic year. Go to classes, read your cases, and begin your outlines before you rush to the school store to pick up every available study aid. You may decide that they are not worth the price.

Some professors are categorically against students purchasing study aids, and with good reason. Some students use study aids as a form of security blanket. If they are struggling in their contracts class, then purchasing a contracts study aid is a quick and easy way to feel that they are fighting back. Quickly, these study aids can begin to take the place of your own work. If your professors recommend against purchasing study aids, then follow their advice. They are your best source of information on passing their classes. If your professors are open to the idea of using study aids, however, here is a brief summary of some of the aids available on today's market.

- **Case briefs**—In many instances, you can purchase a book of ready made case briefs that has been keyed to your particular casebook. Initially, students purchase these books as a way of double checking their own briefs. Over time, however, these briefs become a tempting substitute for your own work. Why bother reading the case if someone else has written up a synopsis of the court's opinions? If you've been reading this book, you already know the answer. Your ability to dissect a case and figure out the court's holding and reasoning is much more important than whether any particular brief is correct. One day, you will be a lawyer who must understand how to effectively read and understand case law. In my opinion, these briefs are the worst study aids on the market, and I do not recommend them to anyone.
- **Flash cards**—This study aid consists of hundreds of questions printed on individual cards with the corresponding answers on the back. Sets of cards are available for all the first-year topics, and for many of the more popular upper-level courses. Typically, this study aid has no index, and you cannot use it to further your understanding of the more complicated issues you will face. Instead, students use this aid to test their knowledge in preparation for exams. It can be useful for this purpose if

you keep a few things in mind. Your essay exams will be much longer than the questions contained within these cards, and therefore the issues will be much harder to find. These cards may be more helpful when preparing to answer multiple choice, short answer, or true/false questions. In addition, the information on the cards may be at odds with your professor's discussion of the same issue. If you find a discrepancy between the cards and something your professor has said, follow your professor's explanation. Of course, be sure that your notes accurately reflect your professor's lecture.

• **Hornbooks**—A Hornbook is a one volume treatise covering a particular area of the law. Although somewhat basic from the standpoint of the legal practitioner, they can be a very useful study aid for students. In fact, hornbooks are sometimes listed as a recommended text for first-year classes. Whenever you have difficulty understanding a legal issue, a hornbook is an excellent place to start your research to further your understanding of the matter. While valuable, this study aid can be as expensive as any of your textbooks. Law libraries often carry hornbooks covering all the first year topics, so start there before investing hundreds of dollars on your own set.

• **Commercial outlines**—A commercial outline is simply a ready made version of the outlines you will be creating for each of your first-year classes, and therein lies the danger. These ready made outlines may be useful when used as a supplement to your own work, but too often they are used to supplant a student's own outline. For this reason, many professors are strongly opposed to students using commercial outlines. As a supplement, however, they can provide additional information and examples that flesh out your developing understanding of a legal topic.

• **Sample examination questions**—As exams approach, students begin looking for old examination questions on which to practice. Some professors make old questions available, while others do not. Regardless, every student wants as many practice questions as they can find. For this reason, publishers have begun issuing study aids containing sample exam questions, both essay and multiple choice, along with sample answers. As we will discuss in the final chapter of this book, practice exam questions are an excellent tool for preparing for finals. As with all of these study aids, however, sample exam books are not geared toward your individual classes. The questions may contain issues related to areas of the law that were not covered by your professor or may state an idea using unfamiliar terminology. On the other end of the spectrum, the questions may provide brief treatment of an issue that was important in your class.

There are other study aids that combine some of the aspects of the ones I have already discussed. Regardless of which study aid you are contemplating, just remember that they are all tools. They can help clear up your understanding of the law or prepare you for final exams, but none contain the magic formula for success. A study aid is only as good as the student reading it, and cannot take the place of your own work.

Creating a Study Schedule

If you've been paying attention throughout this book, then you realize that I believe in an organized approach to law school. In the early chapters, we discussed reading and briefing cases, taking notes, reviewing those notes, and then creating a course outline. It can be helpful to take this organized approach one step further and actually create a study schedule. A study schedule will take into account the various aspects of the study methods we have already discussed, and will give you a visual representation of what you should be doing during any given point in the day. Without a study schedule, you are more likely to fall behind or even forget to complete an important task.

There is a blank study schedule for you to use on the next page, and I recommend that you make several copies. Of course, you may opt for a more technological approach and purchase a personal organizer. Regardless, you will have to engage in some trial and error before you end up with a schedule that works well for you. In addition, your study schedule will likely change from week to week because the work load in each of your classes will not remain static throughout the semester.

There are a few aspects of my blank study schedule that you should be aware of before using it. First, I have included 10 minute breaks for every hour block of time. I have done so because these short breaks are an important way of staying fresh and focused throughout a long study day. Also, my schedule starts at 9:00 AM and it ends at 9:50 PM, which is in keeping with my belief that you should treat law school like a job. Some folks may be able to start studying earlier in the day, but I strongly recommend that you end your day no later than 9:50 PM. You need time at the end of the day to relax and unwind *before* going to bed.

Blank Study/Class Schedule

	Sunday	Monday	Tuesday	Wednesday	Thursday	Friday	Saturday
9:00–9:50							
10:00–10:50							
11:00–11:50							
12:00–12:50							
1:00–1:50							
2:00–2:50							
3:00–3:50							
4:00–4:50							
5:00–5:50							
6:00–6:50							
7:00–7:50							
8:00–8:50							
9:00–9:50							

I have included a filled in version of a study schedule on the next page to give you some sense of what a typical law school week will look like. As you review the schedule, a few things should jump out at you. For example, I am relatively specific when I schedule study time. In addition to scheduling specific study time for each class, I have differentiated between time spent reading cases, reviewing notes, and creating course outlines. I have also attempted to create some balance in my schedule by leaving open blocks of time for relaxation and physical exercise.

My sample schedule only includes activities that are strictly law school related. I encourage you, however, to schedule in time for the other aspects of your life. If you don't schedule time for other activities such as food shopping, exercising, bill paying, and relaxation, they will not get done. Also, you will have to create a study schedule based on your own life, your own classes, and your own abilities. For example, I have included a single hour of reading time for every hour of class. In some instances, more time may be necessary to complete your reading assignments.

You should also note that my sample schedule starts relatively early in the morning and ends in the late afternoon or early evening. This leaves me with a solid block of time for rest and relaxation, but it is not absolutely essential that you schedule this time at the end of your day as I have. Scheduling downtime for the evening can be a nice way to reward yourself after a hard day's work, but you may prefer to have mornings free on the weekends. Also, you will have to take into account other schedules when creating your own. For example, your best friend is unlikely to get married in the evening in order to better accommodate your study schedule!

Finally, don't be intimidated by the number of scheduled work hours. Admittedly, law school will require a lot from you. In most instances, you will have to study for approximately three hours for every hour of class time in order to perform up to your potential. By scheduling your time effectively, however, you will be able to stay on top of your studies and enjoy the other aspects of your life.

Sample Study/Class Schedule

	Sunday	Monday	Tuesday	Wednesday	Thursday	Friday	Saturday
9:00–9:50	Outline Contracts	Read Contracts	Read Con. Law	Read Contracts	Read Con. Law	Read Contracts	Outline Torts
10:00–10:50	Outline Contracts	Contracts	Constitutional Law	Contracts	Constitutional Law	Contracts	Outline Torts
11:00–11:50	Outline Property	Read Civ. Procedure	Torts	Property	Torts Class	Property	Outline Civ. Procedure
12:00–12:50	Outline Property	Lunch	Lunch	Lunch	Lunch	Property	Outline Civ. Procedure
1:00–1:50	Lunch	Civil Procedure	Review Con. Law	Civil Procedure	Legal Writing Homework	Lunch	Lunch
2:00–2:50	Legal Writing Homework	Legal Writing	Review Torts	Review Contracts	Legal Writing	Civil Procedure	Read Torts
3:00–3:50	Legal Writing Homework	Review Contracts	Read Contracts	Review Civ. Procedure	Review Con. Law	Review Contracts	Read Con. Law
4:00–4:50	Read Contracts	Review Civil Procedure	Read Property	Review Property	Review Torts	Review Property	Outline Con. Law
5:00–5:50	Read Civ. Procedure	Read Con. Law	Read Civ. Pro.	Read Con. Law	Read Contracts	Review Civ. Pro	Outline Con. Law
6:00–6:50		Read Torts	Legal Writing Homework	Read Torts	Read Property		
7:00–7:50					Read Civ. Procedure		
8:00–8:50							

CHAPTER XII

Law School Exams

Taking a law school exam can be an intimidating experience. As I've noted elsewhere, your grades in most of your classes will come down to how you perform on one or two exams. In addition, many schools require the faculty to employ some type of curve when assigning grades. For these reasons, final exams generate a great deal of competition and stress among law students. Thankfully, I have some good news for you.

If you follow the advice contained within this book, you will be ready to perform at peak efficiency come exam day. Everything we have discussed so far has been preparing you for your exams. In law school, you don't begin studying for finals a week or two before the examinations. By following my study methodology, you began studying for finals on your first day of classes.

Each week, you diligently read cases, reviewed notes, and worked on your outlines. In addition, you synthesized rules, created your own hypotheticals, and performed legal analysis. All this work ensured that you understood, at a nuanced level, every topic you covered throughout the academic year. After all this hard work, it is time for the big payoff.

While you will still have to prepare for finals, all nighters and marathon cram sessions will not be required of you. For the most part, you will not be learning new ideas as you prepare for finals. Instead, you will be reminding yourself of ideas that you already know. Therefore, the same 8–10 hour day that you employed during the school year will be sufficient time to prepare for finals.

There won't be many new ideas in this chapter. Instead, I'm going to remind you of the things we have already discussed and show you how these ideas apply in the context of your final exams. There are few common mistakes that students make when preparing for and taking law school exams, and I will address these as well.

Reading Days

In most law schools, you will have a number of reading days between the last day of classes and the beginning of final exams. You will devote your reading days to studying for exams, and if you are fortunate you will have additional free days between each final. Although studying for exams is a year long process, certain aspects of your studying will change during this reading period. You won't be going to classes, you won't be outlining, and you won't be reviewing your class notes. You've been doing these things all semester, and now it's time to reap the benefits of all that hard work. Between the last day of classes and the beginning of exams, you will devote your study time to three things: reviewing your outlines, answering sample exam questions, and meeting with your review group.

During the first days of the reading period, your task is a simple one—read your outlines. If you have outlined correctly, your outlines will be thorough but short enough to read through several times in a given day. Again, if you have approached your studies correctly throughout the year, you will not have to learn any new ideas.

Initially, just read through the outline without trying to memorize the concepts. As you read, you will probably notice that you already know many of the ideas contained within the outline. More than this, you will have already committed many of the ideas to memory. All those days of reading, reviewing, and outlining were not in vain! As you work through the outline, note any concepts you are struggling with. Later, go back to these concepts and reread these portions of the outline more carefully. On occasion, you may have to consult an outside study aid like a hornbook to clear up any confusion, but this should be the exception and not the rule.

Once you feel confident about the concepts contained in your outline, it is time to test your knowledge by taking a sample exam. Avoid the impulse to answer a sample exam at the beginning of the reading period. Your performance is likely to be less than stellar, and will only cause stress. Answering a sample exam after reading through your outlines will give you a more accurate assessment of how well you know the subject matter.

Some professors will provide old or sample exams for this purpose, and some may even offer to review these sample exams with you. If a professor offers to review a sample examination answer with you, jump at the opportunity. Considering the number of students in your class, do not be surprised if few professors make this offer. More typically, professors will hold review sessions prior to exams for the entire class. If you can't obtain old or sample exams from your professors, you may consider purchasing commercially available exam questions.

Be sure to mimic exam conditions whenever answering a sample exam. For one thing, this means taking the exam under time constraints. Your ability to produce a brilliant answer in six hours is irrelevant if your exams will be three hours long. In addition to time constraints, turn off your phone, television, and any music. Music and contact with the outside world are not allowed during exams. Also, be sure to write or type out your answer as you will during the examination. Avoid simply outlining your response or using incomplete sentences. After completing the exam, use your course outline to review your answer. This will give you a good idea of areas of the law that require additional review on your part.

The next step is to meet with your review group to review your exam answers. In fact, be sure to contact your study group at the outset of the reading period to schedule these meetings. Be clear about the meeting date, time, and subject matter. Most importantly, be clear that *everyone* must complete their own exam answer in order to take part in these sessions. Otherwise, you may end up helping everyone else, but receive little assistance of your own.

These group meetings are a very important part of the study process. Invariably, you will encounter some thorny issues in these sample exams. As a group, it will be easier to review these issues and come up with accurate solutions to the problems. Time permitting, repeat these steps—reviewing your outline, taking sample exams, and meeting with your study group—up until the day before your exam.

The Day before Your Exam

Try to have a relatively light study session the day before exams. This may seem counterintuitive, but remember how much work you have been doing all year. You are unlikely to learn anything new the day before exams, so avoid scrambling to find the perfect study aid, a classmate's outline, or that fantastic sample exam you have heard about. Instead, put in a solid 6–8 hour day and try to relax, and then go to bed early. At this point in the year, a good night's sleep is more likely to improve your exam performance than would another hour of studying.

Organizing Your Answer

Organizing the approach to your exams begins before you ever enter the examination room. To begin with, you should consider whether to use an organizational formula like IRAC. Some professors dislike the IRAC structure because it can lead to a somewhat formulaic way of answering law school exams. Obviously, do not use the formula if your professors warn against it. Other professors prefer the formula or are ambivalent as to whether you use it. In these instances, I recommend using IRAC.[1] A formulaic approach has its drawbacks, but it helps ensure that you address each important aspect of every issue you encounter.

Another pre-examination aspect of exam organization is the **skeletal outline**. A skeletal outline is simply the broadest structural level of the course outlines you've been working on all semester. To get a better sense of what I'm talking about, refer back to the sample torts outline in *Chapter VI—Creating A Course Outline.* In these sample pages, I organized and defined several different torts concepts. Where necessary, I illustrated these principles by including short descriptions of certain cases or with brief hypotheticals. When completed, this outline will provide an organized explanation of every idea discussed in my torts class, and I will be able to use it as my primary study aid come exam time.

Now, take those sample pages and remove the hypotheticals, definitions, and case descriptions. When you are finished, your modified outline will look something like this.

Sample Skeletal Outline for Torts

I. Intent—volitional act and knowledge to "substantial certainty"
   A. Malice Unnecessary
   B. Transferred Intent
II. Intentional Torts
   A. Assault—Awareness, not fear required
   B. Battery—Must touch victim or something "closely associated"
   C. False Imprisonment—Victim must be aware of imprisonment
   D. Trespass to Land—Defendant does not have to be aware of trespass
   E. Trespass to Chattels—interference—includes damage—with another's property
   F. Intentional Infliction of Emotional Distress—Conduct must be "extreme and outrageous"
   G. Conversion—"serious interference" with another's property. Remedy is full value of chattel

---

1. Review Chapters VIII, IX, and X for a refresher on IRAC and other organizational formulas.

I have reduced those three sample pages down to these essential concepts. Also, I have chosen to include key ideas and legal buzz words for each concept, although these are not absolutely required. If you were trying to turn a completed torts outline into its skeletal version, it would end up being no more than 1–2 pages long. This final skeletal version of the outline should be the last thing you memorize before taking the exam. Then, this will be the first thing you write or type once the exam begins. The skeletal outline isn't part of your exam answer, so write it out on some scrap paper or even on the back pages of the exam question itself.

This skeletal outline will serve three purposes. First, it will give you a basic way of organizing your response to the issues you encounter on the exam. Second, the skeletal outline acts as an exam checklist. As you write out your answer, you can refer back to the skeletal outline to ensure that you haven't forgotten to address an important concept due to time pressure or stress. Third, it gives you a simple, focused task to complete at the outset of an examination when stress will be most pronounced. Once you have finished writing out your skeletal outline, you are ready to start reading the examination questions.

Be sure to read the directions carefully. Failure to read and follow the directions can lead to disastrous results. For example, your exam might include ten different questions, but the directions require that you answer only six of them. Even if you miraculously answer all ten, the quality of your responses will not compare favorably with those of your classmates.

Next, review the call of the question. In some instances, the call of the question will be quite general. A general question might read "address the rights and liabilities of all the parties," and will not require any special organization or approach on your part. In contrast, your professor may ask you to answer the question as if you are the defendant's attorney. Imagine what your grade will look like if, by mistake, you approach the question in a more objective fashion.

After reading through the directions, you may begin reviewing the fact pattern. As you read through the question, your first task is to list the issues generated by the fact pattern. Your list of issues should identify the legal principle involved and make some reference to the facts. For example, a notation that reads "John battery of Ed, intent a problem" will help you keep the issues straight as your list gets longer. This list will form the basis of your examination outline.

You are organizing your answer to the question through an examination outline. An outline allows you to approach the answer clearly and efficiently, and avoids needless duplicity or awkward jumps in logic. Without some form of outline, you will be tempted to answer the first issue you see on the first line of the exam. This issue might be relatively minor, or could be a smaller part of some larger aspect of the exam. It certain courses, contracts and civil procedure in particular, the order in which you address the issues is an important aspect of your overall answer.

Most law school educators agree that students should outline their examination response before writing out the completed answer. These same folks disagree, however, as to how much time one should spend outlining a response. Some would suggest that you should merely list the issues as you find them, while others recommend a detailed outline that might take 1/3 of the exam period to complete. Either extreme, and everything in between, can work, so I recommend practicing with different outlining forms to see what you're most comfortable with. At a minimum, however, I suggest listing the issues as you find them and then reviewing the list to differentiate between the minor and major issues.

Exam Stress

To varying degrees, every student is nervous prior to taking their first law school examination. You will hear from multiple sources that the exams will be more difficult than any test you have ever taken. On top of this, your final grade in most classes will depend on how well you perform on one or two examinations. An entire year's worth of work eventually comes down to a fairly small block of time. It is not surprising that some students freeze up as soon as they here proctor say "begin."

Like most aspects of law school, preparation is the key to minimizing your stress on exam day. Exam stress is at its worst during the first several minutes of the examination period, so you should have a clear plan of what to do once the clock starts running. It may surprise you to hear that one thing you shouldn't do is immediately start answering the first question. With your stress likely at its peak, trying to respond to a complicated set of facts will only make things worse.

Instead, follow the advice I gave you in the previous section, *Organizing Your Answer*. First, write out your skeletal outline. It is something concrete that won't depend on the content of the question. The idea here is to relax your mind by working through something familiar, giving yourself time to relax. After completing the skeletal outline, you are ready to move onto the directions and then the first fact pattern.

On occasion, you may encounter a question that seems incomprehensible even after you review your skeletal outline. On the surface, it may appear unrelated to anything covered in class and you won't even know where to start. This is where panic can truly set in. If you find yourself in this situation, take a deep breath and look at the situation logically. Your professor isn't out to get you, and the exam must be based on ideas covered in class. In addition, every other student taking the exam is dealing with the same thing. If the question is difficult for you, and you have diligently prepared throughout the year, then the question has to be difficult for your classmates as well. As you work through these ideas, you should begin to relax enough to begin answering the question. If you still find yourself anxious, then simply move onto the next question. Just be sure to leave yourself sufficient time to go back to the difficult question later.

Time Constraints

Even the best students have difficulty completing their law school exams on time. As your understanding of legal analysis improves, you will see more and more issues in even the simplest fact patterns. As Professor Glannon of Suffolk University Law School likes to say, the issues in an essay exam are like the layers of an onion. Each time you peel one issue away, it creates another issue in need of resolution. These factors highlight the need for an organized approach to answering essay questions.

I recommend that students adopt a mathematical approach to allotting their time. For example, let's say that your three hour essay exam has three separate questions, and that each questions is worth 1/3 of your final exam score. Unless your professor suggests otherwise, you should spend one hour on each question. This may seem obvious, but it is quite common for students to run out of time on an individual question before they have addressed all the issues. As they try to complete their answer to the first question, they are robbing themselves of the time necessary to complete the next answer.

One way to avoid running out of time is to, once again, be mathematical in your approach. Simply add up the number of issues and divide this number into the time you have to complete the question, but be sure to differentiate the major issues from the minor ones. Minor issues are straightforward problems that you can resolve in a few sentences. The major issues involve a larger number of facts and are much more difficult to resolve. For every point of view in a major issue, there will be a compelling opposing point of view that will require a great deal of discussion. Typically, major issues will take you three or four times longer to answer than minor issues, so be sure to take this into consideration when allotting your time.

This mathematical approach is not perfect, but it will give you a rough idea as to how much time you have to answer each issue. You may discover additional issues as you move through the problem, or a few minor issues will turn out to be major headaches. Still, this approach will ensure that you answer the greatest number of issues in the time allotted, and treat the major and minor issues appropriately. In addition, remember that no one receives a perfect score on a law school exam. Even the best students will miss issues on their exams, so do not panic if your exam answer is not perfect.

The Issue Spotting Exam

The most common type of final exam in law school is the issue spotting essay exam. Each essay question in an issue spotting exam will tell a story. In these stories, a variety of people will do any number of things. As you read the story, your first job will be to spot the legal issues and then analyze the potential outcomes created by the facts. In many ways, this is what you did in class almost every day. Each time your professor laid out a new hypothetical for discussion and analysis, she was preparing you to answer similar questions on your exams. There are, however, a few important differences between your classroom hypotheticals and the issue spotting fact patterns used in exams.

First, when responding to a classroom hypo, you will have some idea as to what rules of law are in play. Typically, classroom hypos revolve around the legal rules extracted from the day's reading. This won't be true when dealing with an exam fact pattern. Part of your job on the exam is to figure out which legal rules are applicable to the various issues you find. Another important difference between classroom hypos and issue spotting exams is the number of issues you must address. Depending on the length of the question and on the complexity of the fact pattern, you may encounter anywhere from a few to over a dozen different issues. All of these issues must be answered thoroughly, but succinctly, if you expect to complete the exam in the allotted time. Typically, each final exam will last three hours. For these reasons, an organized approach to your exams is essential.

Multiple Choice Exams

Too often a student's grade is adversely affected by poor performance on the multiple choice component on a law school examination. Even worse, many of these same students will fall back on the easy excuse, "I've always had problems with multiple choice questions and I always will." This is a danger-ous attitude to have when you consider that 50% or more of your bar exam-ination is likely to be made up of multiple choice questions. If you perform poorly on the multiple choice component of the bar exam, you are likely to fail the test. To better prepare you for the bar examination, many professors have begun to incorporate multiple choice questions into their final exams.

Multiple choice questions can pose a somewhat unique problem for law students. Your answer on a multiple choice question will either be right or wrong, while essay questions give you the opportunity to explain yourself and receive some credit for your response. Students who have spent the better part of the year developing a nuanced approach to the law can struggle when sud-denly required to pick a single answer to a lengthy question.

Despite these issues, *any* student can perform well on a multiple choice exam. To achieve this goal, you must: (1) understand the various parts to a multiple choice question, (2) learn how to avoid making the most common mistakes, and (3) practice.

The Parts of Any Multiple Choice Question[2]

Every multiple choice question consists of three parts—the root, the stem, and the options.

The root creates the universe for the question. Most multiple choice question will be based on a universe, or set of facts, that may be anywhere from a few sentences to several paragraphs long. The longer fact patterns typically create the universe for several questions. You must place yourself in the universe cre-ated by the fact pattern, and avoid adding your own beliefs and assumptions. Then, you have to leave the old universe as soon as your professor provides you with a new set of facts.

The sample on the next page is a relatively short example of the root to a multiple choice question. Notice that the root does not contain a question. From the facts as given, most law students can discern that this fact pattern is raising an issue regarding the intentional tort of false imprisonment. It can be helpful to spot issues in the fact pattern before you even reach **the stem**, which

---

2. Some of the terminology used in this section originated in Michael Josephson, *Eval-uation and Grading in Law School, AALS Section on Teaching* (1984).

Paula vs. Donna
Sample Root for Multiple Choice Question

Paula has a job interview with the DynaGlobe Corporation. When she arrives at the corporate headquarters, Donna the receptionist brings her to a conference room to wait. Donna has been instructed to wait with the candidates so that they don't wander unescorted around DynaGlobe's offices. After waiting with Paula for a few minutes, Donna gets restless and decides to take her afternoon break. She excuses herself and leaves the conference room, but she locks the door behind her so that Paula can't roam the corridors. Donna knows that the conference room has a clearly marked emergency exit that Paula can use in case she needs to leave the building. Unbeknownst to Donna, however, the emergency exit door has been locked. There have been several thefts at DynaGlobe in recent months, so security personnel have started locking all emergency exits. Locking the emergency exits violates a state statute and is against company policy. After 20 minutes of waiting, Paula gets up to go to the bathroom. She tries the main door and then tries the emergency exit, both of which are locked. Paula suffers from claustrophobia and the realization that both doors are locked brings on a panic attack. When Donna finally returns from her break, she finds Paula sobbing in the corner of the room. Paula cannot continue with the interview and the job goes to one of the other candidates.

is the actual question your professor is asking you to answer, but a well written root may contain many issues.

In addition, be sure to leave your emotions and personal biases behind as you read through the root for each question. For example, your professor may create a universe full of loathsome characters and then ask you to represent one of them. Similarly, the root may involve sensitive subjects on which you have very definite opinions. Presidential powers during a time of war and same-sex marriage are topics that are fair game for a multiple choice exam question. Be sure that you answer these types of questions based on the current state of the law and not on what you believe the law should be.

After you have finished the root, the stem is the next part of every multiple choice question. While the root provides you with the facts that form the universe for a multiple choice question, the stem is the actual question. Stems can vary significantly from question to question. Some will be written as relatively straightforward questions while others will read more like statements with which you will have to agree or disagree. Complicated stems may suggest that more than one of the responses is correct, while still others may change certain aspects of the root by adding to or modifying the facts.

Once you have finished reading the stem, you are finally ready to move onto the question's options. The options are the various answers you have to select from when answering the question. Typically, you will be able to exclude one or more of the options quite easily. These easy to exclude options may misstate the law or the facts in an obvious fashion. In other instances, these options will correctly state a legal principle but that principle has no bearing on the question being asked. Your task becomes much harder once you have excluded the obviously wrong responses.

The remaining options will be difficult to choose between because they often contain a grain of truth. For example, the answer may be correct but for the wrong reason. In other instances, the professor will provide you with an emotionally compelling option that is wrong on the facts or the law. Thus, multiple choice questions allow your professor to test you on many levels— whether you have memorized the law, whether you can accurately analyze a factual scenario, and whether you can dispassionately choose the correct answer even if you are unhappy with the outcome.

Step by Step

To perform well on multiple choice exam, there are certain steps that you must follow. Some of these steps will seem almost obvious, but I am including them due to the types of errors I typically see when reviewing multiple choice questions with my students.

- **Step 1: Do the Math**—Before you read the first root, you must determine how much time you have for each question. This will depend on the number of multiple choice questions and on how heavily they are weighted as compared to the other aspects of the exam. For example, assume that your final exam is three hours long and that the multiple choice questions are worth 33% of your final grade. Unless instructed otherwise by your professor, this means that you should spend 1 hour answering the multiple choice questions. If there are 20 questions, you have no more than 3 minutes to answer each one.
- **Step 2: Stick with Your Schedule**—Once you have determined that, for example, you have 3 minutes to answer each question, stay on schedule. At the end of the 3 minutes, you must select one of the options. It is time to move on even if you are unsure of your response. If you don't,

you will be using time that you may need to answer the next question. This makes little sense where the professor has weighted each multiple choice question equally.

- **Step 3: Carefully Read the Root**—As you read through each root, be on the lookout for material facts. You may even circle or underline facts that seem particularly important. Remember that a single root may be relevant to more than one stem, so a reading error may impact your response to more than one question. Do not make unwarranted assumptions regarding the root or add to the facts. Your professor has constructed each question carefully and you may be changing the question in an important way by adding any information to the root.
- **Step 4: Carefully Read the Stem**—The stems can modify the facts from the root, place you in a certain procedural posture, or require you to adopt a specific role when answering the question. A question that asks you to play the role of defense counsel may require a very different answer than one that asks you to act as the judge. In another example, a question that requires you to choose the "best" response is suggesting that more than one answer may have some merit.
- **Step 5: Remove Obviously Incorrect Options**—Removing the obviously incorrect options is the easiest part of answering any multiple choice question, so do it first. Be sure to exclude answers containing incorrect principles of law or misstatements of fact. I suggest placing a line through these options so that they do not distract you when you move to the next step.
- **Step 6: Choosing Between the Difficult Options**—This is the most difficult part of answering any multiple choice question. To simplify the process of choosing between the remaining options, look for any hint that might remove an answer from consideration. For example, the law rarely deals in absolutes so you should view suspiciously any answer that contains words like "always" or "never." Then, the remaining option must be your answer. To paraphrase Sir Arthur Conan Doyle's sleuth Sherlock Holmes, once you have removed the impossible, whatever remains, no matter how improbable, must be the truth.
- **Step 7: Answer Each Question in Order and Guess if You Have to**—Guessing should be a last resort, but it may be required when you are running out of time. Even if you are unsure of an answer, you must select one of the options during the time you have allotted yourself. Do not skip a question with the intention of returning to it later because you may not have the time to do so. Even worse, you may forget to skip the question on the answer sheet making your answers out of sync with

the questions. You may, however, place some sort of identifying mark beside answers you are unsure of. If you have time at the end of the examination, you may then reconsider your answer to these questions.

- **Step 8: Leave the Previous Question Behind**—Once you answer a question, leave it behind unless the new question requires you to do otherwise. Some questions may modify the fact pattern by adding or subtracting information from it. Again, unless otherwise instructed, these additions or subtractions are not part of next question.

The following sample multiple choice questions are based on the "Paula vs. Donna" fact pattern listed above. Through these examples, I am illustrating the various styles of multiple choice questions you might see on an examination. In order to better follow the questions along with my accompanying explanations, here are the legal principles you would have to be familiar with in order to choose the correct answer. I have tried to create questions that you might see on a law school examination, so do not be surprised if you have difficulty answering them even after reading the relevant legal principles.

False imprisonment (intentional tort)—The intentional confinement of another within boundaries by acts or threats of action and without legal justification. The plaintiff has not been confined if he has a reasonable and safe alternative avenue of escape. Also, to succeed in an action for false imprisonment, the defendant may not have consented to the confinement.

Negligence—An individual is negligent when that individual has a duty to protect another from reasonably foreseeable harm or loss, the defendant breaches that duty through some action (or in some instances inaction), and the actions cause the plaintiff's harm or loss. The plaintiff's harm may be physical, mental, or financial.

Respondeat Superior—An employer may be liable for the wrongs of an employee where the negligent conduct took place within the scope of the employee's employment duties. Generally, an employer is not liable for an employee's intentional wrongs because these acts are typically outside the scope of employment. In some instances, however, even an employee's intentional torts can be within the scope of employment.

Violation of Statute as Some Evidence of Negligence—In some jurisdictions, the defendant's violation of a statute or ordinance may be considered by the fact finder as some evidence of negligence. A court will apply this rule if the plaintiff establishes that: (1) she is a member of the class of persons the statute was intended to protect; (2) the injury is the type that the statute was intended to prevent; and (3) the violation of the statute is the legal cause of plaintiff's injuries.

1. Did Donna act negligently in locking Paula in the conference room?
   A. Yes, because Donna caused Paula's injuries.
   B. Yes, because you should not lock a door when another person is in the room.
   C. No, because panic attacks can never be harm.
   D. No, where state law and company policy required that all fire doors remain open, no reasonably prudent person could foresee a likelihood of harming Paula based on locking one of the doors to the conference room.

This is the most straightforward type of multiple choice question. In order to answer correctly, you must understand the rule of negligence. Answer "A" is incorrect because to say that Donna caused Paula's injuries addresses only one of the elements of negligence. Answer "B" is much too inclusive, and does not take into account instances where it might be appropriate to lock a door behind you even if another person is in the room. Answer "C" is wrong because mental suffering may be considered harm in the appropriate circumstances, and this answer excludes panic attacks from ever being harm. This leaves us with "D" as the correct answer. "D" is correct because Donna cannot be negligent unless a reasonably prudent person would not have locked the door, and here Donna had no way of knowing that she was endangering Paula.

2. Paula's false imprisonment action against Donna will fail because:
   A. Panic attacks are not legally recognized harm.
   B. Paula did not know that it was Donna who locked one of the doors to the conference room.
   C. Donna intended to keep Paula from walking unescorted around the office building, but did not intend to lock her in the conference room.
   D. The conference room's emergency exit was an alternative reasonable avenue of escape for Paula.

Question 2 is also fairly simple, but stylistically distinct from question 1. Instead of asking the question, the stem lays out a proposition that you must follow in reviewing the options. The proposition here is that the Donna's action for false imprisonment will fail. Here, options "A" and "D" are easy to dispose of. As previously noted, mental anguish may be harm in the appropriate circumstances, which makes answer A incorrect. Option "D" simply misstates the facts. The emergency exit was not open and therefore could not be an alternative means of escape from the room. This leaves us with "B" and "C" as possibly correct responses. Option "B" correctly states that Paula was unaware that Donna locked one of the doors, but this isn't one of the elements of false imprisonment, which leaves "C." Option "C" touches on the most fundamental aspect of all intentional torts, that the defendant must act intentionally. While Donna intended to lock the door, she did not intend to lock Paula in the conference room against her will. Importantly, Donna believed that there was another means of egress from the conference room.

3. Assuming that Donna is guilty of false imprisonment, what is the most likely outcome if Paula sues DynaGlobe under a theory of respondeat superior?
   A. The action will succeed if Donna's actions are deemed to be within the scope of her employment.
   B. The action against DynaGlobe will fail because false imprisonment is an intentional tort and the doctrine of respondeat superior does not apply to an employee's intentional, wrongful conduct.
   C. The action will succeed because Donna falsely imprisoned Paula.
   D. The action will fail because corporate entities like DynaGlobe are immune from civil lawsuits.

Now the questions are getting a bit harder! The first thing to note about this question is the phrase "most likely outcome." The phrase is a not so subtle reminder to choose the best answer, but that the best answer may not be the only possible answer. Also, the stem requires you to assume that Donna is guilty of false imprisonment. Regardless of whether you agree with this assertion, it is true for purposes of this question. Here, you may quickly dispose of both choices "C" and "D." Answer "C" boldly asserts that Donna falsely imprisoned Paula without any explanation. More importantly, "C" fails to address the doctrine of respondeat superior in any fashion. Option "D" is wrong for the simplest of reasons—corporations are not immune form civil lawsuits. On the surface, options "A" and "B" are difficult to choose between. Option "B" asserts that the action will fail because the doctrine of respondeat superior does not apply to intentional wrongs. This is a difficult choice to exclude because intentional wrongs generally cannot serve as a basis for the vicarious liability of an employer. However, where the intentional act is within the scope of employment, like when a bouncer intentionally harms a patron, the doctrine may apply. Therefore, "B" should be excluded because it overstates a generally correct legal proposition. This leaves us with "A" as the correct choice. Note that response "A" does not require us to believe that Donna's actions are within the scope of her employment.

4. If Paula brings an action for false imprisonment, which of the following statements is (are) correct?

I. Paula's action will fail because she would have been a trespasser if she left the conference room and trespassers may be imprisoned.

II. Paula's action will fail because she was a trespasser onto the property and is therefore not owed the same duty of a care as would be owed to an invitee.

A. Answer 1 is correct.

B. Answer 2 is correct.

C. Both answers 1 and 2 are correct.

D. Neither answer is correct.

This is an example of everyone's least favorite multiple choice question! The question is designed so that either answer may be correct, neither answer may be correct, or both answers may be correct. There is no special magic involved in answering these questions except reminding yourself that more than one response may be correct. Of course, in the end you still must choose between A, B, C, or D. Other than the format, this particular question is relatively simple. Option I is incorrect for two reasons. First, it is not clear that Paula would have been a trespasser if she left the conference room. More importantly, you may never falsely imprison another person. If you legally detain someone, then you are not imprisoning them falsely. Option II again suggests that Paula is a trespasser and is not owed the same duty of care owed to someone invited onto the property. This option is also incorrect on multiple levels. Paula was invited onto the property and the legal concept of "duty of care" applies to negligence actions and not to the intentional torts. Therefore, neither answer is correct and "D" is the correct choice.

5. Assume that a fire occurs while Paula is in the conference room and that she cannot exit from the room. As a result, she is seriously injured in the blaze. Also, assume that in Acadia, the state where the office is located, the fact finder may consider the violation of a state statute as some evidence of negligence. If Paula brings a negligence action against the security personnel who locked the emergency exit, is their violation of a state statute likely to bolster Paula's case?

A. No, because the security personnel were simply following instructions.

B. Yes, but only if the legislature passed the statute in order to protect people like Paula from experiencing the kind of harm she suffered.

C. Yes, but only if Paula is a resident of Acadia.

D. Yes, because the law holds security personnel to a higher standard of care.

In this example, it is the stem that alters our facts and not one of the options. Therefore, be sure to apply these new facts to all four of our choices; however, do not use them when answering subsequent questions unless instructed otherwise.

Here, the correct answer is "B." Notice that this option uses the equivocating language "but only if." You may disagree as to whether the legislature passed this statute to protect plaintiffs like Paula from this type of harm. The words "but only if" require you to treat the statute as applicable to this situation. Once you are over this hurdle, this turns into a fairly easy question. Option "A" is wrong because it doesn't matter whether the security guards were following instructions. As for option "C," Paula's residential status is irrelevant. Option "D" is essentially a nonsense answer. Even if the law held security personnel to a higher standard of care, this fact would play no role in the applicability of the statute.

Practice, Practice, Practice

If you have properly prepared for an essay examination, then you know the law well enough to excel on a multiple choice examination. The only additional thing you need to do is practice taking multiple choice exams. Learning to allot your time properly, carefully read the questions, and accurately analyze the options takes time and practice. While you may have experience with multiple choice exams, the questions tend to be much more difficult in law school. If you do not practice, you are likely in for a nasty surprise come exam time. Finding sample questions, however, is no easy task.

It takes a great deal of time to create fair multiple choice questions. Professors must consider issues like cultural and regional bias, the complexity of the questions, and the amount of time students will have to complete the examination for every question they create. After students have taken the examination, there is still work to be done.

Typically, professors perform a statistical analysis of their class' performance on the multiple choice portion of the examination. On occasion, a disproportionately large percentage of the class will perform poorly on a given question. This may indicate a problem that the professor will have to address through additional editing or possibly removal of the offending question. It takes a great deal of time, but eventually professors develop a bank of clear, fair, and trustworthy questions. Once a professor decides to show a question to the class, that question may never be used in an examination again. Doing so could compromise the integrity of the entire exam. For these reasons, professors tend to release very few of their own multiple choice questions. Thankfully, you may turn to other sources for help.

In addition to materials provided by your professor, there are three good sources for practice multiple choice questions. First, a growing number of publishers sell books containing sample multiple choice and essay questions.

Another excellent source is the National Conference of Bar Examiners ("NCBE"). In their own words, part of NCBE's mission is to "assist bar admission authorities by providing standardized examinations of uniform and high quality for the testing of applicants for admission to the practice of law." For our purposes, this means that they create the multiple choice questions used in most state bar examinations. These questions are particularly useful because many professors attempt to follow a similar format when creating their own multiple choice questions. Once you access the organizations web site, http://www.ncbex.org/, you will be able to find old bar examination questions for sale.

Finally, some bar preparation companies offer sample multiple choice questions and other study aids. These companies are in the business of preparing students to take the bar examination, and they may require you to sign up for all their services prior to offering any materials. These courses can be quite expensive, especially when you consider that you won't need most of their services until after you have graduated from law school. I am not advocating that you sign up for a bar preparation course, but most students do pay to take these classes prior to their bar examination. By signing up in advance, you may be able to obtain study aids during your first year of law school.

If you obtain questions from any source other than your professor, and this applies to both multiple choice and essay questions, beware of their limitations. Only your professor can provide you with questions geared toward his or her class. For example, you may answer a question incorrectly because your professor used different terminology than was used in another source. In addition, you might encounter questions from areas of the law you never covered in class. Finally, be sure to consider the age of the questions and whether they accurately reflect the current state of the law. This tends to be more of problem with older questions, but the law is in a constant state of evolution. Therefore, even relatively new questions may no longer reflect current legal thinking.

Final Tips for Your Law School Exams

If you have read the earlier chapters of this book, then you already understand how important your analytical skills are to success in law school. As a reminder, this skill is just as important to your final exams as it was to writing a legal memorandum or resolving a classroom hypothetical. Law school exams do require a certain amount of memorization because you cannot the applicability of a legal rule if you do not remember its elements. While the memorization of legal rules is important, a significant percentage of your grade will depend on the strength of your legal analysis. As you analyze the examination issues, keep a few things in mind.

You will be nervous when the examination proctor says "Begin," so the worst thing you can do is to start writing out your answer immediately. Instead, consider writing out your skeletal outline as soon as the exam begins. A skeletal outline is merely an organized list of principles and issues, created by you, which relates to a given area of the law. Think about the outline you have been creating all semester, but now reduce it down to a page or two—this is your skeletal outline. Writing out this list will give a few moments to compose your thoughts before digging into the exam.

Read the instructions! This is the most obvious advice imaginable, but every exam period several students will, for example, answer 3 short exam questions, only to discover that the instructions said "provide an answer to 1 of the following 3 hypotheticals." Most students get flustered at the start of an exam, so this type of mistake is more common than you might imagine. When the exam starts, take a deep breath, slow yourself down, and read the instructions.

Before answering an essay question, you must outline and organize your response. When the proctor says "Begin," too many students read the first sentence in an essay exam question, recognize an issue, and are so overjoyed at finding an issue that they spend the next 20 minutes responding to it. The problem with this approach is that the fact pattern was probably over a page long, and the writer just spent more time than was necessary in responding to a relatively straightforward issue. While different students outline differently, students who perform well on law school exams take the time to read through the entire essay question, create a list of the various issues contained therein, and then take a few more minutes to separate out the major issues from the minor ones. This approach will give you a better sense of how much time you have to complete your entire answer.

The first part of any law school exam is a math test. You must look at the amount of time allotted for the question, then consider the number of problems you must resolve in that time, and finally do the math to determine how much time you have per issue.

This is easier when dealing with multiple choice exams where the number of questions is clear at the outset. Still, students will often spend too much time on a single multiple choice question, thereby reducing the amount of time they have to complete the other questions. Remember, unless the instructions indicate otherwise, each multiple choice question is worth exactly the same amount as the next multiple choice question. So, spending more time than you have on any one question does not make any sense.

In terms of an essay question, determining the number of issues that require resolution is a little more complicated. This is where outlining your response, a recently discussed exam tip, comes in. Once you have read an entire essay question, and then listed all the issues, you will have a much better sense of how much time you can allot to each problem

You cannot perform legal analysis without discussing the facts. There are few absolutes in law school, but including the facts in your answer to essay questions is one of them. Remember, most law school essay questions are written in the form of a lengthy fact pattern or story. The facts within these stories create the issues that you must discuss. Almost every fact in these stories must be reproduced and discussed in your examination answer. While it is true that your professors will know the facts in the problem, we do not know whether you understand which facts are relevant to resolving each issue. Including the facts in your answer does not guarantee success on your law school exams, but excluding the facts guarantees that you will perform below your capabilities.

To ensure that the facts are making their way into your essay answers, place a line through each fact as you use it. Do not cross the fact out so that it becomes illegible, however, because a single fact may be relevant to more than one issue. After you finish your essay answer, look back at the fact pattern. If there are facts left over, one of three things has occurred: (1) the facts are truly irrelevant and do not need to be discussed (unlikely!); (2) the facts are relevant to an issue or issues that you have already discussed; or (3) the facts are relevant to an issue that you have not addressed at all.

As for supposedly irrelevant facts, professors rarely place information into their fact patterns that does not need to be discussed. Most "irrelevant" facts are there so that you can explain why they are irrelevant.

Listing facts is not the same thing as discussing them. True legal analysis occurs when you explain to a reader <u>why</u> a fact (or facts) leads to a legal conclusion. Consider the following examples.

Example 1—For purposes of an assault, there is an issue as to whether John's statement and actions amounted to an imminent battery. John told the plaintiff "I will hit you if you come around here again." Therefore, the battery was not imminent.

Example 2—For purposes of an assault, there is an issue as to whether John's statement and actions amounted to an imminent battery. John told the plaintiff "I will hit you if you come around here again." Generally, words alone cannot satisfy the imminence element of an assault. More specifically, these words merely inform the listener that he might be "hit" at some point in the future. The words "at some point in the future" placed a condition on the plaintiff being struck, which means that the plaintiff might never be struck by John. The fact that John might never strike the plaintiff means that the battery cannot be imminent. Also, note how I weave the legal principle back into my discussion of the facts.

Your analysis is the most important thing that goes into a law school exam, so make sure it is in there! Much of what students write when answering a law school exam is not legal analysis. The issues you will be dissecting were created by your professors and are contained within the examination fact patterns. The same is true of the facts you will be discussing in your answer; they were created by your professor. The law you will be relying on to resolve these issues originated in the cases and statutes you read during the course of the semester. The only part of an essay answer unique to you is your commentary on WHY certain facts lead you to believe that a legal issue should be resolved in a particular way. As professors, we value the answer to the question "why" above everything else in your essay answer because it is unique to you and demonstrates how deeply you understand the law. This is why solid legal analysis is the difference between the grades of "C" and "A" on law school exam.

Analyze each element of the relevant causes of action in your examination answer. For example, an Assault is often defined as the intentional placement of another in apprehension of an imminent battery. If the fact pattern on your torts exam raises the possibility of John assaulting Fred, then you MUST address all the elements of an assault. Was the defendant's conduct **intentional**, was the plaintiff placed in **apprehension**, and was that apprehension of an **imminent** battery? While you must address all of these elements, the depth of your analysis regarding each element will depend on the complexity of the problem. For example, it might be quite obvious that the defendant was acting intentionally, but the real question is whether the plaintiff's apprehension was of an imminent battery. In this instance, your analysis of imminence will likely be longer than your analysis of intent. Forcing yourself to analyze every element will accomplish two things: (1) it will let the professor know that you understand that every element of a cause of action must be proven; and (2) it will force you to consider whether each element has been satisfied, thus avoiding the mistake of failing to discuss a complex problem that, at least on the surface, seemed quite obvious. Another way to conceptualize this advice is to consider the I-R-A-C formula many students use when answering examination questions. In reality, you are writing a mini I-R-A-C for each element of every cause of action being discussed as opposed to a large I-R-A-C of, for example, of the tort of assault.

Avoid starting your analysis with a conclusion. Instead, the first sentence of your discussion of each issue should identify the problem in need of resolution. For example, you might begin your analysis of a torts problem by noting that "John may have battered Fred when he threw a stick over the fence that struck the plaintiff." In contrast, avoid writing "John battered Fred when he threw the stick over the fence." While beginning with a conclusion may be acceptable when writing a memorandum, keep in mind that your conclusions in a memorandum are usually based on a great deal of thoughtful reflection. When writing an examination answer, time is of the essence and you may be incorrect regarding your initial belief as to how the problem will come out. Beginning each problem with an issue statement, as opposed to a conclusion, addresses two related problems. First, it provides you with the flexibility to look at all sides of a problem before coming up with an answer. Second, it helps you to remain objective. When you start with a conclusion, the tendency is to support that conclusion even in the face of strong opposing arguments.

Objectivity and indecisiveness are not the same thing. When students attempt to perform objective legal analysis, they often fall into the trap of being indecisive as opposed to objective. When performing objective legal analysis, you must still come to a conclusion. It's just that your conclusion is the product of carefully considering all reasonable alternatives. Lawyers rarely face issues where the conclusion is obvious. Often, our advice is based on choosing between multiple flawed alternatives. So, you have to get in the habit of picking an answer that you are less than 100% sure of. Telling the reader that a problem could be resolved in two ways, but that the final answer will "depend on what the court thinks" is tantamount to telling the reader "this is hard, so you figure it out!"

Be sure to address all reasonable alternative points of view. Most students use the I-R-A-C formula when writing the answers to their law school exams. This formula, which is quite similar to the C-R-E-A-C paradigm often used in legal writing classes, stands for: state the issue, provide the law, analyze the applicability of the facts to this law, and come to a conclusion. Because addressing counter arguments is such an important part of legal analysis, the formula might be more accurately written as I-R-A1 (state the argument)-A2 (state any reasonable counterargument)-Conclude, or resolve which argument is better and WHY it is better. In other words, I-R-A1-A2-C. So what is a reasonable a counterargument? A counterargument is reasonable if it is based on the facts in the problem or reasonable inferences from those facts. If you find yourself creating facts, then the counterargument you are creating is unlikely to be a reasonable one.

Sample Law School Exam

The following material is a sample civil procedure examination and an accompanying answer. I will comment in italics at various points in the material to draw your attention to particularly important ideas. I have included this material in order to illustrate what an examination question and answer might look like, and not as the final word on the legal issues discussed. As always, defer to your professor's expectations if anything in these materials differs from what you are told in class.

I have designated this as a 90 minute question, which is reasonable considering the number of issues contained in the material. The answer, however, is likely beyond what any law student could generate in 90 minutes. A good student would be capable of producing portions of this answer in the time allotted, but not the entire answer. While I could have written a more "realistic" answer, I chose to create a professor's version of the right answer.

Fact Pattern
CompuFix vs. Jones and Smith
90 Minute Question

Fred Jones and Ron Smith worked for CompuFix, a computer consulting company incorporated in the state of Acadia. Their duties required them to travel throughout the country, consulting in the computer departments of major corporations. They specialized in offering network solutions to companies with over 500 employees. Both Fred and Ron had three year employment contracts with CompuFix. The parties negotiated the contracts while Fred and Ron were traveling around the country, but both men signed the agreements in CompuFix's main and sole office in Springfield, Acadia. Under the terms of the agreement, the men could not engage in any other computer-related business that placed them in competition with CompuFix. As part of the agreement, both men were required to seek out new clients for the company. The prohibition against working in another computer-related business terminated on the same day that the three year employment contracts ended.

Eventually, Fred became disenchanted with all the travel required by his job and decided to open a business of his own. Fred loved his home state of Verhampshire, so it was an easy decision to locate his new business there. Fred

opened DigiCare the day after his employment contract ended with Compu-
Fix, and he lived in a small apartment on top of his office. Fred's new business specialized in offering computer assistance to companies that were too
small to have an Information Technology department of their own, but he was
willing to take on larger clients if any decided to sign on. On occasion he
helped companies with networking problems, but most of his work was much
more basic. More typically, he would do things like advise his clients about
new hardware purchases, update software as needed, and fix damaged computers. To date, Fred's clients are all located within the state of Verhampshire.
While he hopes to have more of a national presence one day, today his business is confined to his home state.

Fred's business thrived from the outset. Within the first month, he signed
on over 36 new clients and his revenues projected out to be over $500,000 for
the year. By the end of the month he was able to sign on one of Verhampshire's most exciting new businesses, Ultrafine Coffees, as a new client. Ultrafine operated a chain of coffee shops in Verhampshire and had over 300
employees. The company planned on going national at the end of the year and
anticipated doubling in size by that time.

Fred loved his new business, but missed his friend Ron. Ron was still employed by CompuFix, but his employment agreement was scheduled to end
in a few months. Fred decided to contact Ron, who lived in the neighboring
state of New London, to see if he would be willing to leave CompuFix and
work for DigiCare. Fred dialed Ron's cell phone number and began discussing
his business proposal. Ron happened to be driving through Acadia when he
received Fred's phone call. Ron was worried about leaving an established company like CompuFix, so Fred suggested that they start working together for a
few hours a week just to see whether Ron liked the new arrangement. He
wouldn't have to leave CompuFix, and could sign a new agreement with them
if things didn't work out with Fred. Ron reminded Fred about the clause in
the employment contract that prevented him from working for another computer-related business that was in direct competition with CompuFix. Fred
didn't think this was a problem because DigiCare did not have any large clients
and most of his work had nothing to do with computer networking. Ron decided that he had little to lose. Before he hung up the phone, he told Fred that
he would see him on Saturday.

One Saturday while Ron was at DigiCare, he received a call at home from
Samantha Lecroix, the president of CompuFix. She wanted to discuss the pos-
sibility of Ron signing up with CompuFix for another three year agreement.
Ron's wife answered the phone and she told Samantha to try calling over at
DigiCare where Ron was working. Incensed, Samantha hung up the phone.

Immediately she began researching DigiCare and quickly concluded that the company would one day become one of CompuFix's strongest competitors. She was particularly upset that no one in her company had tried to sign on Ultrafine Coffees as a new client, and decided that Ron had been shirking his duties. She also decided that Ron was violating his employment agreement and that Fred was partially to blame.

The next week Ron was served with a civil complaint and summons while he was at his home in New London. A process server similarly served Fred with a summons and complaint while Fred was at his office in Verhampshire. Both men were properly served under the laws of Acadia. Ron was being sued by CompuFix for breaching the terms of his employment contract. Compu-Fix was suing Fred for tortious interference with its contractual relationship with Ron. CompuFix, the plaintiff in both actions, is seeking damages of $250,000 from each defendant.

The above fact pattern is typical of what you can expect on a civil procedure examination. It is full of factual information that will generate a large number of issues for your discussion. Before you begin outlining a response, however, be sure to read the question associated with the fact pattern. The question may be extremely broad and require you to address "the rights and liabilities of all the parties." If so, then you must discuss every issue you find. A narrower question may require you to emphasize certain issues and even disregard others.

As you outline your answer, be sure to differentiate between the exam's more difficult issues, those that may be resolved more quickly, and any issues that do not require discussion. For example, the final paragraph of facts indicates that Fred and Ron "were properly served under the laws of Acadia." Thus, there is no need to discuss this issue on the exam.

Finally, did you happen to notice that this is a "90 Minute Question"? Spending more than 90 minutes here means less time spent on the other equally important parts of the examination.

I. Does the Acadia Trial Court have subject matter jurisdiction to hear these claims and personal jurisdiction over each defendant?

II. Assuming that the Acadia Trial Court does have jurisdiction over this matter, will the defendants be able to remove the case to federal court? If so, which federal court? Assume that the defendants agree that they want to remove the case to federal court and that Acadia has only 1 Federal District Court.

The above two questions serve to the narrow the focus of your answer. For example, you are not required to discuss the possibility of the defendants filing a motion to dismiss or a motion for summary judgment in response to plaintiff's lawsuit. Also, note that there are two questions to answer. Be sure to clearly iden-tify which question you are responding at the outset of each answer.

Applicable Law
Acadia Long Arm Statute[3]
Transactions or conduct for personal jurisdiction

Section 1—This statute is intended to reach to the limits of due process. A court may exercise personal jurisdiction over a person, who acts directly or by an agent, as to a cause of action in law or equity arising from the person's:

>   (a) transacting any business in Acadia;
>   (b) contracting to supply services or things in Acadia;
>   (c) causing tortious injury by an act or omission in Acadia;
>   (d) causing tortious injury in Acadia by an act or omission outside Aca-dia if he regularly does or solicits business, or engages in any other per-sistent course of conduct, or derives substantial revenue from goods used or consumed or services rendered, in Acadia;
>   (e) having an interest in, using or possessing real property in Acadia.

In some instances, your professors may include a statute or even a case to use when answering a question. The inclusion of a long arm statute like this one is a particularly common on civil procedure exams. Keep in mind that this statute is not the only law you will use when responding to the question.

Model Answer to Civil Procedure Problem

Question I
Subject Matter Jurisdiction in Acadia Trial Court

The Acadia Trial Court is likely to have subject matter jurisdiction over both the breach of contract claim brought against Ron and the tortious interfer-ence with contract claim brought against Fred. Subject matter jurisdiction refers to the power of a court to hear a particular type of lawsuit. Unlike fed-eral courts, which have relatively limited subject matter jurisdiction based on either diversity or matters arising under federal law, state courts have broad subject matter jurisdiction over most civil claims. There are a few instances where the federal government has placed the power to hear certain cases en-tirely within the federal courts, but these exceptions do not apply here. The suit against Ron is a garden variety breach of contract action, and the Acadia

---

3. This language is based on the Massachusetts long arm statute. Mass. Gen. Laws ch. 223A, §3 (2005).

Trial Court certainly has the power to hear this lawsuit. Similarly, the action against Fred is based on tort law, and the trial court also has the power to hear this type of lawsuit. Personal jurisdiction over the parties is not so clear cut, and must be analyzed separately as to each defendant.

Notice that I clearly identify which question I am responding to at the outset of my answer. In addition, I have included a subheading to make it clear that I am addressing the issue of subject matter jurisdiction. Subheadings are not mandatory, but they are an excellent way of identifying each issue as you move through an exam. With so many issues in a typical law school examination, you should make your answers easy to follow.

The above analysis to subject matter jurisdiction is quite brief in comparison to the personal jurisdiction analysis to come. The analysis is brief because the issue is quite simple to resolve. Be sure to treat each issue fairly, but not necessarily equally. Some issues will take much more time to resolve.

Personal jurisdiction in state court — general considerations

The Acadia Trial Court ("State Court") is likely to have personal jurisdiction over Ron. As for Fred, it is a somewhat closer call, but the court is likely to have personal jurisdiction over him as well. There are 4 ways that a state court can have personal jurisdiction over a defendant. They are: (1) when that defendant is a citizen of the forum state; (2) when the defendant is served in the forum state; (3) when the defendant waives a personal jurisdiction argument by appearing in the forum state to argue any issue other than personal jurisdiction; or (4) through use of the state's long arm statute.

Citizen of Forum State and Personal Jurisdiction — Here, neither Fred nor Ron is a citizen of the forum state, Acadia. The facts indicate that Fred lives in Verhampshire and Ron lives in New London. Therefore, Acadia does not have personal jurisdiction over these defendants based on their citizenship.

Service in Forum State — Typically, a state court will have personal jurisdiction over any defendant who is served in the forum state. In this context, "service" is a reference to service of process. At the commencement of an action, the defendant must be served with a copy of the complaint and a summons. This serves to make the defendant aware of the action against him. While in hand service of process in the forum state is a way of obtaining personal jurisdiction over a defendant, here the defendants were served outside of Acadia. The facts make it clear that Ron was served while at his home in New London and Fred was served at his office in Verhampshire. Therefore, the Acadia court does not have personal jurisdiction over Fred and Ron based on service of process.

Waiver of Personal Jurisdiction—The Acadia court can have personal jurisdiction over a defendant where that defendant appears in the forum state to argue any aspect of the lawsuit other than personal jurisdiction. By choosing to appear in the forum state and argue some aspect of the lawsuit, the defendant is deemed to have waived any argument regarding personal jurisdiction. Here, both Fred and Ron have just been served and neither has appeared in court in conjunction with this lawsuit. Therefore, the Acadia court does not have personal jurisdiction over these defendants based on a waiver of that argument. This answer could change, however, should Fred or Ron choose to appear in an Acadia court at some point in the future.

These first three aspects of a court obtaining personal jurisdiction—citizenship, service, and waiver—are clearly inapplicable in this instance. For that reason, a student might decide to mention these ideas even more briefly than I have or to exclude them altogether. If you make a decision to exclude essentially unimportant ideas from your description, be sure of two things: (1) that they are truly unimportant; and (2) you are using the time saved to delve more deeply into the exam's meatier issues

Long Arm Statute—On these facts, Acadia long arm statute is the only way for an Acadia court to have personal jurisdiction over these defendants. Analysis of whether a state court has personal jurisdiction based on its long arm statute is a two step process. First, the complained of conduct must fall under some provision of the forum state's long arm statute and the plaintiff's claim must arise from this contact. Second, the assertion of jurisdiction must comport with the due process considerations expressed by "minimum contacts" analysis and *International Shoe.* Where the defendant has continuous and systematic contact with the forum state, a court may have personal jurisdiction over the individual even when the contacts are unrelated to the subject of the lawsuit. This is known as general in personam jurisdiction. Otherwise, the plaintiff's claim must arise from the contacts used to establish personal jurisdiction. For example, sporadic contacts with the forum state will not support personal jurisdiction where those contacts are unrelated to the subject matter of the lawsuit. However, even a single contact with the forum state may be sufficient under minimum contacts analysis where that contact is strongly related to the plaintiff's lawsuit and the court's assertion of jurisdiction would not offend "traditional notions of fair play and justice." This is known as specific in personam jurisdiction.

In this sample answer, I have decided to lay out several general legal considerations before analyzing the issues in greater detail. These general points are now out of the way and will not have to be repeated as to each of the defendants in the lawsuit. Also, I have referenced International Shoe, an extremely important case that you will spend several days discussing in your civil procedure class. Naming cases is rarely required on law school exams, but the names of the more important cases have become a short hand way of referencing the legal principle the case stands for. If you remember the name to one of these cases, then feel free to use it on your examination answer.

Personal jurisdiction over Ron Based on Long Arm Statute
Clause 1(a) of Statute

The State court is likely to have personal jurisdiction over Ron based on clause 1(a) of Acadia's long arm statute. Clause 1(a) allows the court to assert personal jurisdiction when a person has "transacted any business in Acadia." Here, Ron signed his employment contract with CompuFix in the state of Acadia. While it is unclear whether Ron ever worked in Acadia, his act of signing the contract in the forum state would likely fall under the very broad provision of the long arm statute "transacting any business in Acadia." Just as important, this contact would likely satisfy due process considerations and the minimum contacts analysis required under *International Shoe.*

Due process concerns are satisfied when the defendant's contacts with the forum state are sufficient so that he or she can expect to be brought into court there. Here, Ron's main, and possibly only contact with Acadia, was the signing of the contract there. While it is possible that Ron transacted other business in Acadia related to his employment contract, such as picking up checks, dealing with insurance matters, etc, the facts are silent on these issues. Therefore, Ron's contacts with Acadia are not so significant or continuous as to support an assertion of general in personam jurisdiction—meaning that an Acadia court will not have personal jurisdiction over him for any and all lawsuits. The signing of the contract, however, is sufficient to support personal jurisdiction for a lawsuit based on an alleged breach of that very agreement. Ron knowingly signed the contract in Acadia, and should not be surprised to be haled into the courts of Acadia to defend a lawsuit based on breach of that contract. Therefore, due process considerations would support the Acadia Trial Court's assertion of personal jurisdiction over Ron if it is based on Clause 1(a) of the long arm statute.

I have concluded that the Acadia Trial Court will have personal jurisdiction over Ron based on clause 1(a) of the state's long arm statute. Despite this conclusion, I will still address the applicability of the remaining sections of the long arm statute. It isn't that I doubt my conclusion; it is that my answer would be in-

complete if I didn't analyze the other clauses. In the examination context, you must analyze every reasonably applicable issue. Even if you were performing this analysis for your legal employer, you would address the other clauses of the long arm statute. In either context, your goal is to provide the reader with a complete answer.

Clause 1(b) of Statute

It is possible but unlikely that Clause 1(b), "contracting to supply services or things in the state of Acadia," could also support an assertion of personal jurisdiction over Ron. The answer to this issue depends on how one interprets the words of the long arm statute. Under one view, Ron's job requires him to work as a computer consultant "throughout the country," but the facts are silent as to whether he supplied these services in Acadia. It seems unlikely that Ron's contract would require him to provide computer networking services throughout the country, but that this would not include the very state where CompuFix was headquartered. Under this interpretation of the statute, it is impossible to determine whether Ron supplied goods or services in Acadia without more information. There is, however, an alternative point of view.

As I have already mentioned, Ron's contract required him to supply computer consulting services. Because he signed the agreement in Acadia, this could be viewed as "contracting to supply services or things" in the forum state. This point of view has serious flaws. First, it requires a somewhat tortured reading of the statute. The relevant language requires the defendant to contract to supply services in Acadia. Importantly, the words do not read "contracting in Acadia to supply services." Also, it seems more likely that the legislature contemplated goods or services coming into Acadia under this clause of the statute. Therefore, Clause 1(b) is unlikely to apply here unless Ron actually provided consulting services to clients in Acadia.

Even if this language is deemed to apply here, it seems unlikely that jurisdiction under Clause 1(b) would comport with due process and the minimum contacts analysis required under *International Shoe*. If Ron supplied computer services in Acadia and his contacts in Acadia were systematic and continuous, then the court may have general in personam jurisdiction over him. Unless this is the case, the court will not have specific personal jurisdiction over him for a lawsuit based on the alleged breach of his employment contract under Clause 1(b) of the long arm statute. Broadly, one could argue that his employment contract required him to provide consulting services and therefore these contacts would support an assertion of personal jurisdiction for a lawsuit based on a breach of that agreement. Simply put, however, this lawsuit is not based on whether Ron supplied consulting services in Acadia. It is about whether he breached that agreement when he took on additional employment. Not only is it unclear whether Ron engaged in any sales activities in Acadia, these possible contacts are essentially unrelated to the subject of this lawsuit. The only clear contact with Acadia, the signing of the employment contract, is not sufficient to satisfy the minimum contacts analysis of *International Shoe* for an assertion of jurisdiction based on Clause 1(b) of the long arm statute, "contracting to supply services … in Acadia."

Other Clauses of the Statute

It is quite clear that Clauses 1(c), 1(d), and 1(e) of Acadia's long arm statute do not apply here. Clause 1(c) involves "causing tortious injury … in Acadia," and there is no allegation that Ron caused any tortious injury. For the same reason, Clause 1(d), which also involves causing tortious injury, does not apply. Finally, Clause 1(e) involves the defendant having some interest in real property in Acadia, and the facts do not indicate that Fred has any property interests in the forum state.

There are several things to take note of in the above answer. First, I continue to use subheadings in order to maintain order. Second, this aspect of my answer pertains solely to Ron. When there are multiple parties in your examination, carefully consider whether you should analyze their actions separately or together. Where there is no difference in the analysis, then you can analyze the parties together in order to save time. More typically, the analysis will differ as to each party. This will require you to address each individual separately.

Also, notice that my analysis is lengthier when discussing certain clauses of the long arm statute. The basic organization of my analysis as to each issue, however, remains the same. As for the organization, note that I use my subheadings to state the issue I will be discussing, but that I sometimes begin my sections with a conclusion. This is my preferred method of answering a question, but don't make the mistake of analyzing to your conclusion. Let the conclusion proceed naturally from your analysis.

As for the analysis itself, take note of my approach to Clause 1(b). I lay out two possible interpretations of the language of the statute, and then proceed to analyze the pros and cons of each approach. Remember, you are not undercutting your analysis be discussing alternative points of view—just the opposite. Good analysis requires you to discuss all reasonable alternatives in coming to your answer.

Finally, note that the strength of my conclusions differs as you move from issue to issue. I modify my conclusion to Clause 1(a) with the word "likely," but the conclusion to the last issue begins with the words "it is quite clear." These differ-

ences are meant to convey at the outset how strongly I feel about the answers to each issue. Just be careful when using words like "clearly" or "obviously" when responding to most issues. Your professors will spend a great deal of time constructing nuanced examination questions so that the answers to most of the issues will not be clear or obvious.

Personal jurisdiction over Fred
Clause 1(c) of statute

As for Fred, the long arm statute may support personal jurisdiction over him, but it is a much closer call than with Ron. Most aspects of Acadia's long arm statute require that the defendant perform some act within the state. For this reason, Clause 1(c), "causing tortious injury by an act or omission in Acadia" may not apply. Fred's "interference" with the contract was in the form of convincing Ron to work for him. Fred phoned his friend and tried to convince him to work at DigiCare, and importantly Ron received the phone call while driving through Acadia. Also, Ron made his decision to work with Fred during this phone conversation. For this reason, it is possible that Fred's actions satisfy Clause 1(c) of the long arm statute. I say "possible" because Fred was not in Acadia when he made the phone call to Ron. Therefore, it would seem odd to describe Fred as "causing tortious injury ... in Acadia" if he was never in the forum state during the phone call.

However, the counter argument would be that Fred did cause injury in Acadia regardless of his location when he made the call. If Fred and Ron were standing in Acadia during their conversation, this contact would support personal jurisdiction over Fred based on Clause 1(c) of the long arm statute. While Fred was not physically present in Acadia during the conversation, in a sense he was there through his voice and words coming through the telephone line. Importantly, the specific language of Clause 1(c) does not require the defendant's presence in Acadia. Thus, the idea of Fred causing tortious injury in Acadia while he is physically present elsewhere is not so farfetched. Therefore, Clause 1(c) arguably applies.

Minimum contacts analysis, however, is unlikely to support personal jurisdiction over Fred even though he called Ron in Acadia. Similar to the situation with Ron, Fred's contacts with Acadia are fairly minimal. He also signed an employment contract with the state, and did reach into the state to call and encourage Ron to come work with him. These contacts are not so significant or continuous as to support the Acadia court's general in personam jurisdiction over him. However, his single phone call into Acadia to convince Ron to work with him is an extremely significant contact. This contact is the basis for the very lawsuit that CompuFix is bringing against him. It was during this contact that he engaged in the behavior that may amount to tortious interference with Ron's contractual relationship with CompuFix. On a surface level, this contact is a sufficient minimum contact to support personal jurisdiction over Fred.

There is, however, a strong argument against this single contact being sufficient to satisfy due process. The facts are unclear as to whether Fred was aware that he was calling into Acadia when he dialed Ron's cell phone number. On the one hand, whether he was aware of Ron's location or not does not alter the fact that he reached into Acadia and caused tortious injury there. On the other hand, if Fred was unaware as to Ron's presence in Acadia, then he would be surprised to be brought into an Acadia court based on this single contact. Of course, when Fred dials a cell phone number, he should know that the recipient of the phone call could be in any state. But, Fred is not trying to reach into the forum state when he makes his phone call. Essentially, the court would be basing personal jurisdiction on happenstance—that Ron happened to be in Acadia when Fred made the phone call. Basing personal jurisdiction on happenstance would not comport with "traditional notions of fair play and justice" that are the hallmark of minimum contacts analysis under *International Shoe*. While it is a relatively close call, an Acadia court is unlikely to have personal jurisdiction over Fred if he was unaware of Ron's location when he called.

In my estimation, this is the most complicated issue in the exam. Not surprisingly, it is my lengthiest answer. Despite the complexity of my answer, the basic organizational structure of my response remains the same. I lay out the issue, I provide the applicable law, I analyze the issue, and then I conclude. While the basic structure remains the same, the analysis becomes significantly longer than the other sections when discussing more complicated issues. For example, my minimum contacts analysis alone is three paragraphs long.

Clause 1(a)

Clause 1(a), "transacting any business in Acadia," may also apply to this situation. Initially, this clause seems inapplicable due to the cause of action being alleged by the plaintiff, tortious interference with a contractual relationship. However, one could argue that Fred was conducting business in Acadia when he called Ron there. More specifically, he wanted Ron to come work with him in his new business, and this certainly sounds like "transacting any business" in Acadia.

As for due process considerations, the same issues that I referenced in my analysis of Clause 1(c) of the statute apply here as well. Again, if Fred was aware that he was calling into Acadia when he called Ron, then he should not be surprised to end up in an Acadia court to defend against an action for tortious interference with a contractual relationship. If he was unaware that he was calling into Acadia, the same issues discussed above apply. Please refer to my above minimum contacts analysis for additional details.

The one unique aspect of my answer to this issue is that I have incorporated by reference the analysis to the previous issue. Here, the analysis of this aspect of the issue is the same in both instances. Referencing an earlier portion of your answer can save time, but it also can create confusion for the reader. Before using this device on your exams, ask your professor for guidance.

Clause 1(d) of Statute

Clause 1(d) of the statute does not support personal jurisdiction over Fred. Clause 1(d) allows the court to assert personal jurisdiction over a defendant who causes "tortious injury in Acadia by an act or omission outside Acadia." If Fred called Ron in Acadia, then the alleged tortious interference with contractual relationship fits this clause. Importantly, however, Clause 1(d) goes on to say that the defendant must regularly do business in Acadia. The facts indicate that Fred wants to go national one day, but for right now all of his clients are located in his home state of Verhampshire. Further, clause 1(d) would only apply if the defendant derived "substantial revenue" from goods or services provided in Acadia. Fred is a long way from deriving "substantial revenue" in Acadia, making Clause 1(d) inapplicable.

Clauses 1(b) and (e) of Statute

It is unlikely that any other clause within the long arm statute applies to Fred's situation. Fred has not provided any goods or services in Acadia and does not own any property there either. Therefore, Clauses 1(b) and (e) would not apply.

Question II
Removal to federal court

These defendants will be able to remove this case to the federal district court for the district of Acadia. A defendant may remove a case to federal court if that case could have been brought in federal court initially. A case may be brought in federal court when it arises under federal law or where there is diversity between the parties. As no federal law is involved, the parties will have to base federal jurisdiction on diversity.

A federal court may have subject matter jurisdiction over a lawsuit where there is diversity between the parties. To establish diversity, all defendants must be domiciled in different states from all of the plaintiffs. In determining diversity, courts apply the notion of domicile. Simply put, a person is domiciled in a state if they reside in that state and intend to remain in that state indefinitely. An intent to remain permanently is not required.

A corporation is domiciled in both its state of incorporation and in the state which represents the company's principal place of business. A corporation can have multiple domiciles where the state of incorporation and principal place of business are different. Here, CompuFix is domiciled in Acadia because it was incorporated in that state.

Courts apply different tests to determine a corporation's principal place of business. For example, the nerve center test focuses on the location where major corporate decisions are made. Other courts utilize a center of corporate activities test which emphasizes the location where production operations are centered. Finally, some courts combine these tests under a total activities approach to determining a corporation's principal place of business. Regardless of which test is applied, CompuFix's principal place of business is Acadia. Not only is the "main" office in Acadia, it is the company's only office. Therefore, for diversity to exist, neither defendant can be domiciled in Acadia.

Based on these facts, Fred is domiciled in Verhampshire and Ron is domiciled in New London. Regarding Fred, the facts clearly state that he does business and lives in his "beloved" Verhampshire. His home is located on top of his business, and there is nothing in the facts to suggest that he is even considering living elsewhere. This satisfies both the presence and intent to remain indefinitely requirements of domicile.

In regard to Ron, he appears to be a domiciliary of New London. He lives in New London, which satisfies the presence element of the domicile test. As for an intent to remain indefinitely, there is nothing to suggest that Ron plans to leave New London at any point in the near future. He currently commutes to DigiCare's offices in Verhampshire, and he should be able to do this even if works with Fred on a more permanent basis. Importantly, Ron's domicile will not change until both the presence and intent to remain indefinitely requirements come together in another location. Therefore, Ron's domicile is New London. Because both defendants are domiciled in states other than Acadia, they are diverse from the plaintiffs for purposes of subject matter jurisdiction.

Amount in controversy

To complete the diversity analysis, we must review whether the amount in controversy requirement has been satisfied. The amount in controversy requirement is satisfied unless it appears to a "legal certainty" that the plaintiff can only recover $75,000 or less. The court will apply this standard to each defendant. Here, the plaintiff has sued each defendant for $250,000. At trial, the plaintiff will allege the Ron was shirking his duties when he started working with Fred. More specifically, Fred was able to bring Ultrafine Coffees on as a new client. This company has 30 coffee shops in Verhampshire and has plans to go national. If Ron had brought Ultrafine in as a client for CompuFix, it would likely have meant a great deal of revenue for the company. While the exact amount of revenue is unclear, there is no way we can say that the amount will be $75,000 or less to a legal certainty.

For similar reasons, the amount in controversy requirement is satisfied with respect to Fred. Fred allegedly interfered with CompuFix's employment relationship with Ron. Ron was working with Fred when, allegedly, he should have been working for CompuFix. Without Fred's interference, CompuFix might have signed on a lucrative new client. This does not mean that CompuFix will win this lawsuit against Fred. Ultimately, CompuFix will have to show that Ron's actions violated the terms of his employment contract and that Fred was partially responsible. At this stage, however, we are only concerned with whether diversity jurisdiction is appropriate. We cannot say to a legal certainty that CompuFix will recover $75,000 or less, therefore the amount in controversy requirement is satisfied as it pertains to Fred. Therefore, the defendants could remove this matter to federal court because the lawsuit could have originally been brought there based on diversity jurisdiction.

In question II, I continue to use the same organizational devices that I began with. Once again, I use subheadings, where applicable, to separate the issues. Also, I analyze each issue as to Fred and Ron separately because certain facts apply to one but not the other.

One final note of caution. Be sure that you reference the parties, places, and events correctly and consistently throughout the examination. In this example, I chose to refer to the defendants by name, but I could have used the first letters of their names. Just be sure to make a choice and stick with it. As for the names of the two computer companies, CompuFix and DigiCare, they are somewhat similar. They may not seem all that similar now, but consider the stress and excitement you will feel during your civil procedure examination. Make a quick notation somewhere on the examination question to keep the parties clear in your mind.

CHAPTER XIII

Résumés and Writing Samples

One day, you will graduate from law school. Intellectually you all realize this, but there are times during law school when graduation may seem like it is decades off into the future. Graduation, however, is coming sooner than you think. Graduating from law school is certainly something to celebrate, but it also marks another important transition in your life—going from being a law student to a lawyer. This transition will be exciting and at times a little frightening because there are a whole new series of unknowns to face.

One of these unknowns is the process of getting your first job as a lawyer. Thankfully, almost all law schools have a "Career Development" or "Placement" office that can help. Despite the assistance offered by these offices, you are ultimately responsible for writing your own résumé and creating your own writing sample.

Résumé Basics

If this is your first attempt at writing a résumé, I have several pieces of good news for you. First, some of the most important aspects of writing a solid résumé are no different than writing any other legal document. Just like a legal memorandum, your résumé must be clear, well organized, and free of typographical errors. Second, the basics of persuasive legal writing are also applicable when writing a résumé. When well written, your résumé describes your accomplishments accurately, but in the best possible light. Finally, your law school's career development office may very well have professionals on staff who can provide you with guidance before applying for a job. So, this discussion of creating a résumé is only a first step.

Formatting Your Résumé

There is no one perfect format for a résumé that guarantees you will receive an interview, much less a job. That being said, there are a number of common mistakes that, if made, will seriously decrease your chances with a prospective employer. While you do have some leeway in terms of fonts and organization, your résumé should project a professional image. For that reason, certain résumé conventions have developed over time, and you should not deviate from them without a very good reason.

- **Paper**—Use standard letter-size paper—8.5 x 11—you might want to use slightly heavier paper because it stands up better and suggests that the sender has put some thought into their application packet. Avoid card stock or any similar heavyweight paper that will not fold easily or fit into a standard envelope. As for color, stick with more conservative choices like white and ivory. Other colors may stand out in a pile of résumés, but can project a less than professional attitude to potential employers. If you plan on scanning your résumé into a computer, then use plain white paper for the best results.
- **Font Size and Style**—With today's word processing programs, you can choose from literally hundreds of fonts when creating a document. Many are fine for purposes of a résumé, but others look **cartoonish** at best. Avoid using *script*, or any other font that will be difficult for the potential employer to read. As for font size, most of the text should be at 12 point, although your name (16 point) and other contact information (14 point) may be slightly larger. Finally, use fonts and typefaces consistently throughout the document. For example, it is fine to use **bold** or *italics* when listing the name of a company for whom you once worked, but be sure to list all company names in the same fashion.
- **Margins**—The best practice is to maintain standard margins—1 inch both left and right and between 0.5–1 inch top and bottom—throughout the document. Avoid the temptation to reduce the margin size in order to accommodate more information on a single page. Too much text on a single page will make the document difficult to read. Do not justify text on the right side of the document as this can create awkward gaps between words.
- **Length**—For most students, a résumé should be one page long because they lack the relevant job experience that would necessitate a lengthier document. Students with a more extensive work background may create

a two-page résumé. If your résumé is going to be two pages long, be sure that you break the pages at a logical location. For example, if a job description starts moving onto page 2 of your résumé, then break page 1 earlier so that the entire description moves to page 2.

- Sections—All résumés should contain the following sections: contact information, education, and experience. In addition, many résumés contain at least one additional section titled "Additional Skills" or "Interests," and the content of this section varies extensively depending on the individual.

Contact Information

Provide the employer with the contact information they will need in order to reach you. At a minimum, this section must include your name, address, and a phone number. Today, it is quite common to include multiple phone numbers and an e-mail address. You want your name to jump out at the reader, so consider using a larger point size for your name and contact information. For example, writing your name in 16 point and your contact information in 14 point makes sense if the remainder of the document is written in 12 point.

Listing both a home and cell phone number is quite common, but be sure to consider your living arrangements before choosing to do so. Would you want a potential employer to speak with your roommates or members of your family? Do you typically receive messages or do they get lost when people call your home number? If the answer to these questions is "no," consider listing your cell number exclusively.

In regard to your address, many students have both a "local" and "permanent" address to choose from. You may include both, but do so with good reason. If your permanent address is in another part of the country and the potential employer is located there, then include the address in order to create a connection to the area that can work in your favor.

As for electronic communication, be sure that your e-mail address is professional and not a humorous nickname that you used while in college. Do not include links to your Facebook or MySpace page, but assume that potential employers will look you up on their own. For that reason, review these pages and remove any information that portrays you in anything other than a professional light. When in doubt, take the information out.

Education

For students, the Education section of the résumé should appear immediately after their contact information. List the schools you attended in reverse chronological order, which means that law school will likely be the first thing noted. Include the colleges and universities where you received any undergraduate and graduate degrees, but do not list your high school unless it is a prestigious school or you are trying to create a connection to that part of the country.

When listing each institution, be sure to include the name of the institution, the city and state where the school is located, the degree and any honors you received, and the important activities you took part in. Class rank and GPA may also be included, but only do so if they reflect positively on you. If your GPA is below a 3.0 or if you rank outside of the top 1/3 of your class, you may want to exclude this information. Also, be scrupulously accurate when providing this information on your résumé, which means that you should not round numbers in your favor. For example, you are not in the top 10% of your class if you rank 21st out of 200 students.

Experience

List your employers in reverse chronological order, and be sure to include your title, the city and state where you were employed, and the length of your employment. In regard to the duration of your employment, include both the month and year you started and stopped working for each employer. Potential employers are always on the lookout for gaps in an applicant's résumé, and a failure to include the months you started and finished with an employer may suggest you are trying to hide such a gap.

The style used when describing work experience is somewhat unique in résumés. For example, there is no need for the personal pronoun "I." This is your résumé, so readers will assume that you are the one who did the work. Also, most sentences should be quite short, almost to the point of being sentence fragments, and should begin with action verbs in order to create a more dynamic and easily read product. To illustrate, compare the following job descriptions.

Version 1

I wrote legal memoranda for the appeals court judges in which I assessed the strengths and weaknesses of each party's argument and suggested possible questions that could be asked during oral argument. I also wrote draft decisions for my judge and performed legal research into evolving areas of the law. Finally, I was a member of a several person team assigned to write new model jury instruction.

Version 2

Prepared bench memoranda assessing strengths and weaknesses of each party's arguments. Authored draft decisions. Created questions that judges used during oral argument. Conducted research into evolving areas of the law, including the contractual rights of surrogate mothers. Assisted in the development of model jury instructions currently being used in Acadia courts.

Version 3

- Prepared bench memoranda assessing each party's arguments.
- Authored draft decisions.
- Created questions that judges used during oral argument.
- Conducted research into evolving areas of the law, including the contractual rights of surrogate mothers.
- Assisted in developing model jury instructions currently being used by Acadia courts.

The above descriptions all refer to the same exact work performed by the same individual. The first job description is reasonably well written, but fails to follow the stylistic conventions appropriate to résumés. The writer uses the personal pronoun "I" extensively, which tends to create a fairly repetitive sentence structure. Further, the absence of the action verbs at the beginning of each sentence makes for somewhat dull reading.

Versions 2 and 3 are both acceptable, and the only meaningful difference between them is the use of bullet points in Version 3. Bullet points may make the document a little easier to read, which is important considering how little time prospective employers spend reviewing each individual résumé. Also, note that the use of action verbs makes for more dynamic reading. While the content of the three versions is largely the same, most employers would be more interested in meeting the author of Versions 2 or 3. Feel free to employ the following list of action verbs when writing your own résumé.

Action Verbs

accelerated	composed	formulated	produced
accomplished	conducted	fostered	programmed
achieved	constructed	found	projected
acquired	conserved	gathered	promoted
adjusted	consolidated	guided	proposed
administered	consulted	handled	prosecuted
advised	contracted	heightened	provided
aided	controlled	highlighted	purchased
analyzed	convinced	identified	received
applied	coordinated	implemented	recommended
appointed	corresponded	improved	recorded
appraised	counseled	initiated	referred
arbitrated	created	inspected	reported
argued	critiqued	instructed	represented
arranged	debated	instituted	required
assembled	decided	interpreted	researched
assessed	defined	interrogated	resolved
assigned	delegated	interviewed	revealed
assisted	delivered	invented	reviewed
assumed	demonstrated	investigated	scheduled
audited	designed	launched	selected
authored	determined	lectured	served
authorized	developed	licensed	solved
awarded	devised	located	specialized
began	directed	maintained	streamlined
bolstered	discovered	managed	strengthened
boosted	dispensed	maximized	studied
briefed	documented	modified	suggested
budgeted	drafted	monitored	summarized
calculated	edited	motivated	supervised
catalogued	elected	negotiated	supplied
chaired	enlarged	observed	supported
charted	enlisted	obtained	surveyed
checked	ensured	operated	targeted
classified	established	organized	tracked
cleared up	estimated	participated	trained
closed	evaluated	performed	transformed
collected	examined	persuaded	translated
combined	executed	planned	traveled
commented	expanded	prepared	uncovered
communicated	expedited	prescribed	updated
compared	familiarized	presented	welcomed
compiled	filed	processed	worked
completed	forecast	procured	wrote

Additional Résumé Sections

Beyond the three required sections of a résumé—contact information, education, and experience—some students require at least one additional section for information that does not fit neatly into the other categories. For example, some students are published authors, and for these students a "Publications" section makes sense. Publications that appear exclusively on the Web may be included, but this does not necessarily mean providing a link to a personal blog because not all blogs are created equal. A blog where I occasionally bemoan the state of my favorite sports team or mention a great new recipe I tried is not worth listing. Before listing your blog, or any publication for that matter, ask yourself this simple question. Is a potential employer more likely to hire me after reading it?

In addition to "Publications," some students include an "Additional Skills" or "Interests" section if they have more information that they want to convey to an employer. An "Additional Skills" section is where you would list, among other things, fluency in a foreign language or significant computer skills. Keep in mind that most law students know how to perform computer-assisted legal research using Westlaw® or Lexis®, so listing these skills is unnecessary.

A section entitled "Interests" typically contains information regarding activities that you enjoy but that are not necessarily related to the legal profession. Activities like scuba diving, travel to exotic locations, or automobile restoration may resonate with a prospective employer and can be good conversation "ice breakers" at the beginning of an interview. Of course, for every person who might be interested in your hobby, there are others who could not care less about what you do in your spare time. In fact, some employers may find the entire notion of listing one's interests as less than professional, so the choice is yours. My suggestion is to include your interests, but only if they are truly unique and real conversation starters.

Sample Résumés

Below, I have provided you with three sample résumés to consider. As to content, they are almost identical. I have, however, changed the fonts and other formatting to give you some sense as to how different the same information can look in different formats. I do not view any one of these samples as superior to the others, and you should feel free to adopt aspects from all of them when creating your own résumé.

Mark L. Justice
1 Lawyer Drive • Springfield, Acadia 01234
(617) 123-4567 (H) • (617) 321-7654 (M)
mjustice@gmail.com

Education

University of Acadia Law School • Springfield, Acadia
Candidate for Juris Doctor, May 2010

Class Rank:	Top 5% (10/207)
GPA:	3.78/4.0
Honors:	Acadia University Law Review, Staff Member
	Deans List, 2008 and 2009
Activities:	Environmental Law Society

University of Acadia • Newtown, Acadia

Dual Major:	Bachelor of Arts in English and Education, May 2003
Honors:	Magna Cum Laude
	University Honors Program

Experience

Commonwealth of Acadia Appeals Court • Springfield, Acadia
Summer Clerk • May 2009–August 2009

- Prepared bench memoranda assessing each party's arguments.
- Authored draft decisions.
- Created questions that judges used during oral argument.
- Conducted research on evolving areas of the law, including the contractual rights of surrogate mothers.
- Assisted in development of model jury instructions currently being used by Acadia courts.

Marshburg High School • Marshburg, Acadia
English Teacher • July 2003–May 2007

- Created lesson plans for three different levels of sophomore English.
- Administered program that contributed to improved standardized test scores on English portion of exam from 75% in 2003 to 84% in 2007.
- Developed and administered after school ESL program.

Interests

- International travel, particularly in South America
- Writing short stories.

Mark L. Justice
1 Lawyer Drive • Springfield, Acadia 01234
(617) 123-4567 (H) • (617) 321-7654 (M)
mjustice@gmail.com

Education

University of Acadia Law School　　　　　　Springfield, Acadia
Candidate for Juris Doctor, May 2010
Class Rank: Top 5% (10/207)
GPA:　　3.78/4.0

Honors:　　Acadia University Law Review, Staff Member
　　　　　　Deans List, 2008 and 2009

Activities:　Environmental Law Society

University of Acadia　　　　　　　　　　　Newtown, Acadia
Dual Major: Bachelor of Arts in English and Education, May 2003
Honors:　　Magna Cum Laude
　　　　　　University Honors Program

Experience

Commonwealth of Acadia Appeals Court　　Springfield, Acadia
Summer Clerk　　　　　　　　　　　　May 2009–August 2009

Prepared bench memoranda assessing strengths and weaknesses of each party's arguments. Authored draft decisions. Created questions that judges used during oral argument. Conducted research on evolving areas of the law, including the contractual rights of surrogate mothers. Assisted in the development of model jury instructions currently being used in Acadia courts.

Marshburg High School　　　　　　　　Marshburg, Acadia
English Teacher　　　　　　　　　　　　July 2003–May 2007

Created lesson plans for three different levels of sophomore English. Administered program that contributed to improved standardized test scores on English portion of exam from 75% in 2003 to 84% in 2007. Developed and administered after school ESL program.

Interests
International travel, particularly in South America.
Writing short stories.

MARK L. JUSTICE

1 Lawyer Drive • Springfield, Acadia 01234 • (617) 321-7654 •
mjustice@gmail.com

EDUCATION

University of Acadia Law School   Springfield, Acadia
Candidate for Juris Doctor, May 2010
Class Rank: Top 5% (10/207)
GPA: 3.78/4.0

Honors: Acadia University Law Review, Staff Member
              Deans List, 2008 and 2009

Activities: Environmental Law Society

University of Acadia   Newtown, Acadia
Dual Major: Bachelor of Arts in English and Education, May 2003
Honors: Magna Cum Laude
                University Honors Program

EXPERIENCE

Commonwealth of Acadia Appeals Court   Springfield, Acadia
Summer Clerk   May 2009–August 2009

Prepared bench memoranda assessing strengths and weaknesses of each party's arguments. Authored draft decisions. Created questions that judges used during oral argument. Conducted research on evolving areas of the law, including the contractual rights of surrogate mothers. Assisted in the development of model jury instructions currently being used in Acadia courts.

Marshburg High School   Marshburg, Acadia
English Teacher   July 2003–May 2007

Created lesson plans for three different levels of sophomore English. Administered program that contributed to improved standardized test scores on English portion of exam from 75% in 2003 to 84% in 2007. Developed and administered after school ESL program.

INTERESTS

International travel, particularly in South America.
Writing short stories.

Creating a Writing Sample

I cannot overstate the importance of creating a strong writing sample. You spent a great deal of time in law school learning to think analytically—or think like a lawyer. The ability to think analytically is useless, however, if you cannot communicate what you know to another person. Much of what we do as lawyers involves the written communication of our thoughts, ideas, and

> **Herb's Hints**
> ———
> Always bring extra copies of your writing sample, résumé, and list of references with you to an interview. It never hurts to be prepared!

arguments to colleagues, clients, opposing counsel, and judges. In fact, employers have rated legal research and writing as the most important skills that graduates should possess upon entering their offices, rating them more highly than knowledge of the law![1] Employers understand that you will not know every imaginable legal principle when you start working for them, but they do expect you to be able to learn those principles through legal research and then communicate what you have found in the written form.

Eventually, almost all employers require that applicants submit a writing sample. Even if you performed at the top of your class in law school, employers will have résumés from many others who have performed similarly. Your law school grades may get you an interview, but your writing sample will help land you the job you want. Even if an employer does not request one during the initial résumé gathering stage, you will need a writing sample should you be called in for an interview. However, I recommend against sending out a copy of your writing sample along with each résumé. Instead, follow the employer's instructions.

Choose Wisely

While there are no absolutes when choosing a document to use as a writing sample, potential employers will scrutinize every aspect of it so choose wisely. In addition to your writing ability, your writing sample sends a message to employers about your judgment. Each year I review writing samples that, unintentionally, imply the following negatives about the writer:

---

1. Bryant G. Garth and Joanne Martin, *Law Schools and the Construction of Competence*, 43 J. Legal Educ. 469, 490.

- The applicant is not a good legal writer
- The student has yet to learn about confidentiality and professional discretion
- Legal analysis must be a foreign concept to this student
- The writer has avoided writing anything since the first year of law school

Please note that these are negative inferences that may be drawn, not from your writing ability, but from the document you have *chosen* as a writing sample. Knowing that an employer may draw these negative inferences from your writing sample is not even half the battle. Now you need to know which aspects of a writing sample might generate these negative inferences and how to avoid them. Even more importantly, you need to know how to turn these negative inferences into positive ones.

You Are Not in College Anymore

One of the more common mistakes I see students make is using college papers for their writing samples. Students make this choice for a very simple reason—legal writing is hard. Every 1L knows this fact. Even for students with strong basic writing skills, the structure and step-by-step approach that is required in analytic writing can be difficult to master.

Therefore, students who do not feel entirely comfortable with their legal writing skills—which is just about everyone—will use a document they feel better reflects their writing abilities. The rationale behind this decision certainly has a surface level appeal, and goes something like this: (1) I'm not a very good legal writer; (2) I didn't do all that well in my legal writing class; (3) but, I did receive a good grade on that research paper I wrote for Anthropology 303; and (4) that paper better reflects my writing ability and will hide the fact that my legal writing is a work in progress.

When written out in the above fashion, I hope that the flaws in the above reasoning jump out you.[2] First and foremost, you are interviewing for a job in the law. Why would an employer care how well you wrote an anthropology, English literature, or political science paper? Even worse, your choice of a college level paper implies one of two things; either you are mentally still in college and have yet to fully transition into law school or you believe yourself to be a poor legal writer. Neither is a message that you want to convey.

---

2. As an aside, the very act of writing out one's thought process in an orderly fashion—one of the hallmarks of good legal writing—helps us to confront the weaknesses in arguments we might have otherwise missed.

Never forget that *everyone's* writing skills are a work in progress. In fact, legal writing is a skill that will continue to evolve over your entire career. Besides, being ashamed of your own abilities suggests a distinct lack of confidence on your part—a character trait that is not in high demand among legal employers.

Instead of a college level paper, use a legal memorandum that you wrote for a class or for a summer employer as your writing sample. Legal memoranda are among the more common documents that attorneys write, so it only makes sense that you demonstrate your ability to write one. Just as importantly, a legal memorandum requires the writer to perform legal analysis. Remember, legal analysis is your prediction as to how a set of facts might be resolved based on the current body of law. Above all else, employers want to read a writing sample that demonstrates strong analytical skills.

Because analytical skills are in such high demand among legal employers, students should be hesitant to use seminar papers or law review articles as writing samples, even if they were completed while a law student. Lawyers rarely write in this style, and applicants are unlikely to impress prospective employers with their ability to do so. More important, writing samples should highlight your analytical abilities, and seminar papers are a poor vehicle for doing so. In addition, writing samples should be relatively short, and seminar papers or law review articles are difficult to follow in anything other than their complete form. An exception to this general rule would be a seminar paper or law review article on a topic that would be of particular interest to an employer. For example, if the employer engages in a great deal of intellectual property work, a piece on the Digital Millennium Copyright Act may be an appropriate choice for a writing sample.

Picking My "Best" Memorandum

Even 1Ls are likely to have multiple legal memoranda to choose from, so here are a few things to keep in mind when choosing between them. Most employers judge writing samples based on the strength of the legal analysis. Therefore, it does not make a difference whether you choose a document written from an objective and persuasive standpoint, as both are acceptable for purposes of a writing sample. Simply pick the memorandum that best demonstrates your analytical abilities.

A good rule of thumb is to choose a document you wrote recently as opposed to one you wrote earlier in the year or even longer ago. As I noted earlier, writing is a skill that continues to evolve and improve throughout one's career. The most dramatic improvements, however, occur during the earliest stages of our careers. Therefore, your most recent memo likely represents your best writing, making it the best choice for a writing sample.

In addition, I recommend that you grab every opportunity to work on your writing. With so much room for improvement early in your career, each project or class you take will help produce a better writing sample. If possible, you want to avoid being a third year law student who has to use a memorandum from a first year class as a writing sample. Additional writing opportunities will not only improve this critical skill, but they will also send the message to employers that you understand the importance of writing like a lawyer.

Another consideration when choosing a document to use as a writing sample is the practice area of the prospective employer. Employers like to read memos on topics they recognize, so it is always a good idea to dovetail the writing sample to a prospective employer's area of practice when possible. This shows the writer has spent time researching the firm as opposed to simply sending out résumés to every potential employer. Early in your career, however, you are unlikely to have memoranda that might appeal to every possible employer. If not, do not worry because this will be true of all of your law school peers. That being said, it is not a bad idea to have a second document ready to use as a writing sample. In doing so, you will have at least two chances of coming close to the employer's area of interest.

A great choice for a writing sample can be a document you wrote while working as a summer associate for a law firm or even a judge. These documents remind employers that your experience is not limited to law school and demonstrate your ability to work without the safety net of a professor's guidance. Documents written while working for an employer, however, do raise a few concerns that must be addressed before using them as writing samples. Chief among these concerns is the issue of client confidentiality.

Generally, documents submitted to a court are a matter of public record, but this does not apply to internal office memoranda where issues regarding client confidentiality, or even trade secrets, may arise. If you intend to use an office document as your writing sample, the best first step is to contact the employer to discuss the matter. The best time for doing this is while you are still working for the employer and have built up a reservoir of good will. You may be able to address an employer's or client's concerns by simply changing the names of the parties throughout the document. If you do so, be sure to note this fact in your cover sheet. Doing so marks you as a professional who understands the value of discretion.

Once you have chosen a document to use as a writing sample, the next thing you must do is read every word of it from beginning to end. This is the first step in the editing/

> "There is no great writing, only great rewriting." — Justice Louis D. Brandeis.

proofreading process. As I have already noted, your writing skills will improve dramatically during the early stages of your career. Take advantage of your improved writing skills and rewrite as much of the document as is necessary to place your writing sample in the best possible light. In addition, you probably wrote the original document under time constraints, making it the best you could have done *in those circumstances*. Now you have the time to do things right, so take advantage of the opportunity. This holds true even if you received an "A" on the document from your writing professor. Typically, an "A" on a first-year writing assignment means that you performed better than the vast majority of your peers. It does not mean that the document was perfect.

Formatting Considerations

The format for an office memorandum is fairly similar from office to office, and this is the format that most legal writing professors require in class. Use basic fonts such as Times New Roman, keep one-inch margins all around, and be sure that the font size is large enough to read easily but not so large that it looks amateurish. Times New Roman, for example, works best using a 12 point size.

> ### Herb's Hints
>
> A header that includes your name is a nice "subtle" way of reminding an employer who you are every time they turn the page of your writing sample.

Using a basic font is particularly important if the employer requests an electronic version of your writing sample. The more basic the font, the more likely your document will look as you intended when printed out by a prospective employer. It is also a good idea to create a header for the document that provides your name and the words "writing sample" at the top of the page.

While the sample should provide employers with enough writing so that they may accurately judge the writer's abilities, most employers do not have the time to read long writing samples. Therefore, try to keep the sample between 5 and 10 pages long. Keeping your writing samples relatively short will also make the document easier to edit and proofread. Fewer mistakes in your final draft means you are more likely to impress an employer with your attention to detail. If the original memo is more than 5–10 pages long, simply choose to include one or more of the better arguments and leave out the rest. If the sample is something less than the entire memo, be sure that the material provided makes sense without the excluded sections.

Employers want to see how well you explain the law and analyze the facts, and this type of writing occurs in the "Discussion" or "Argument" sections of a memo. While other sections of your memo, like the "Questions Presented" and the "Statement of the Facts," are important, you may leave them out of your writing sample. In addition, you likely spent the most time reworking the "Discussion" or "Argument" sections of your memos, so they usually represent your best work. This is a particularly important consideration once you realize that many employers will form their opinions of your writing ability within the first page or two of the document. If you include all of the other sections of the memo in your writing sample, the sample will be several pages long before the reader reaches your best work.

Once you have removed the other sections of the memorandum, you will need to create a cover sheet that helps set the context for the reader. The cover sheet should include the following information: (1) for whom the memo was written (professor vs. summer employer); (2) if the memo was written for a class, which class; (2) a quick summation of the factual scenario and the area of law analyzed in the document; (3) whether the sample is solely the student's work or has been edited;[3] (4) whether the document is written objectively or persuasively; and (5) an offer to provide the entire memo to the reader. Optional information includes the grade received, whether an employer submitted the document to a court, and the outcome of the case if the memo was written in an office setting.

Notice a few additional things about my sample cover sheet. I have written it in a memo format, which I feel is appropriate considering the fact that the writing sample itself is an office memorandum. In addition, I have taken the time to address the memorandum to a specific individual within the law firm. A small touch like this helps reflect positively on your professionalism. Finally, I have provided the reader with a contact number at the end of the document. This is not absolutely necessary, especially considering the fact that a cover letter will accompany my writing sample. Still, I am anticipating the possibility that my writing sample may be copied and distributed among various members of a hiring committee, and done so without my cover letter. Therefore, I have just made it easier for any member of the hiring committee to contact me.

---

3. If the memo was written for a legal writing class, then it has been edited by another. Similarly, if your office supervisor suggested changes to a document that you then incorporated, it is not solely your work.

Sample Cover Sheet

To: John Smith, Hiring Partner
        Smith, Jones, and Harper, LLC
From: Herbert Ramy, applicant for summer associate's position
RE: Attached Writing Sample, <u>State v. Baxter</u>
Date: April 25, 2010

I completed the following memorandum during my first year of law school for Professor Barfield's class, Introduction to Legal Research and Writing. This is the final draft of the memorandum I submitted and I revised it based on comments and suggestions I received from Professor Barfield. I received an "A" on the assignment and the "Best Memorandum" award for this work.

For purposes of this memorandum, Prof. Barfield placed me in the role of an Assistant District Attorney in the mythical state of Acadia. At trial, the state had secured a conviction against Ted Smith for assault and battery by means of a dangerous weapon, with the weapon in question being the defendant's shoes. The defendant and the victim had been drinking in a bar when a disagreement over the defendant's girlfriend occurred. The defendant followed the victim out of the bar where he punched and kicked him several times.

The defendant appealed his conviction, arguing that the District Attorney's Office failed to submit sufficient evidence to the jury and that the trial court should have allowed the defendant's Motion for a Judgment as a Matter of Law. More specifically, the defendant attacked two aspects of the prosecution's case. First, Baxter contended that the description of the defendant's shoes was too vague to support an inference that they caused the victim's injuries. Second, the defendant argued that the victim's injuries were not so significant that they could support the jury's finding that the defendant used a weapon.

In my role as an Assistant District Attorney, the DA asked me to assess the strengths and weaknesses of the defendant's appeal. Therefore, I wrote the memorandum from an objective rather than persuasive standpoint.

For the sake of brevity, I have only included the discussion section of the memorandum. I can provide you with the other sections of the document—facts, brief answer, and question presented—upon your request.

If you have a question about my writing sample or any other aspect of my application, please feel free to contact me at (617) 555-5555.

Sweat the Small Stuff

"Little things" like grammar, punctuation, and word choices are much more important than students tend to realize. Employers will often receive dozens, sometimes hundreds, of résumés for a single job opening. With that many résumés, the employer needs a quick way to shorten the list of prospective candidates. Obviously, grades and class honors play an important role in this decision, but another way to shorten the list is to remove candidates whose writing samples have grammatical, punctuation, and citation errors. The law is a very detail-oriented profession. If job applicants make errors that are easily avoided, why should an employer trust their judgment on larger issues?

A Few Final Do's and Don'ts

In addition to the work I do with students on their writing samples, I have also been the recipient of many job applications at various points in my legal career. Over time, I have noticed several common mistakes made by students and lawyers alike. On their own, these errors may not seem all that important, but place yourself in the position of a hiring partner. If you had a stack of 100 applications that needed to be cut down for 20 interview slots, and several of the writing samples contained errors, what would you do?

- **Maintain the highest level of professionalism in your documents.** This means avoiding slang—including internet slang like LOL—or other informal language.
- **Do not use words that are not words.** This may seem obvious, but a number of these "words" have slowly crept into every day speech and must be avoided. For example "irregardless" is not a word, and is often confused with irrespective.
- **Know the difference between "infer" and "imply."** Some students use these words almost interchangeably even though they have very distinct meanings. Imply means to provide information indirectly. Therefore, one who provides information—the writers of documents, for example—may be implying additional information in an indirect fashion. The word infer, on the other hand, means to draw additional conclusions from the provided information. Only the recipients of information—those reading a document, viewing a scene, or hearing information (jurors)—may infer. Consider the statement "I brought

my umbrella with me today." The speaker may be implying that it is likely to rain later in the day, a point that the listener may very well infer.

- **Correctly use all legal terminology.** Words like finding (found, find), holding (held, hold), and reasoning (reasoned, reason) all have specific legal meanings and should not be used interchangeably.
- **Cite correctly.** Be aware that Bluebook citation form is not necessarily used by legal practitioners within your jurisdiction. Look to local court rules to determine what citation rules are followed. When in doubt, remember the primary reasons to cite in legal documents: to provide support for legal assertions and to direct the reader to that support. If a reader might want to view the material that supports a conclusion or assertion, then cite it.
- **Quotation and citation are not the same thing.** Placing material in quotation marks does not relieve the writer of the obligation to provide the reader with a citation to where the quoted material first appeared. Similarly, citing at the end of the sentence is not enough if that sentence contains information lifted directly from another source. In this instance, use quotation marks *and* cite in order to avoid a charge of plagiarism.
- **Avoid quoting too extensively in documents.** Employers want to see how well an applicant writes, and they will not get a true sense of this ability if most of the sample consists of quotations. It may feel like it is safer to quote, but the job of the writer is to explain the relevant legal principles to the reader. As a senior partner once told me, "If I wanted to read the case I would have pulled it off the shelf myself." Of course, one should quote when the failure to do so might change the meaning intended by the original author, but this occurs much less frequently than many students think.
- **Consider changing the "funny" names used by your writing professor.** If your writing sample is based on an assignment created by your legal research and writing professor, the parties and places may be based on characters from television or the movies. While you may have laughed when reading about how "Spock" slandered "James T. Kirk" or when "Homer" battered "Bart," references of this sort may make your document look unprofessional. Not all employers will feel this way, and some may even enjoy the references so the choice is yours. Whenever I am in doubt in situations such as this one, I am reminded of the advice given to me by a more senior colleague—"you will never offend by dressing too conservatively or by being overly professional."

Writing Sample—Example

The following example of a writing sample is based on the memo appearing in Chapter X, "Legal Writing." I have attempted to incorporate all the suggestions given in this chapter, so there are differences between this version of the memorandum and the one contained in Chapter X. For example, I have started the writing sample with the "Discussion" section of the original memo, leaving out the "Question Presented" and "Facts" section. In addition, I have changed the font from Helvetica to Times New Roman, and I have altered the name of the defendant and many of the case names. In the original, I used characters names from "The Mary Tyler Moore Show" when choosing the names for my cases.

To: John Smith, Hiring Partner
         Smith, Jones, and Harper, LLC
From: Herbert Ramy, applicant for summer associate's position
RE: Attached Writing Sample, <u>State v. Smith</u>
Date: April 25, 2010

I completed the following memorandum during my first year of law school for Professor Barfield's class, *Introduction to Legal Research and Writing*. This is the final draft of the memorandum I submitted and I revised it based on comments and suggestions I received from Professor Barfield. I received an "A" on the assignment in addition to the "Best Memorandum" award for this work.

For purposes of this memorandum, Prof. Barfield placed me in the role of an Assistant District Attorney in the mythical state of Acadia. At trial, the state had secured a conviction against Ted Smith for assault and battery by means of a dangerous weapon, with the weapon in question being the defendant's shoes. The defendant and the victim had been drinking in a bar when a disagreement over the defendant's girlfriend occurred. The defendant followed the victim out of the bar where he punched and kicked the victim several times.

The defendant appealed his conviction, arguing that the District Attorney's Office failed to submit sufficient evidence to the jury and that the trial court should have allowed the defendant's Motion for a Judgment as a Matter of Law. More specifically, the defendant attacked two aspects of the prosecution's case. First, Smith contended that the description of the defendant's shoes was too vague to support an inference that they caused the victim's injuries as opposed to merely the blows themselves. Second, the defendant argued that the victim's injuries were not so significant that they could support the jury's finding that the defendant used a weapon.

In my role as an Assistant District Attorney, the DA asked me to assess the strengths and weaknesses of the defendant's appeal. Therefore, I wrote the memorandum from an objective rather than persuasive standpoint.

For the sake of brevity, I have only included the discussion section of the memorandum. I can provide you with the other sections of the document—facts, brief answer, and question presented—upon your request.

I. Discussion

Smith is likely to prevail on his appeal of the trial court's denial of his motions for a directed verdict and judgment notwithstanding the verdict. The Acadia Court of Appeals will apply the *de novo* standard of review in determining whether our office presented sufficient evidence at trial for the jury to find the existence of a weapon beyond a reasonable doubt. See State v. Sloane, 199 Acadia 216 (1995) (noting *de novo* standard appropriate when reviewing denial of motion for required finding of not guilty). Acadia's Assault and Battery by Means of a Dangerous Weapon ("ABDW") statute actually contains two separate definitions of a weapon. First, an item is a weapon if it is specifically designed to cause harm. 30 Acad. Stat. Annot. § 17(A). Obviously, shoes are not designed to cause harm, making § 17(A) of the statute inapplicable to this case. Under, § 17(B) of the statute, however, any item may be a weapon if it is intentionally used to cause harm and it has the "capability of causing serious bodily harm." 30 Acad. Stat. Annot. § 17(B). Importantly, the item, and not just the blow to the victim, must be capable of causing the requisite harm. *Id.* The state may establish an item's ability to cause "serious bodily harm" either through a sufficient description of the item or based on the severity of the victim's injuries. State v. Carlton, 88 Acadia 77 (1952); State v. Jones, 98 Acadia 17 (1950). In this instance, the description of the defendant's footwear as "shoes" or "sneakers" is insufficient to establish their ability to cause serious bodily harm. In addition, the bruising over much of the victim's body was serious, but still not sufficient evidence to establish that the defendant's footwear was a weapon.

Description of Defendant's Shoes Insufficient

The jury did not hear a sufficiently detailed description of Smith's shoes to find that they were a weapon. Under Acadia's ABDW statute, an item may be a weapon only if it is capable of "causing serious bodily harm." It is difficult for a jury to make this finding without an adequate description of the item in question. 30 Acad. Stat. Annot. §17(B); see State v. Carlton, 88 Acadia 77 (1952); State v. Jones, 98 Acadia 17 (1950).

If the jury receives a relatively detailed description of the item in question, they may be entitled to find that it was used as a weapon. In State v. Jones, a jury convicted the defendant of using her shoes as a weapon. Jones, 98 Acadia at 19. During trial, a witness described the shoes as "sharp and pointy." Id. at 18. In addition, the defendant's shoes punctured and broke two bones in the defendant's hand. Id. From this evidence, the court concluded that a reasonable jury could find that the shoes in question had the "capability of causing serious bodily harm." Id. at 19. The Jones Court went on to reason that it was irrelevant whether the injuries were more severe than could have been accomplished without a weapon. Id. The key was whether the weapon, in this case the defendant's shoes, *could* cause more harm than could the blow by itself. Id. In contrast, the Court in Sloane held that the jury had not received a sufficient description of the defendant's weapon, again a pair of shoes, to determine that they were capable of causing serious harm. State v. Sloane, 199 Acadia 216 (1995). In Sloane, the state failed to introduce any description of the defendant's shoes. Id. at 218. From the evidence at trial, the jury could have inferred that the defendant was wearing some type of footwear. Id. Yet, the court reasoned that any additional inference as to the type of footwear would be "tantamount to guesswork" and impermissible. Id.

In the instant case, the prosecution failed to introduce a sufficient description of the defendant's shoes to warrant the jury finding they were a weapon. Initially, the victim testified that the defendant was wearing "shoes" during the attack, but later modified his testimony on cross examination. On cross examination, he admitted that he had used the term "shoes" as another word for footwear, explaining that he "just meant that [the defendant] wasn't barefoot." Reviewing the evidence in a light most favorable to the prosecution, the district attorney established that the defendant was wearing shoes, but this description is little more than what was presented in State v. Sloane. 199 Acadia at 218. In both instances, the evidence required the jury to infer that the term "shoes" described an item capable of causing serious bodily harm. The drawing of such an attenuated inference amounts to the kind of guesswork proscribed by the Sloane court. Further, the term "shoes" is extremely general as compared to the description of the weapon in State v. Jones. 98 Acadia at 18. In Jones, the Court emphasized the specific description of the shoes as "sharp and pointy" in upholding the defendant's conviction. Id. When one considers the broad range of footwear that could be described as shoes, this description standing alone cannot establish their capability of causing serious bodily harm. However, the jury is allowed to review evidence beyond the description of the shoes in determining whether they were used as a weapon.

Severity of Defendant's Injuries

The jury may use the severity of the victim's injuries as some basis for establishing that the defendant used an otherwise innocent item as a weapon. In State v. Carlton, the court looked to a general description of the defendant's footwear as well as the extent of the victim's injuries in upholding the defendant's conviction. State v. Carlton, 88 Acadia 77, 78 (1952). The jury heard sufficient testimony for a finding that the defendant was wearing "shoes," but the Court reasoned that, without more, this description was insufficient to uphold the conviction. Id. The jury did hear more, however, in the form of testimony that the victim suffered from broken ribs and a dislocated shoulder as a result of the defendant's kicks. Id. In contrast, another victim, who had not been kicked with shod feet, sustained a few bruises. Id. The Carlton Court held that the severity of these injuries allowed for a jury finding that the defendant was armed with a weapon that was capable of causing serious bodily harm.

Slaughter's injuries were not sufficiently severe to establish that the defendant's shoes were a weapon. Unlike the broken bones sustained by the victim in Carlton, our victim merely sustained severe bruising over his entire body. While these injuries are not to be minimized, it is doubtful that they support a finding that the shoes were used as a weapon. Our office needed to prove that the shoes had the capability of causing more harm than would the kicks alone. Without some additional details regarding the extent of the victim's injuries, no reasonable jury should have found that these bruises established the presence and use of a weapon.

II. Conclusion

The court is likely to agree with the defendant's contention that the jury did not hear sufficient evidence to find that he was armed with a weapon. While the jury could have inferred that the defendant was wearing shoes during the attack, they did not receive enough of a description of the shoes to determine they were capable of causing "serious bodily harm." Similarly, the defendant's injuries were not sufficiently severe to warrant a finding that they could only have been caused by a weapon, defendant's shoes, as opposed to the blows themselves.

CHAPTER XIV

Acing Your Job Interview

Regardless of the strength of your grades, the brilliance of your writing sample, or the praise lavished upon you by your references, every legal employer will want an interview—possibly multiple interviews—before offering you a job. Even if you have never been on an interview, do not panic. Acing an interview is a lot like performing well on your law school exams. All it takes is confidence, a smidgen of common sense, and a great deal of preparation.

The first thing to remember is that the prospective employer already likes you well enough to ask you in for an interview. Lawyers are busy people, and they would not waste their time inviting a person in for an interview who had no chance of securing the job. However, this also means that everyone being invited in for the interview has what it takes, at least on paper, to do the job. With so many applicants to choose from, how do employers choose between a large number of worthy candidates?

Up until this point, the employer has relied on documents in making its choices. First, they reviewed your résumé and cover letter. If they liked those documents, then they possibly asked for a writing sample. Even if an employer loved these documents, however, they would be left with a problem. These documents will not tell them everything they need to know about you.

Lawyers work with other people all day—clients, colleagues, judges and administrative staff—and documents are a poor vehicle for assessing your interpersonal skills. To better determine whether you would be an appropriate fit for their office, they need to assess your people skills in the best way available to them, and that is through an interview. Your job during the interview is to communicate the intelligence, good judgment, and positive character traits that make you the best candidate for the job. To do this, however, you are going to have prepare as if you were getting ready for a final exam.

> **Herb's Hints**
> ───
> If you are given the option, try scheduling your interview for late in the morning—10:00 or 11:00 AM. Commuting should not be a problem at this time of the day, and both you and the interviewer are likely to be fresh and ready to go.

Preparation

Your preparation begins the moment a prospective employer calls to schedule an interview. You are likely to be both nervous and excited, which is normal. Just be sure that you calm yourself down sufficiently in order to write down some important information. By the way, did you notice that I said "write down" the information? In your excitement, you do not want to forget an important part of the message, which would necessitate an embarrassing phone call back to the employer. In addition to the obvious—the date and time of the interview and the location where the office is located—here is a list of additional information you will want before hanging up the phone.

- The *exact* location where the interview will take place. This includes the floor of the building and the office number. You may simply end up waiting in a reception area, but it is nice to know where you are going if you need to ask for directions.
- A contact person and phone number. If you need to call back for some reason, you want to know who will be answering the phone. If the number belongs to a secretary or administrative assistant, you might be more inclined to call for additional information but do not be a pest! A negative word from a highly thought of administrative assistant can ruin your chances for the job before the interview has even begun.
- Do they want a writing sample or list of references in advance or is it OK to bring these items with you to the interview? Even if they want these materials prior to the interview, be sure to bring additional copies of your writing sample, reference list, résumés, and business cards (if you have any) with you. If you are interviewing with a group, one person is bound to need a copy of your résumé. Having these documents with you is a simple way of showing that you take this opportunity seriously and that you are prepared.
- An e-mail address and FAX number. If they want your writing sample and list of references in advance of the interview, ask how you should send them the information. If they offer, an e-mail or FAX is a satisfactory way of providing the employer your information. Once again, be sure you know who will be receiving these materials so that you may address them appropriately. As always, be professional and courteous in your communications.
- The names of all people with whom will you be interviewing. This information will help you conduct research on your interviewer. Although

not absolutely necessary, it is nice to know the interviewer's area of specialization and even where they went to school.
- **The URL (web address) for the law firm's web page.**
- **The approximate duration of the interview.** This information can help with your commuting plans, including where you may want to park your car. You do not want to be anxiously looking at your watch during the interview because your car is about to be towed away!

With this information, you are now ready to begin your research in earnest. Broadly, this research can be divided into two categories—information about the law firm and information about the interviewer. Do not discount the importance of conducting this research. Prospective employers often complain that job candidates come to interviews knowing nothing about the law firm. This lack of preparation indicates a lack of professionalism and interest in the job. Thankfully, there are a number of sources you may turn to in order to obtain the information you need.

Researching the Law Firm

Researching a prospective employer is a lot of work, but there are multiple reasons to extend yourself in this fashion. Obviously, you are trying to impress potential employers with your professionalism. Your research also implies that you want the job, otherwise why would you have gone to the trouble of doing the additional work? There are two subtler reasons, however, why you should conduct this research. First, it will help you decide whether working for a particular law firm is in your best interests. Sometimes applicants are so excited at the prospect of getting a new job that they fail to consider how happy they would be at a particular law firm.

Second, if you truly want the job, your research can help you find connections with your interviewer. Maybe you went to the same university or took evidence with the same professor in law school. Maybe you grew up in the same part of the country, and frequented the same beaches or parks when you were growing up. Connections like these may not seem important, but they help turn you into a real person in the eyes of an interviewer as opposed to simply another candidate looking for a job.

One of the first places to turn to for information regarding an employer is their web site. At one time, only the largest law firms maintained their own web sites. Today, more and more law firms understand the importance of having an internet presence they can control. If you are interviewing with a larger law firm, look for the "mission statement." A mission statement can tell you a great deal about how the lawyers in the firm see themselves, but keep in mind that these statements are often aspirational in nature. At the very least, a web page is likely to include information about the firm's areas of practice and a list of the lawyers working there. Keep in mind, however, that the law firm controls the content of these web pages. The information is still quite valuable, but you may need to turn to other sources for a less biased view of what the law firm is truly like.

As you review the web page, look for the bios of lawyers who will be interviewing you. If you were unable to obtain this information when you scheduled the interview, then look for lawyers who are on the firm's hiring committee. When reviewing the bios, pay particular attention to areas of practice and any major cases in conjunction with the lawyer's name. If one of the parties appealed a listed case, then head to the applicable reporter and read the decision.

In addition to a law firm's web page, there are other internet based sources that you can turn to for information about a law firm. Lexis® and WestLaw® are useful for looking up cases the firm litigated, particularly if you use the lawyer's name as a search term. For example, you may use an attorneys name in a field restricted search—AN (lawyer's name)—in WestLaw®. Most students are at least somewhat familiar with WestLaw® and Lexis®, but they are less familiar with another excellent source for information regarding lawyers and their law firms—Martindale-Hubbell®. In the words of the web site's creators, martindale.com[1] is the "Premier Destination for Sophisticated Buyers of Legal Services." Of particular value to job seekers, the web site's main page includes a search engine dedicated to finding lawyers and law firms.

Although web-based researching is a must when seeking out information on a potential employer, do not discount the value of "human-based" sources of information. For example, most law schools have an office of professionals dedicated to helping students and alumni with their job searches. The professionals who staff your Career Services office often have a wealth of information regarding employers, particularly those in your local area.

Your Career Services office is also a great source for the names and contact information of alumni and current students who have worked for the law firm where you are interviewing. A quick e-mail to these individuals is a great way to introduce yourself, but I recommend scheduling a face to face meeting or telephone conversation if you truly want candid information about the law

---

1. The martindale.com® web site is owned by LexisNexis®.

firm. Many lawyers are leery of using e-mail, particularly an office e-mail address, to candidly communicate with others.

Reviewing Yourself

Once you have researched your potential employer, you have to take a hard look at yourself as the next phase of the preparation process. For example, when was the last time you reviewed your résumé? While many job seekers update their résumés on a regular basis, this often consists of merely adding new information to the document without reviewing older entries. Even if you did review the entire résumé for accuracy and timeliness before sending it out—a process I wholeheartedly endorse—you must reread the document with the eyes of an interviewer. Be aware that every document you submit to the employer contains information that is fair game for a question during the interview.

If you mentioned "creating" a new system for tracking clients in one of your job descriptions, are you ready for a question about what this work entailed? Does your former employer still use your system? How did it differ from the old system? Were you assigned this task or did you create the system without direction from your boss?

If you listed making the dean's list during your first three semesters of law school, are you ready to explain why you failed to make the dean's list during the other semesters? How many students make the dean's list and what is the cumulative average required to be on the dean's list? Remember, your materials will generate many of the questions asked by the interviewer, so there is no excuse for not being prepared.

Dressing for Success

Your personal appearance is the first impression the interviewer will have of you when you walk into their offices, so you have to look your best. Starting with your clothing, a business suit is a must for men, and a pantsuit or jacket and skirt is required for women. A blue blazer and khakis simply will not cut it, even if your research indicates that the firm's lawyers dress in business casual attire. Business casual may be fine once you have the job, but you must put your most professional foot forward during the interview.

If you do not have conservative business attire, make the investment and do not wait. You may need to have your clothes tailored, so buy them well before interview season begins. If you already have more conservative clothes, do they still fit? When was the last time you tried them on? Weight loss or gain is often a part of the first year of law school, and the day of the interview is not the time to find out that your clothes no longer fit.

Your attire for the interview, however, goes beyond the suit or skirt and jacket you wear. It includes your tie, jewelry, cologne, and other details that will not be relevant in most other contexts. For example, both men and women should limit the amount of jewelry they wear to the interview. I recommend against earrings for men, multiple sets of earrings for women, and no tongue studs for either. In fact, when considering all aspects of how you present yourself during an interview, less is more. Use less cologne, wear fewer pieces of jewelry, cut your hair shorter (for men), and choose a less flamboyant tie if you want to be sure of making a good impression.

Admittedly, not everyone will agree with the above recommendations. Some might legitimately argue that you should not work for a law firm that requires you to dramatically alter your appearance in order to get the job. These same people would argue that a departure from who you are and what makes you comfortable likely means you will be unhappy working for the firm. Ultimately the decision is yours, but consider the following:

We all alter our appearance depending on where we are going and what we are doing. I dress differently when I attend a wedding as opposed to working in the yard. I might be more comfortable wearing torn jeans and a sweatshirt to a wedding, but it would be disrespectful to the bride and groom. More importantly, I would look ridiculously out of place! Admittedly, there is a certain amount of "fitting in" that occurs when you work in a law firm. Your supervisors and colleagues will expect it, and your clients will as well. And do not worry, you can wear your torn jeans and sweatshirt once you open your own law office.

Into the Lion's Den

You made it to the interview on time, but not too early. You look good in your best business attire, and you brought extra copies of your writing sample, résumé, and list of references with you to the interview. You researched the law firm, prepared for your interviewer's questions, and came up with questions of your own. In short, you are ready for the interview.

As you enter the law firm's office, there are a few additional things to keep in mind if you want to make a great impression. First, be cordial and respectful to everyone you meet. While this advice obviously applies to the interviewer and all the law firm's lawyers, it applies equally to the administrative staff and paralegals. These people are essential to the success of any law office, a point that your interviewer certainly knows. In fact, the support staff will know more about the practice of law than you do, especially during the early stages of your career. Finally, it is not unheard of for interviewers to touch base with administrative assistants to get their take on how candidates comported themselves while waiting for the interview to begin.

Once the interviewer comes out to meet you, make eye contact and shake hands firmly. Be sure to remember the interviewer's name, which may be difficult to do if you are meeting with a group of lawyers as opposed to a single individual. Unless instructed otherwise, refer to interviewers by their last names. While the interviewer may suggest that you use a first name, it never hurts to be overly respectful.

In the interview room, try to make yourself as comfortable as possible. If there are other interviewers in the room, be sure to shake everyone's hand and do your best to remember all the names. If you can remember the names, you will be able to address each interviewer individually when they ask a question. In addition, the names will be important later when you compose "thank you" notes—a point I will discuss more fully later in this chapter.

If offered, it is fine to accept a glass or water or something else to drink. Interviews can last for a long time, and you will be doing a great deal of the talking. A sip from a glass of water will help if your mouth gets dry, and is also a great way of buying yourself a few moments to think of an answer to a difficult question.

> **Herb's Hints**
>
> When dealing with multiple interviewers, shift your gaze between people from time to time so that they all remain engaged in the conversation.

Initially, you will probably be a little anxious, but your nervousness should disappear as the interview progresses. Also be on the lookout for nervous habits or gestures. Hair twirling, fast talking, and nail biting are all examples of nervous habits that can be distracting during an interview. Personally, I have to control my hands when I talk! I used to wonder why interviewers would break eye contact when I would answer a question, and then I realized that their eyes were being drawn to my hand gestures.

If you find yourself getting nervous, try to keep two things in mind. First, interviews proceed more smoothly when you treat them like conversations. A speech has to be memorized or read from a script, and it will always sound rehearsed. In contrast, a conversation is a much more natural form of communication.

Second, even though interviewers have something you want—a job—they also need something—an employee. Convince yourself that the interviewer needs you as much as you need them, and be confident that you are the best applicant for the job. The interviewer will pick up on the confidence you are exuding, making you a stronger candidate.

Interview Questions

While your résumé and other submitted materials may dictate the specific questions asked during the interview, there are questions that are staples of almost every interview that you should be prepared for. Do not, however, equate preparation with having a canned speech ready for each question. Remember, an interview should be a conversation between you and the interviewer. The more you try to memorize lengthy responses to specific questions, the more likely you will flub your response. Instead, read these questions so that none of them catch you unprepared.

In addition, always be truthful when answering questions. Good trial lawyers are quite adept at catching witnesses in half truths and inconsistent statements, and this applies to candidates during an interview. Of course, there is a difference between being truthful and sabotaging your chances at getting the job. For example, let us say that an interviewer asks the following question—"I noticed that you received a C+ on your criminal law final. Why was that?" If you were the interviewer, which of the following truthful responses would you prefer.

> *Answer 1 — That final took place at the end of the first semester, and unfortunately I was still in college party mode when I started law school. I was going out with my classmates most nights, and my criminal law class took place at 9:00 AM. I made it to class on most days, but I was pretty rough around the edges if you know what I mean. All things considered, I was pretty happy with my C+.*

> *Answer 2 — If you notice, criminal law was my first law school final exam and I did not prepare for the exam as I should have. I did attend class and do the reading, but at that time I was not aware that doing well in law school required quite a bit more. That C+ was a wake up call. If you look at my transcript, you will notice that my grades improved considerably from that point on.*

Sample Interview Questions

As you review these questions, consider how many of them contain more than meets the eye.

1. Tell me a little bit about yourself. *This is one of those interview icebreakers that is intended to get the conversation rolling. Information about where you grew up, where you went to college and your recent job experience are all acceptable topics for discussion. When discussing the more personal information—like where you grew up—be brief.*

2. What was it like growing up in _____. *Another ice-breaker question and one that is more common when the candidate has grown up outside of the United States or in another part of the country.*

3. Why did you decide to go to law school? *An innocent enough question on the surface, but one that can tell the interviewer more about you than you may realize. Law school did not have to be your childhood dream, but avoid an answer that implies a lack of focus or indecision.*

4. Why did you choose to go to law school at _____. *The only bad answer to this question is "[b]ecause I couldn't get into my other five choices."*

5. What was your favorite (or least favorite) class in law school? Why? *If you are interviewing for a position as a litigator, then the interviewer may expect you to mention classes like evidence or trial practice.*

6. Who was your favorite (least favorite) professor in law school? *It is better to be positive with questions like this one. Negative answers can make you sound petty and immature. Also, be aware that interviewers who attended your law school will have their own opinions of the faculty that may be quite different from yours.*

7. Have you always wanted to be a lawyer? *This is merely a variation on the "why did you decide to go to law school question." This is a great question for listing skills that you had upon entering into law school—like a strong writing ability or a knack for seeing both sides of a problem.*

8. We are interviewing a number of qualified applicants. Why would you be a better fit for this law firm than everyone else? *The trick with a question like this one is sounding confident without crossing the line over into arrogance. Do not be embarrassed to toot your own horn. If you do not believe in yourself, then why should the interviewer believe in you?*

9. What are your major strengths and weaknesses? *Another great question for referencing important lawyering skills. As for weaknesses, avoid noting that you work "too hard," as every interviewer has heard this response before.*

10. Where do you see yourself in 5 years? *Avoid answers that suggest you are using this job as a stepping stone onto bigger and better things.*

11. Have you ever been fired from a job? *A very tough question, particularly if you were fired for poor performance. It is fine to give your version of events, but keep in mind that the interviewer may end up calling your old employer.*

12. What practice areas are you most interested in? *If you have done your homework, then you should be able to dovetail your interests to the firm's practice areas.*

13. Are you willing to work in a different practice area if that is what our needs are? *A "no" to this question may end your chances of getting the job, so choose your answer carefully. Keep in mind that new lawyers often end up working in a number of different areas before they settle on a specialty. In fact, developing an expertise in multiple areas of the law make will make you a better lawyer and more marketable in the future.*

14. Do you have any role models? *Do not feel compelled to choose a lawyer as your role model.*

15. I noticed that you received a "C+" in _____. Why did that happen? *As I noted above, be honest but put a positive spin on what happened.*

16. Do your grades accurately reflect your abilities? *An easy question if you are at or near the top of your class. If your answer to this question is "no," then be prepared to explain why your grades were not better. Avoid complaining about your professors, particularly if most of your grades fall into the same range.*

17. Do you see yourself as a leader? *Do not worry, they interviewer is not assessing your potential to be the managing partner. Still, even new lawyers need the strength of personality to manage their cases, deal with their clients, and work effectively with the administrative staff and other attorneys.*

18. Do you prefer to work unsupervised or with a lot of guidance? *Be careful with this question because no supervisor needs employees who need constant supervision or guidance. In addition, feel free to change the tenor of the question by using a phrase that is a favorite among lawyers—"It depends." For example, "I would expect more guidance from a supervising attorney when dealing with unfamiliar areas of the law. While I am certainly capable of re-*

searching new topics on my own, there is no sense in reinventing the wheel and wasting valuable time."

19. When wouldn't you take on a client's case? *Through this question, the interviewer is trying to determine how well you understand the rules of professional responsibility and the business of being a lawyer.*

20. Are you willing to do *pro bono* work? *In some states, lawyers are required to perform* pro bono *work each year, so know the rules in your jurisdiction.*

21. What did you think of the workload in law school? *If you thought the workload in law school was overwhelming, then you are not ready for what it really takes to be a lawyer.*

22. What was the most important skill you learned in law school? *Remember that employers highly value the ability to research and write effectively.*

23. Was there a favorite case you read as a law student? *Try and stay away from politically charged cases, like* Bush v. Gore, *where you have a 50-50 chance of offending the interviewer. Instead, try and find cases that interested you, and that are also in the law firm's practice area.*

24. Since you entered law school, have you had any doubts about joining the legal profession? *Many students have momentary doubts at some point during the first-year of law school, but would you want to hire a person who still wonders whether they made the correct career choice?*

25. How do you handle working under pressure and with deadlines? *If you wilt under pressure and deadlines, then you may want to consider a different profession.*

26. Describe your dream job. *Even if interviewers use the term "dream job," they are looking for a more prosaic job description. Even if you want to make lots of money for doing very little, and who doesn't, that is not the answer the interviewer is looking for. Being more realistic, aren't we all looking for work that is challenging, interesting, and fulfilling?*

27. Looking back, would you have done anything differently during your first-year of law school? *It is perfectly OK to acknowledge that you could have done things differently. Acknowledging one's mistakes shows maturity and the ability to learn, but do not be too hard on yourself.*

28. I noticed that you worked as a summer associate with the law firm of
    _____. Why didn't they offer you a job after law school? *This question
    is more common for 3d year and graduating law students. As always, be honest
    but avoid bad mouthing a past employer. You are likely to have learned
    something, even with the worst employer, so focus on this fact when coming
    up with an answer.*

29. Are you interviewing with other law firms? *If you are being courted by other
    firms, great!*

30. Has law school changed you? *Many students feel that law school has
    changed them in some way. As always, use positive language when describing
    these changes. For example, "I became more outgoing and likely to debate
    others after my first year of law school." This sounds better than describing
    yourself as argumentative.*

31. Tell me about a time when you faced a difficult situation and how you
    handled it. *A very open-ended question, but one that is much easier to answer
    if you consider a response before the interview.*

32. What kind of salary are you looking for? *Here is your first foray into the art
    of negotiating. If you give a number at this point, rest assured that your salary
    will not be any higher than this amount. Particularly during a first interview,
    it is appropriate to defer your response. One way to defer your response is to refocus
    the question. For example, "At this point, I am more interested in the type
    of work done by your firm than I am in the salary." If the interviewer presses
    you on this point, then have a figure in mind that is based on your research of
    what associates make in similar law firms—just don't sell yourself short.*

33. What is your favorite hobby? *Almost any answer works here, as long as you
    have some outside interests. A person with no outside interests is likely to
    burn out quickly, making that person a poor choice for an employee.*

34. How do you unwind or de-stress after a day at work or school? *"With 3
    martinis" is not the best answer to this question.*

35. Why do you think you would be a good lawyer? *Again, try to dovetail your
    answer to the skills law firms are looking for.*

36. What is your greatest personal accomplishment to date? *Another question
    that is easier to answer if you think about it before hand. Have you received
    any awards that were important to you? Did you conquer a perceived limi-*

tation through the force of your own will? Are you the first person in your family to obtain a college degree or get into law school? Just have an interesting story to tell.

37. Are you willing to move for a position? *If there is no possibility of you moving, then say so. There is no sense in wasting your time, or the interviewer's, if the only job opening is in another part of the country. If there is a chance that you would be willing to move, however, then say so and defer the final decision to another day.*

38. I assume you've done some research on us. What can you tell me about our law firm? *Another easy question if you have done your homework. References to the firm's mission statement, major cases they have won, or their positive reputation in the legal community are all acceptable responses to this question.*

39. Do you have any questions for me? *Traditionally, all interviews end with this question. The only bad answer here is to have no answer at all. You must have questions for your interviewer. Your questions show your interest in the job and your listening skills. In addition, your questions can hint at the amount of research you have done on the firm.*

Here are a few general questions to get you thinking, but try to make your questions specific to the law firm you are interviewing with and to the conversation you just had with interviewer. Also, avoid asking questions whose answers were readily available elsewhere, like the law firm's web site.

Questions for Your Interviewer

1. What level of supervision do you provide to your associates?

2. What about this law firm makes it a strong place to work?

3. Do you expect new hires to specialize immediately, or will they have an opportunity to work in different practice areas?

4. What skills are the most important for a new hire to succeed in this job?

5. How would you describe your ideal new hire?

6. In order to best prepare for my job responsibilities, are there any courses that you recommend I take during my remaining time in law school?

7. How would you describe your management style regarding new associates?

8. How are new hires evaluated?

9. When can I expect to hear back from you?

10. May I contact you should I have any additional questions?

Illegal Interview Questions

It is possible that your interviewer will ask you an illegal question. This may be surprising considering the fact that you are applying for a job in the law, but it does happen. Many illegal questions touch on issues of race, gender, and family or marital status. Questions of this type are illegal because an employer may not refuse to hire a candidate based on these factors.

When asked an illegal question, you have three options. You may answer the question, refuse to answer the question, or answer the essence of what the interviewer is asking without directly addressing the illegal aspects of the question. For example, if the employer asks whether you are disabled, the underlying question is likely about your ability to perform the job in question. That being the case, you can choose to ignore the specific question and respond that you "are healthy enough to perform the job with (or without) a reasonable accommodation."

Before deciding on a course of action, you should know that a refusal to answer a question can impact whether or not you are offered the job. Of course, you may not want to work for a law firm that would hold such a decision against you.

Also keep in mind that the interviewer may not be aware that certain questions are illegal. Many interviews are conducted by lawyers, not by human resources professionals who are well versed in employment discrimination issues. In addition, there can be a fine line between an illegal and an illegal question. For example, an employer may not ask you whether you are married or whether you plan to have children. The interviewer may, however, inquire as to your availability to work overtime or to take extended business trips.

In the end, the choice of how to proceed when asked an illegal question is yours, and your options do not end when the interview is over. You still have the option of refusing a follow up interview or not taking the job at all. In addition, you may contact your law school's office of career development if they invited the employer onto the campus. Finally, if you feel that you have been discriminated against, you could contact the United States Equal Opportunity Commission (EEOC). For more information, check out the EEOC web site at www.eeoc.gov.

Wrapping Up the Interview

Once you have asked your last question, it is time for a few final "housekeeping" measures. If the matter has not come up yet, you should ask whether the interviewer would like a copy of your writing sample or a list of your references. Also, be sure to ask when you can expect to hear from the law firm again, assuming you have not done so already. With these last points out of the way, shake everyone's hand and be sure to thank the interviewers for their time and consideration. Even though interviews can be a nerve-wracking experience, it is important for you to remain composed and pleasant through these final moments of the process.

> ### *Herb's Hints*
>
> Ask your interviewers for their business cards. The cards will help you get the names and addresses correct if you call with questions and when you send out "thank you" notes.

The final handshake is your last opportunity to get everyone's name before leaving the interview. These names are important so that you can send out "thank you" letters or e-mails to each of the interviewers. While letters are a bit more formal, it has become more acceptable to use e-mail for this sort of correspondence. The important thing is that you send the interviewer the "thank you" note. In addition to being polite, "thank you" notes are a great way of differentiating yourself in a positive way from the other applicants. The note does not have to be very long, but you should address a separate one to every interviewer. If possible, you can also refer back to some aspect of the interview as a way of personalizing your note. There is no such thing as a perfect thank you note, but the following example will give you some sense of what one should look like.

Sample "Thank You" Note

Herbert N. Ramy
120 Tremont St.
Boston, MA 02108
(617) 573-8000
hramy@suffolk.edu

Dear Ms. Jones,

I just wanted to thank you for the opportunity of interviewing for a summer associate position in your litigation department. I particularly appreciated the tip you gave me about cross-examining an expert witness. I will be sure to use the information in my trial practice class next semester.

If you have any additional questions, please do not hesitate to contact me at the above listed cell phone number or e-mail address.

I look forward to hearing from you in the near future.

Sincerely,

Herbert N. Ramy

Herbert N. Ramy

Interview Checklist

A Week or More before the Interview

- ❑ Review and edit all materials before sending them in.
- ❑ Conduct research into law office.
  - ○ Review firm web site.
  - ○ Check services like Lexis®, Westlaw®, and Martindale-Hubbell® for information about the firm and its attorneys.
  - ○ Read recent cases litigated by law firm.
- ❑ Try on my interview clothing to make sure that it still fits and that it will look appropriate in a professional environment.
  - ○ Clean and press all clothes I plan on wearing to the interview.
  - ○ If necessary, buy new interview clothing.

❑ Get haircut.

❑ Contact my references to let them know they may be receiving a phone call from a particular law firm.

❑ Reread my résumé with an eye towards questions that it might generate on the part of the interviewer.

❑ Review list of potential interview questions.

❑ Prepare several questions of my own.

    ○ Some general questions (level of supervision, is specialization required, etc.).

    ○ Based on my research, at least one or two questions specific to the law firm.

The Day before the Interview

❑ Lay out clothes for interview.

❑ Make a trip to the interview location to make sure that I know where I am going and where I can park.

❑ Make additional copies of my résumé, writing sample, and list of references to bring with me to the interview.

❑ Review potential interview questions.

❑ Review questions that I have for the interviewer.

❑ Avoid a late night out and excessive alcohol consumption.

The Day of the Interview

❑ Eat a light meal before the interview.

❑ If possible, have someone else check my appearance before I leave for the interview.

❑ Confirm that my briefcase contains extra copies of my résumé, writing sample, and list of references.

❑   Give myself plenty of time to reach my destination.

❑   If I arrive more than 10 minutes before the scheduled interview, wait before entering the office.

❑   Once I enter the office, turn off my cell phone in order to give the interviewer my undivided attention.

❑   Be confident!

Answer Key

Chapter I

True or False

1. The United States Supreme Court is always the final word on matters of state and federal law.

False—United States Supreme Court decisions are the final word on matters of federal law, but state appellate courts are free to resolve matters of state law without interference from the federal courts. The United States Supreme Court may address a matter of state law if the state court's resolution of the issue is somehow at odds with the Supreme Court's interpretation of the United States Constitution.

2. Federal trial courts are referred to as United States District Courts.

True—This is the general designation for federal trial courts. Individual trial courts are also identified by the state, and possibly region of the state, where the court sits. For example, the federal trial court in Massachusetts may be referred to as the United States District Court for the District of Massachusetts.

3. Appellate courts resolve questions of fact, not questions of law.

False—Appellate courts resolve questions of law and not questions of fact. The trier of fact, typically the jury, directly heard the evidence at trial and was in a far better position to resolve factual questions. The appellate court may, however, readdress questions of law to assure that the litigants received a fair trial.

4. A *pro se* litigant is one who has decided to handle his case without the assistance of a lawyer.

True—Parties who choose to represent themselves in a legal matter are said to be proceeding pro se. *Note that this is true in both civil and criminal cases.*

While the government has the obligation to appoint an attorney to indigent criminal defendants, the defendant may decline the offer and choose to handle the case for himself.

5. All litigants in civil trials have a right of appeal.

True—In the both the federal and state systems, litigants have a right to appeal their cases to a higher court. Depending on the jurisdiction, the appeal will go to an intermediate court of appeals or, if the jurisdiction does not have an intermediate appellate court, to the jurisdiction's court of last resort.

6. In the federal system, the court of last resort is the United States Supreme Court.

True—The United States Supreme Court is the highest level appellate court in the federal system. In the state systems, courts of last resort goes by a variety of different names.

7. A litigant unhappy with a decision handed down by one of the United States Circuit Courts of Appeals has a right to have the matter heard by the United States Supreme Court.

False—In general, the United States Supreme Court hears appeals a matter of discretion as opposed to as a matter of right. A litigant unhappy with a decision of one of the United States Circuit Courts of Appeals must petition the United States Supreme Court to hear the matter through a **writ of certiorari.** *The Court will then decide whether or not to hear the matter by granting or denying* **certiorari.**

8. All state court systems include a trial court, an intermediate court of appeals, and a court of last resort.

False—While this is true in the federal court system and in some state systems, a number of states have a single appellate court. In states with a single level of appellate court, appeals proceed directly to the state's court of last resort.

9. Primary persuasive authority is not law.

False—All primary authority is law. Primary persuasive authority is simply law that originates in a jurisdiction other than where the dispute is being handled. For example, a decision from the Florida Supreme Court is primary authority and law that must be followed in all Florida courts. In Idaho, this Florida law is persuasive authority that the Idaho court may, but is not required to follow.

10. Generally, courts must follow primary authority that originates in the same jurisdiction where the court sits.

True—When primary authority originates in the same jurisdiction where a court is sitting, it is mandatory or binding authority that the court must follow. In rare instances, a court of last resort may deviate from established precedent and the doctrine of stare decisis *by choosing not to follow the earlier decisions of that court.*

Short Answer

When responding to these questions, provide a brief explanation for your answer.

1. Must the government appoint an indigent defendant counsel in a civil matter?

The government must appoint an attorney to indigent defendants, but only in criminal trials. In civil matters, which cover all non-criminal cases, the government does not have to appoint an attorney for either of the parties.

2. During a trial, the witness tries to testify that she heard the defendant say "I'm going to shoot," but defense counsel objects because the testimony falls under the legal definition of hearsay. Despite the objection, the trial judge allows in the testimony. May an appellate court review the trial judge's decision?

Yes—A trial judge's ruling on the admissibility of evidence is a question of law, and is exactly the kind of dispute that appellate courts address.

3. May an appellate court use case law from other jurisdictions to support their opinions?

In general, courts look to the law in their own jurisdiction to support their decisions. In some instances, there is no law within the jurisdiction that addresses a particular issue. In these instances, the court may rely on the law from other jurisdictions, a form of persuasive authority, in arriving at its conclusions.

4. What is the difference between primary mandatory authority and primary persuasive authority?

Primary mandatory authority is law from the jurisdiction where the parties are litigating the dispute. Primary persuasive authority is also law, but from a different jurisdiction and cannot bind the parties or the court.

5. Under the doctrine of *stare decisis*, must an appellate court always follow its earlier decisions?

Courts generally follow their earlier decisions under the doctrine of stare decisis, *even if the new judges on the court would have ruled differently had the matter come before them originally. Courts may, however, deviate from established precedent when the reasons underlying the original decision no longer apply in the present day.*

6. Name two types of secondary authority.

The most common types of secondary authority include commentary on the current state of the law or articles exploring the future course of the law. These sources include legal treatises, restatements of law, legal encyclopedias, legal dictionaries, and law review articles.

7. May an appellate court use secondary authority as support for its decisions?

Courts may use secondary authority to support their decision. In general, courts only rely on secondary authority in the absence of mandatory primary authority.

Chapter III

Exercise 2: Case Briefing Exercise, *Ransom v. State*

Case Name, Author, Citation: *Ransom v. State*, 460 P.2d 170 (Alaska 1969). Author—Justice Boney.

The reference to "Alaska" in the parentheses tells the reader that the Alaska Supreme Court decided this case. This is only one of the many aspects of case citation that you will learn during the first weeks of class.

Procedural History: Defendant charged with A&B w/ dangerous weapon in joint indictment (Berfield other Defendant). Convicted with weapon being footgear. Appealed to AK Supreme Court.

Notice that I have abbreviated a few of my terms. Case briefs are rarely, if ever, collected by your professors, so feel free to abbreviate terms as you see fit.

Facts: The defendant allegedly kicked the victim while wearing some type of "footgear." However, the witness did not know what kind of footgear the defendant was wearing. The witness testified that the defendant was wearing something on his feet, but nothing more.

Remember to keep your facts section lean and narrowly focused on the issues before the court.

Issue: May a conviction for Assault and Battery with a weapon, with the weapon being a shod foot, be sustained when the only evidence introduced was that the defendant was not barefoot?

Holding: No.

Rule: To establish the existence of a weapon for purposes of Assault and Battery by means of a weapon, the prosecution must submit sufficient evidence from which the jury could determine beyond a reasonable doubt that the item used by the defendant had the capability of causing "serious bodily harm" based on the manner in which it was used.

Notice that I have tried to write this rule in a general fashion so that it may be applicable to future cases. However, I did limit the rule somewhat by specifically referencing Assault and Battery by means of a weapon. While it is possible that the rule from this case would apply to any crime involving a weapon, I did not feel that I had enough information to make that conclusion.

Reasoning: The jury did not have sufficient evidence to determine beyond a reasonable doubt that the defendant was wearing footgear capable of causing harm, and the jury cannot determine whether an object has the capability to cause harm without knowing its physical characteristics. Further, the use of the weapon, rather than just the blow, must have the capability of causing serious bodily injury considering the manner in which it was used. Thus, a more specific description of the item used was required.

Here, I have tried to answer the question "why." A good explanation of the court's reasoning is essential. Without it, you are more likely to apply the rule incorrectly. With the reasoning, you can better determine if the rule fits the facts of a new case.

Disposition: Reversed and remanded

Notes: Voir dire has two definitions. (1) Questioning of potential jurors to determine whether they may serve. (2) Preliminary questioning of witness to determine competency.

When terms like "voir dire" appear in a case, you are obligated to look up their definitions. You will encounter dozens of terms like this during your first year of law school and learning their meanings is all part of becoming a lawyer.

Exercise 3: Discussion Questions, *Ransom v. State*

Question 1—What arguments can you think of, both pro and con, for treating hands and feet as dangerous weapons if the defendant has been specifically trained to use them to harm others (e.g. boxer or martial arts expert)? How do you think the Alaska Supreme Court would rule if they were confronted by these facts?

On the pro side, if an individual has been trained to use his body as a weapon, then he should be liable for assault and battery with a weapon if he uses this weapon to harm another person. This specific training places an enhanced responsibility on these individuals. They have trained themselves to use their bodies as a weapon, so it is fair for the courts to treat these bodies as a weapon when they are used to cause "serious bodily harm."

On the con side, there are several problems with treating the human body as a weapon. On the practical side, how much training is required before an individual's body should be viewed as a weapon. It would be easy to refer to a professional boxer's hands as a weapon. Similarly, a person who has received years of martial arts training might view her entire body as a weapon. What if the person has attended one self-defense class? Also, the court might be dissuading the public from taking self-defense classes because now their bodies have become weapons in the eyes of the law.

Making the body a weapon also has ramifications in the area of self defense. Typically, you may defend yourself from an attack by using like force. If an attacker punches you, you may punch them back. If you escalate the confrontation by using a weapon, however, the defense of self defense may no longer be available to you. Thus, a professional boxer might never be able to defend himself without being charged with the use of a weapon.

Finally, by treating the body as a weapon, the court may be turning the entire definition of weapon on its head. Legislatures typically treat crimes more seriously if the defendant uses a weapon. For example, legislatures usually differentiate between simple assault and battery and assault and battery with a dangerous weapon, treating the latter as the much more serious crime. Allowing the body to become a weapon would effectively erase the lines the legislature has drawn between certain crimes. A proponent of the opposing view would argue that a carefully crafted rule would treat the human body as a weapon only under a narrow set of circumstances. Every punch would not become an assault and battery with a weapon. Instead, if you were trained to use your body as a weapon, then the court could fairly treat these individuals differently.

Do not be concerned if you did not consider all of these ideas in your answer. I have been doing this for a lot longer than you have! The above answer is intended to illustrate the layered approach to analyzing an issue. Each time you think you have the answer figured out, be open to the possibility that there is an alternative point of view. Remember, most law school answers are about discussing the various ways of viewing a scenario as opposed to a single narrow conclusion.

Question 2—If the witness testified that the defendant had been wearing "boots," would this change in the testimony have altered the Alaska Supreme Court's holding? Why?

I do not think that this single change in the witness' testimony, from footgear to boots, would have changed the outcome of the case. In *Ransom*, the appellate court noted that there was insufficient evidence for the jury to determine, beyond a reasonable doubt, that the footgear in question had the capability of causing harm. The court went on to reason that the jury needed information regarding the physical characteristics of the footgear to find them capable of causing serious bodily injury considering the manner in which it was used. Here, the word "boots" is certainly more descriptive than the term footgear. Most boots do have the capability of causing serious harm if an assailant is wearing them as he kicks his victim. Standing alone, however, the description "boots" is not enough evidence from which a jury could find a capability of causing serious harm beyond a reasonable doubt. Without more information, there is no way to know what the witness meant when he used the term "boots." While most boots have the capability of causing serious harm, not all boots fit this description.

The *Ransom* Court did note "under some circumstances a heavy-soled boot ... could be a dangerous weapon," but this statement is full of qualifying language. For example, the words "under some circumstances" imply that boots would not be a weapon in all circumstances. In addition, there is no way to know whether the boots in this instance are "heavy soled," which was part of the description the *Ransom* Court referenced favorably. Therefore, the term "boots" without elaboration is unlikely to meet Alaska's definition of a weapon.

Note the form that I have used in writing the answer to the above question. I have started with the issue, then immediately stated my understanding of the legal premise necessary to resolve the question. Next, I lay out my analysis of the issue, which necessarily includes information both favorable and unfavorable to my conclusion. Notice that I weave the principle of law into the facts material to my reasoning. Finally, I wrap up the answer with a statement of my conclusion. This simple form—Issue, Rule, Analyze (pro and con), and Conclude—is often used to answer even the most complex legal issues. I will discuss this formula, and its variations, in much more detail in later chapters.

Chapter IV

Exercise 1A

In *Garratt v. Dailey*, the court noted that the defendant could still be liable for a battery if he knew to a substantial certainty that his actions would result in an unwanted touching. Does this standard allow the trier of fact to take into account the defendant's age, and if so how?

This standard, knowledge to a substantial certainty, does allow the court to take into consideration the defendant's age. Under this standard, the court must consider whether Dailey knew to a substantial certainty that his aunt would strike the ground when he moved the chair. Dailey, as a five year old child, may not have understood the ramifications of his actions. If not, then he did not form the requisite intent to be liable for a battery.

Exercise 1B

Assuming for a moment that the standard does allow for consideration of the defendant's age, should this be applied objectively or subjectively? In other words, should the trier of fact be asked to determine whether this specific child knew that his actions would result in an unwanted touching (subjective) *or* should the emphasis be on whether an average child of the same age and background should have been aware of the ramifications of his actions? Explain your answer.

A subjective approach is preferable and has one very powerful argument in its favor. The subjective standard emphasizes whether this particular defendant intended the tort of battery. For purposes of assigning liability, it seems fairer to determine whether the individual actually had the mental state necessary to have committed an intentional tort. The one argument in favor of the objective approach is that it is more favorable to the plaintiff. It would be much easier to show that an average person knew to a substantial certainty that his actions would cause an unwanted touching. Plaintiff is suing a specific individual, however, not the average person. Therefore, the subjective approach is preferable. *Please note that this was intended as an intellectual exercise. When addressing intent in the torts context, we employ a subjective approach.*

Exercise 2A

Pretend that you are John's attorney. Based on the law and on these facts, construct an argument as to why John should not have to pay the fine or lose his license. If you come up with more than one argument, list the ones you feel most strongly about first. Remember to fully explain the rationale supporting your conclusion.

John should not have to lose his license or pay his fine because his actions were not what the legislature had in mind when it passed the law he allegedly violated. The law requires drivers to come to a complete stop for 2 seconds at a stop sign before proceeding. John edged his car out slowly but did not stop for the full 2 seconds. Technically he has violated the statute, but only if one reads the statute very narrowly.

The legislature passed this law because drivers were quickly rolling through stop signs and not stopping at all. This behavior resulted in several accidents, some of which were fatal. John, however, was not rolling through the stop sign quickly. Instead, he slowly edged out into the road before proceeding, a fact confirmed by the police officer who cited John. In addition, it was necessary for John to slowly edge out into the intersection because bushes were obstructing his view. Even if he had come to a 2 second stop at the stop sign, it would not have made his subsequent movement into the intersection any safer. John drove safely under the circumstances, which was the legislature's intent when it passed the statute. Therefore, John should not lose his license of pay a fine.

Exercise 2B

Now, switch gears and pretend that you are the prosecutor! This is an old law school trick that is designed to force you to consider all points of view. If you haven't taken the opposing arguments into consideration when coming up with your answer, then your answer is incomplete. This time, come up with an argument as to why John should be treated no differently than anyone else who violated the statute. In your answer, be sure to address the defense arguments and why the prosecutions position should prevail.

John violated the 2 second stop statute and should pay a fine and lose his license. The statute very clearly requires that all drivers stop for a full two seconds at a stop sign before proceeding. John will argue that bushes obstructed his view and that he had to slowly edge out into the intersection before proceeding. This argument fails to consider one obvious point—John could have come to a 2 second stop before slowly edging out into traffic. If he had done so, he would have obeyed the law and been safe. Admittedly John was not driving as recklessly as were the individuals who prompted the legislature to pass the law, but the law does not differentiate between those who drive slowly or quickly through a stop sign. In addition, the state cannot allow those who violate the law to dictate what conduct is proscribed by the statute. If it was impossible for John to proceed safely and obey the statute, his arguments would carry more weight. As noted, John could have done both and is guilty of violating the 2 second stop statute.

Note that in both of the above samples I follow the same basic formula. I lay out my conclusion, address the relevant law, and then analyze how my rationales are supported by the facts before stating my conclusion again at the end. This CRAC approach is used less commonly in law school then IRAC, particularly on law school exams where you must be objective. I chose to use CRAC in this instance because the questions required me to adopt a position, thus making me an advocate. As an advocate, it is appropriate to begin your discussion by asserting your position.

Chapter V

Exercise 1A

Using the above torts hypothetical as a jumping off point, change the fact pattern where the outcome remains the same—John still breaches his duty of care and is negligent.

A change in the weather conditions would not necessarily relieve John of liability. For example, we could change the weather so that the area is not suffering from a drought. Even under normal weather conditions, John is likely negligent if he throws his cigarette butt out the window and it causes a fire. John has still created the risk, and a reasonably prudent person would not throw a fire source out the window even in normal weather conditions. The fact that many people do in fact throw cigarette butts out the window without causing a fire should not protect John from liability. People speed on the highways every day without causing an accident, but this does not mean it is safe to exceed the speed limit. It just means that speeders have chosen to engage in risky behavior and they will be liable if the cause an accident. Similarly, John has chosen to engage in risky behavior, and now must pay the price if his actions cause a fire.

This is merely one example of a change in facts that would not change the outcome. Do not be concerned if you changed a fact other than the one I chose.

Exercise 1B

Now, change the fact pattern enough so that John no longer breaches his duty of care. When attempting this exercise, keep the reasonably prudent person standard in mind. John will no longer be negligent once a reasonably prudent person would act in the same way.

Instead of throwing his butt out the window, John tamps it out in his ashtray. An hour later he stops at a rest area and dumps the contents of his ashtray into a much larger ashtray at the entrance to a restaurant located in the rest area. The larger ashtray was marked "Cigarette Butts Only." After John leaves, another patron throws a paper napkin into the ashtray. John's cigarette has been smoldering the entire time, and now ignites the napkin. The ensuing fire destroys the restaurant.

Under these circumstances, John is unlikely to be liable for negligence. First, he tamped the butt out into his own ashtray and then disposed of it in another larger ashtray. Further, at least an hour passed between John smoking the cigarette and dumping out his ashtray. John did everything he could to be safe. One could argue, however, that it was his still smoldering cigarette that ultimately started the blaze, so he should bear the responsibility. But, keep in mind that John dumped his ashtray into a receptacle designed specifically to accommodate smoldering embers. In addition, the sign warned others that this ashtray was meant for "Cigarette Butts Only." Under these circumstances, John could not be expected to anticipate that another patron would throw paper into the ashtray and start the fire. Further, even if John could anticipate that others would use the ashtray inappropriately, a reasonably prudent person does not have to protect others from every possible harm.

Notice that I still work through a counter argument in my scenario. It is easy to create a fact pattern where the defendant is clearly not liable. The trick is to rework the hypotheticals so that they are somewhat difficult to answer. In this way, the hypotheticals will truly prepare you for the kinds of questions you will see on your exams.

Chapter VII

Synthesis Exercise

Case 1

What principle, or principles, of law does *Commonwealth v. Delgado* stand for?

- *In general, words alone are not sufficient evidence of a weapon.*
- *"Informational" language, however, is an exception to the general rule.*
- *An example of "informational" language is language that tells the victim that the defendant has a weapon and is willing to use it.*

Case 2

What additional principle, or principles, of law does *Commonwealth v. Tarrant* stand for?

- *The defendant does not have to be in possession of a weapon when arrested as long as he had the opportunity to dispose of it prior to arrest.*
- *Informational words in the form of a handwritten note may also be sufficient.*
- *Defendant may still be guilty of possessing and using a weapon even if the victim did not believe the defendant was armed.*

Case 3

What additional principle, or principles, of law does *Commonwealth v. Howard* stand for?

- *The defendant's informational language is not sufficient evidence of a weapon where the defendant was arrested during the commission of the robbery and had no opportunity to dispose of the alleged weapon.*

Final Synthesis of Rule

Now, try to synthesize a rule from the holdings of *Delgado*, *Tarrant*, and *Howard*.

A jury may find that the defendant possessed a weapon based on the defendant's informational language, words spoken or written that communicate the existence of a weapon, unless the defendant is unarmed when arrested and did not have an opportunity to dispose of the weapon.

Chapter VIII

Analysis Exercise

Sample Answer to Analysis Exercise

As you read the following analysis, I will comment in italics at the end of each paragraph to further explain what you are reading. In addition, keep a few things in mind. First, I divide out my analysis so that I am addressing each element independently, even the obvious ones. Make sure you get full credit from the professor for discussing even the most obvious issues.

Second, notice that I use the IRAC formula as I address each element. The formula by itself is not legal analysis. Each letter does, however, stand for a point that you must address within your analysis. The formula merely helps to remind you to address each point, and to do so in a logical order. Personally, I use IRAC or CRAC almost interchangeably. Some professors will prefer one formulation over another, so be sure to follow their instructions.

Third, I use the facts from the problem in my analysis. In legal analysis, you are telling the reader how a future court might treat a particular set of facts. This is impossible to do without actually using the facts in your analysis. One of the most common criticisms students receive about their examinations or papers is that they have failed to analyze the issues. This occurs when students make a vague assertion that "these facts satisfy" a particular rule, without specifying which facts they are referencing.

Finally, notice that I come to a conclusion without being conclusion driven. I allow my analysis to guide me to a conclusion, which means that I objectively lay out alternative points of view where applicable. If there isn't a reasonable alternative point of view, however, I do not create one.

Ed's Words as an Assault of John

The first issue is whether Ed assaulted John when he yelled "[y]ou almost took my head off a few plays back and if you don't watch yourself I'm going to do the same to you." An assault requires the: (1) intentional; (2) placement of another; (3) in apprehension; (4) of an imminent battery. Standing alone, these words fail to satisfy the imminent battery element of an assault.

This first paragraph is essentially an introduction to the remainder of my analysis. In the first sentence, I clearly state that we are dealing with an assault because I do not want to make my reader guess as to the subject of my discussion. In addition, I further refine the issue by identifying the parties and the key facts generating the issue. You might have a dozen individuals in your fact pattern on an examination, so clarity is essential. In this instance I have noted a few key facts because it is possible that Ed has committed another assault elsewhere in the fact pattern, and the reader needs to know which potential assault I am addressing. After the issue, I quickly move into the rule of assault, and then wrap up my introduction with a quick conclusion. This preliminary conclusion is merely acting as a transition into the remainder of my answer and is not required. If you don't come to a conclusion here, however, be sure that you provide the reader with an overall conclusion at the end of your analysis.

Regarding the first element of an assault, Ed did act intentionally toward John. The courts define intentional conduct as desiring to do something or knowing to a substantial certainty that your actions will produce a certain effect. Here, Ed spoke volitionally, and had to know that John would hear the words because the two men would be no more than a few feet apart during a basketball game. It would be hard to imagine any argument that Ed did not intend John to hear his words. Therefore Ed's conduct was intentional.

This is my analysis to the first issue, whether or not Ed acted intentionally when he yelled at John. I start off with a conclusion, but as I noted earlier this first sentence could have been written in the form of an issue. I then state the rule regarding intent before performing some very brief analysis. The question is easy to resolve in this instance, so I do not belabor the obvious and quickly move on to the next element of an assault.

Similarly, Ed's words were clearly directed at Ed, another person, which satisfies the second element of an assault. When Ed stated "you almost took my head off a few plays back," his words were clearly directed at John and referenced an earlier play in the game. Also, the facts do not indicate that anyone else was even present.

This discussion is as short as the first element because it is just as simple to resolve. In order to save time, I have combined my conclusion in the first sentence with the second element, that the assault must be directed at "another."

Ed's words also satisfied the third element of an assault, apprehension. Apprehension in this context requires that the plaintiff be aware of the imminent battery, but fear of the defendant is unnecessary. It is likely that John was aware of Ed's words as the two individuals could not have been more than a few feet apart when Ed yelled. In addition, John responded to Ed's words by telling him to stop being such a baby and play ball. Based on his response, it seems clear that he was aware of what Ed was saying. It doesn't appear that John was placed in fear of Ed's words, but an assault requires awareness and not fear of the imminent battery. Therefore, John was aware, or apprehended, Ed's actions.

Although this is still a short discussion, we are finally getting to the meatier elements of an assault. After concluding that Ed's words satisfy the apprehension element of an assault, I quickly state the rule. I do not simply say that the plaintiff must "apprehend" the imminent battery. Instead, I further refine the definition by noting that apprehension in this context means awareness. This distinction is quite important to my analysis. After stating the rule, I go on to explain why we know that John heard, or apprehended, Ed's words. First, the two were playing basketball together and could not have been more than a few feet apart when Ed spoke. If there was any doubt as to whether John heard Ed's words, it is dispelled by John's response. John's words are clearly responsive to Ed's threat, and a response means he must have heard something that required a response. After my analysis, I briefly note the rule does not require fear. This is a common mistake students make when addressing assault scenarios because one common definition of apprehend is to be afraid. I want my reader to know that I understand the difference. Fear isn't even suggested in these facts, however, so I move quickly to the next element.

Ed's words do not, however, satisfy the imminence element of an assault. In the context of an assault, imminent means that there will be no significant delay between the defendant's actions and the battery. Generally, words alone cannot satisfy the imminence element of an assault. Words without accompanying conduct may be threatening in nature, but do not necessarily indicate that a battery is about to occur. In this instance, Ed merely yelled "[y]ou almost took my head off a few plays back and if you don't watch yourself I'm going to do the same to you." These words indicate the possibility of a battery, but one that might occur at some undetermined time in the future. It is unclear from the statement when this battery might occur. In fact, the possibility that Ed will batter John is predicated on some future conduct from John. Ed does threaten to batter John, but only if John "doesn't watch himself." Therefore, Ed is saying that he might not batter John, meaning that a battery cannot be imminent.

In addition, Ed says that he is going to do the "same" thing to John that was done to him. If Ed is suggesting that he will push John as part of the basketball game, as opposed to pushing him outside of the game, then John may be consenting to the touching. A touching that has been consented to does not amount to a battery. Players frequently come into contact with each other during a basketball game, and it is an aspect of the sport that one accepts when one plays. Ed's anger when he speaks these words, however, makes it more likely that he does intend to batter John outside of the context of the game. Even if Ed is threatening to commit a battery, his words are not clear evidence of an intent to act imminently. Therefore, Ed's words standing alone do not indicate an imminent battery.

By far, this is the longest section of analysis in the memo. It needs to be because this is where we have a tension point in the facts. This means that we have a number of facts on this point and these facts appear to suggest opposite conclusions. Therefore, you as the writer must touch on all of the relevant facts and explain why one conclusion is superior to the others. As you read through the analysis, did you notice that I briefly address a few other sub issues? Good analysis will often expose other issues that you should address to complete your answer. For example, I briefly discuss the possibility that John may have consented to the imminent battery by playing basketball with his friend. Consent is actually a separate issue that could be broken out and discussed independently in its own paragraph of analysis. Instead, I have made the judgment that the issue is relatively minor and could be satisfactorily dealt within the paragraph on imminençe. You will often be called upon to make these types of judgment calls as you perform legal analysis.

In sum, even if Ed's words indicated a future battery, the lack of imminence means that Ed did not assault John when he yelled at him.

Because the analysis of any issue requires the writer to review a number of sub-issues, I like to wrap up my analysis with a brief restatement of my overall conclusion.

Chapter IX

Exercise 1

1. Is Danielle liable for the damage to her neighbor's car?

2. Is she at fault because she reached over to fix the mirror, but ended up putting the car into gear?

3. Is she at fault for simply starting the car without a license?

4. Does she have a learner's permit?

5. If she has a learner's permit, what does it permit her to do behind the wheel of a car?

6. Under the law, was she "driving" the car when the accident took place?

7. Is she guilty of driving a car without a license?

8. The facts indicate that she had taken at least one driver's education class. What did they teacher her in the driver's education class?

9. Was she taught anything in the class that might have contributed to the accident?

10. Was her car's emergency brake engaged?

11. Is there a statute that requires the emergency brake to be engaged when a car is parked?

12. Did her driver's education class teach her about using an emergency brake or making sure that it is engaged before starting the car?

13. Assuming the emergency brake was not engaged, would have it stopped the car had it been engaged when Danielle accidentally put the car into gear?

14. Did Danielle violate any laws by not having her seat belt on?

15. Is Danielle guilty of larceny regarding the keys to the family car?

16. Is Danielle guilty of stealing the family car?

17. Can Danielle argue that the car, as a family automobile, is hers so that she cannot be guilty of stealing the car?

18. Is Danielle liable for the damage to her family's car?

19. Are Danielle's parents, based solely on their relationship with their daughter, liable for the damage to the neighbor's car?

20. Did Danielle's father act negligently by leaving the car keys in an easily accessible location, particularly after Danielle kept asking for driving lessons?

21. Are Danielle's parents liable for the damage to the neighbor's car due to the poor supervision of their daughter?

22. Can Danielle sue her parents for the injuries she sustained in the car accident under a theory of poor parental supervision?

23. Can a state agency charged with the welfare of children charge Danielle's parents with a violation of the law based on her injuries and their alleged poor supervision of their daughter?

Exercise 2

There are a number of different factors—some subtle and some more obvious—that transformed the analysis of *Just Being Neighborly* from objective to persuasive. The differences include:

1. The first sentence of the persuasive analysis lays out a strongly worded conclusion, as opposed to framing the issue as a question in need of an answer.

2. Luke, not Keith, is portrayed as the instigator of the confrontation, despite the fact that Keith threw the first punch. In this analysis, the fight begins when Luke starts yelling and invades Keith's personal space.

3. The time line of the event is stretched out to make it appear that Keith was maintaining his composure throughout much of the confrontation and only threw a punch when it was absolutely necessary.

4. At every opportunity, Keith's actions are described as "reasonable," and this is not coincidence as the law of self defense requires that Keith act reasonably.

5. The word "escalate" is used twice and both times to describe Luke's actions. The one who escalates a confrontation is typically the one who is at fault.

6. Facts that seem beneficial to Luke are turned on their head and now support Keith's position. For example, the fact that Luke is typically a pleasant person would seem to make Keith's decision to throw a punch unreasonable. In the persuasive version of the analysis, this change in Luke's demeanor is used to support Keith's reasonable belief that he was under attack.

7. The analysis still contains a reference to a reasonable counterargument—that the phrase "you will be sorry" could allude to any number of actions on the part of Luke. In this persuasive version, however, the counterargument is much shorter. In addition, the counterargument is itself countered when the writer reminds the reader that the words "you will be sorry" must be viewed in the context of the entire confrontation between the neighbors.

Chapter X

Exercise 1: Mini Brief of *State v. Carlton*

Issue: May a jury find that the defendant's shoes were a weapon based on the victim's broken ribs and dislocated shoulder?

Holding: Yes, a jury may find that the defendant used a weapon if the victim's injuries are serious enough to show that the item in question and not merely the blows caused the harm.

Reasoning: The jury must hear sufficient evidence to find that the defendant used an item capable of causing serious bodily harm. One way to establish an item's capability of causing serious bodily harm is by showing that the victim's injuries were more severe due to the item.

Exercise 2: Mini Brief of *State v. Morgenstern*

Issue: May shoes be a weapon under Acadia law?

Holding: Yes, any item may be a weapon under Acadia law if it is capable of causing serious bodily harm.

Reasoning: Acadia's Assault and Battery with a weapon statute allows that any item may be a weapon if it is capable of causing serious bodily harm. If the description of the item in question indicates that it is capable of causing serious harm, then the jury may find that the defendant used a weapon.

Glossary

Admissions—A request from opposing counsel that a party to the lawsuit declare some facts as true. Admissions are commonly used to narrow the contested issues at trial, and are made under pains and penalties of perjury.

Appellant—The party appealing a case to higher court. The appellant is asking the appellate court to correct some error that occurred in the trial court or in a lower level appellate court.

Appellee—The party opposing the appellant's appeal. Typically, the appellee prevailed in the lower court and is arguing that the original decision should stand.

Beyond a reasonable doubt—The prosecution's burden of proof in criminal trials. The prosecution must prove to the trier of fact every element of the crime beyond a reasonable doubt. This standard is extremely hard to define, however, court's often instruct jurors that they must be sure to a "moral certainty" in order to find guilt beyond a reasonable doubt.

Binding Authority—Legal authority that a court must follow and that controls a case's outcome. Examples include statutes, constitutions, higher level court decisions, and rules of evidence and procedure that originate in the jurisdiction where the court is sitting.

Civil Cases—Any non-criminal case where a plaintiff has filed suit against the defendant for money damages or for enforcement of an agreement. Typically, the plaintiff is seeking money as compensation. In some instances, the plaintiff may ask the court to enforce an agreement between the parties or to force the opposing party to refrain from doing something.

Civil Complaint—The means of initiating a civil lawsuit. Through the complaint's individual numbered paragraphs, the plaintiff lays out what happened and her theory as to why she is entitled to some form of relief.

Civil Motion to Dismiss—A motion brought by the defendant who is asserting that the plaintiff has made some error when initiating the lawsuit. There are several types of motion to dismiss. Among the most common is a motion to dismiss for failure to state a claim upon which relief may be granted. Through this motion, the defendant is asserting that the facts as declared by the plaintiff do not make out a civil wrong and that the court must dismiss the case.

Common law—Judge made law as opposed to law derived from statutes or rules of procedure.

Conclusions of Law—A court's resolution of legal questions that arise during the course of a trial. Typical conclusions of law include evidentiary rulings and decisions regarding the motions filed by the litigants. Appellate courts do not disturb factual findings but may review and modify conclusions of law on appeal.

Criminal Complaint—One of two ways to initiate a criminal proceeding. In most jurisdictions, the state uses a criminal complaint to initiate criminal proceedings when the defendant is accused of committing relatively minor crimes.

Cross Examination—The questioning of the opposing party's witness during a trial.

Counterargument—The legal, factual, and logical support for *an* answer to a problem, just not the answer you adopted.

Defendant—In a civil matter, the defendant is the party against whom the plaintiff has filed suit in order to remedy a perceived civil wrong. In criminal cases, the government has accused the defendant of breaking some law and is seeking to have the defendant incarcerated, pay a fine, or both.

***De Novo* Review**—Latin for anew or beginning again. Standard of review where the appellate court reviews a lower court decision as if the matter was never originally ruled upon below. Other standards of review require the appellate court to be much more deferential to a lower court's decision.

Deposition—A pre-trial discovery device where witnesses are required to answer an attorney's questions. The deponent is typically sworn in at the outset of the deposition and answers counsel's questions under the pains and penalties of perjury. In some instances, counsel may use inconsistencies between a witness's deposition and trial testimony to challenge the witness' credibility.

Directed Verdict—A motion made prior to the jury's deliberations alleging that no reasonable jury could find for the opponent and that the moving party is entitled to judgment. If the court allows the motion, the trial is over and the case is not submitted to the jury. In federal courts and some state courts, this motion is referred to as a motion for a judgment as a matter of law.

Direct Examination—The questioning of a party's own witness during a legal proceeding.

Discovery—Process through which a party to a lawsuit obtains information from the opposing party. Methods of discovery include depositions, requests for production of documents, interrogatories, and requests for admissions.

Diversity Jurisdiction—One type of subject matter jurisdiction in the federal courts. Diversity jurisdiction exists where all plaintiffs to the lawsuit are domiciled in different states from all defendants in the same lawsuit and the amount in controversy exceeds $75,000.

Domicile—A party is domiciled in a state when they are present in a state and intend to remain in that state indefinitely. An individual's domicile will not change until these two elements are both present. This concept is used to determine whether a federal court has subject matter jurisdiction over a civil lawsuit.

Finding of Fact—The trier of fact's conclusion regarding a factual question necessary to the resolution of a legal issue. *Compare, conclusion of law.*

Hearsay—An out of court statement offered for the truth of the matter asserted. Fed. R. Evid. 801. Under the rules of evidence, hearsay statements are inadmissible in court unless they fall under one of many exceptions to the hearsay rule. Under the rules of evidence, verbal, electronic, and written statements all may be hearsay.

Holding—The court's resolution of a legal issue.

Hornbook—A single volume legal treatise. Typically, hornbooks cover the law from a single course in a level of detail that is appropriate for law students.

Indictment—In more serious criminal matters, an indictment is the process whereby the government submits evidence of criminal wrongdoing to a grand jury and attempts to establish that the defendant should be tried. Unlike the beyond a reasonable doubt standard used in criminal trials, the government need only establish probable cause that the defendant committed the crime in question. *See also, True Bill and No Bill.*

Information—Another name for a criminal complaint.

Interrogatories—A pre-trial discovery device that consists of a set of written questions sent to the opposing party in a lawsuit. The questions must be answered under the pains and penalties of perjury. Most jurisdictions limit the number of questions a party may ask using this discovery device.

Judgment as a Matter of Law—A motion alleging that no reasonable jury could find for the opponent and that the moving party is entitled to judgment. If the court allows the motion, the trial is over. *See also Directed Verdict.*

Judgment Notwithstanding the Verdict (also JNOV and Judgment *Non Obstante Veredicto*)—A motion made after the jury returns its verdict alleging that no reasonable jury could find for the opposing party and that the jury's verdict should be disregarded or amended.

Law Review—A legal journal, typically student run, that publishes articles discussing evolving legal issues. In some instances, authors may suggest the course the law should take or warn of the dangers of following a legal doctrine. Most law schools publish at least one law review, and student membership on the law review editorial board is considered an honor. Law review articles are a form of secondary authority, but some law reviews and law review articles are more highly regarded than others.

Legal Treatise—A book, or set of books, that systematically explains an area of law.

Mandatory Authority—*See Binding Authority.*

Material Facts—Any fact that would affect the outcome of a legal matter. Professors often explore the idea of material facts through the introduction of classroom hypotheticals. A professor will change certain facts from a recently discussed case and allow students to analyze whether the changes would result in a different outcome. If the changed fact results in a different outcome, the fact is material.

Memorandum of Law—A document written in which the attorney analyzes the relevant legal issues. In its objective form, attorneys use it internally in a law office to inform colleagues of competing points of view. In its persuasive form, the document is intended to inform the reader of the law and persuade the reader to adopt the writer's point of view.

Motion—The vehicle through which the parties to a civil or criminal matter ask the court to take some action.

Motion for Summary Judgment—Through this motion, a party to a lawsuit is asserting that all issues of material fact have been resolved and that the moving party is entitled to judgment as a matter of law. Because this motion is made prior to trial, the moving party is relying on facts obtained through the various discovery devices in claiming that there are no material facts to be decided at trial.

Notice of Appeal—A document appellant files with the appellate court giving notice of an intent to file an appeal. Typically, a notice of appeal must be filed within 30 days of judgment in the lower court.

Outline—A document through which a student attempts to define and logically organize a course's legal concepts.

Persuasive Authority—Anything that a court relies in coming to its decision other than binding authority from within the court's jurisdiction. Case law from outside of the court's jurisdiction may be persuasive authority because the court may be persuaded to follow these decisions but is not required to do so.

Petition for Writ of Certiorari—When an appeal is discretionary, as opposed to a matter of right, the mechanism through which the appealing party seeks appellate review.

Plaintiff—The party in a civil lawsuit who has filed suit to address some perceived civil wrong.

Pleadings—Documents filed with the court during the course of a lawsuit.

Precedential Authority—A case that has been decided and that future courts may use as a basis for their decisions.

Preponderance of the Evidence—The standard of proof in most civil matters. Although defined somewhat differently from jurisdiction to jurisdiction, it is the trier of fact's conclusion that the evidence weighs more heavily in favor of one party than the other. In weighing the evidence, the trier of fact must carefully review of the quality of evidence, as opposed to merely the amount of evidence, introduced by the parties.

Primary Authority—Law that a court may consider when arriving at a decision. If the law comes from the same jurisdiction as the court considering the issue, then the court may be required to follow this primary mandatory authority. If the law originates in another jurisdiction, or if the law was decided by a court lower in the system's hierarchy, then this law is primary persuasive authority.

Probable Cause—Facts, based on trustworthy information, that would lead a person of "reasonable caution" to believe that a crime has been or is being committed. *See Draper v. United States*, 358 U.S. 307 (1959).

Pro se—Appearing in a legal proceeding without the benefit of an attorney.

Question of Fact (also Issue of Fact)—A fact in dispute that the trier of fact must resolve. For example, a question of fact arises when two witnesses provide conflicting testimony as to the same issue.

Question of Law—A legal issue that is in dispute and will be resolved by the judge. For example, the admissibility of evidence at trial is a question of law for the judge.

Redirect Examination—The re-questioning of a party's own witness during a legal proceeding. Redirect examination occurs after opposing counsel has concluded the cross examination of the witness. On redirect examination of a witness, counsel's questions must relate to issues raised during the opponent's cross examination of the witness.

Request for Production of Documents—A pre-trial discovery device through which litigants seek to obtain documents in possession of the opposing party. Commonly requested documents include business records, pay stubs, and check receipts.

Required Finding of Not Guilty—Motion made by the defendant in criminal trials asserting that, as a matter of law, the prosecution has failed to introduce sufficient evidence to support a conviction for the crime charged.

Rest or Rested—Litigant's decision to discontinue introducing evidence. For example, the plaintiff will "rest" after questioning his witnesses and introducing any other evidence. Once the plaintiff, or prosecution, has rested, the defendant may begin to present her evidence to the trier of fact.

Restatement of Law—A form of secondary authority where the authors discuss the common law of the United States, topic by topic. Restatements are published by the American Law Institute, an organization comprised of noted judges, scholars, and attorneys. While a Restatement is a form of persuasive authority, the opinions contained therein are highly respected. In some instances, courts have adopted portions of a Restatement as the law of that jurisdiction.

Secondary Authority—Anything, other than law, that a court may rely on in its rulings and holdings. All forms of secondary authority are persuasive authority because a court may rely on it in coming to its decision but is not required to do so.

Sequester, sequestered, sequestration—Isolation of the jury during its deliberations and in some instances during the entire trial. A sequestered jury is cut off from all outside sources of information and opinion, which helps to ensure that its decisions are based solely on the evidence submitted at trial and the judge's instructions regarding matters of law.

Skeletal Outline—A one or two page version of a larger outline that students may use to organize their approach to an examination question.

Standard of Review—The level of scrutiny that an appellate court will apply when reviewing a lower court's rulings. Standards of review range from the extremely deferential to a *de novo* review, which allows the appellate court to scrutinize a matter without considering the lower court's decision.

Stare Decisis—Latin for "to stand by things decided." This doctrine requires courts to follow earlier decisions from higher level courts within the same jurisdiction and promotes consistency and predictability within the judicial system. This aspect of *stare decisis* is merely another term for judicial precedent. Courts do depart from the doctrine, but generally only after the passage of time and when the rationale supporting the earlier decision no longer applies.

Subject Matter Jurisdiction—The power of the court to hear a particular case. State courts have very broad subject matter jurisdiction, meaning they have the power to hear most lawsuits. In comparison, federal courts have relatively limited subject matter jurisdiction.

Tort—A civil wrong for which plaintiffs typically seek monetary damages. Examples include battery, false imprisonment, and negligence.

Trier of Fact—The one who makes findings of fact. The trier of fact will either be the jury, or the judge if the parties have agreed to a jury waived trial (also known as a bench trial). The trier of fact must listen to the evidence as presented by the parties to the litigation and then determine what actually occurred.

True Bill—The grand jury's affirmative conclusion that the government has established probable cause that the defendant committed a particular crime.

Index